Emerging Patterns
in Urban
Administration

Emerging Patterns in Urban Administration

Edited by

F. Gerald Brown
Thomas P. Murphy

University of Missouri — Kansas City

Heath Lexington Books
D. C. Heath and Company
Lexington, Massachusetts

Printed in the United States of America

Library of Congress Number: 79-115485

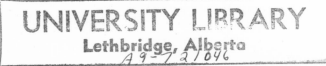

Contents

Preface   vii

Introduction — F. Gerald Brown   3

Part 1:   The Urban Polity   11

    1   The Change Process in Municipal Government —
        Timothy Costello   13

    2   Political Stability in Metro Government — Daniel R.
        Grant   34

    3   Bridging the Gap Between Citizens and City Government —
        Randy H. Hamilton   64

Part 2:   Urbanization and the Federal System   81

    4   Urban Administration and Creative Federalism —
        Edmund S. Muskie   83

    5   State Government and the Urban Crisis — Jesse M. Unruh   100

    6   Executive Leadership in the Urban County — Lawrence K.
        Roos, Thomas C. Kelly   112

Part 3:   **Implications for Metropolitan Planning**   125

7   *The Planning Role in Urban Decision-Making — Robert L. Williams*   127

8   *Future Manpower for Urban Management — Nathan D. Grundstein*   140

9   *The New Technical Competence for Urban Management — T. R. Lakshmanan*   172

Part 4:   **Centralization vs. Decentralization**   193

10   *Councils of Government: The Potential and the Problems — Kent Mathewson*   195

11   *The Decentralization of Urban Government: A Systems Approach — Guy Black*   222

12   *Intergovernmental Management of Urban Problems in the Kansas City Metropolitan Area — Thomas P. Murphy*   248

Notes to Chapters   277

About the Contributors   282

Preface

The essays and discussions in this book are built around two issues that we believe to be basic. These are the need to develop an effective synthesis of theory relevant to urban administration and the need to deal meaningfully with the continuing gap between the state of the art academically and the state of the art as practiced by working professionals. These discussions are offered as a contribution in the direction of a possible joint resolution.

It is usual in a preface to discuss the intellectual origins of the book and the conceptual vicissitudes of the author as he traveled to the point of declaring himself in print and then to bow lightly to a host of other people who have contributed to the enterprise. We would like to reverse this usual order. We do this not through any sense of modesty but because the involvement of a host of people in specific ways in the development of these readings is most relevant to the issue of the linkage between theory and practice.

The focus of the book is on action systems rather than on neat description. The theme throughout is, *how can we get things done in our cities?* How can we raise the level of sophistication and effectiveness of urban action patterns? The book itself is an outgrowth of a linking-up between the university and a set of urban action systems in Kansas City, Missouri.

We began by asking around among our contacts and acquaintances in the city, "Who are the movers in this town? Who are the people usually found behind the scenes when things really happen relating to urban problems?" We then asked the same questions of the people whose names were given in answer. Many readers will recognize this as roughly similar to the reputational approach for identifying a community power structure. But what we had was not the power structure of Kansas City. It was a rough approximation of the "action structure." Most of these people were rather experienced and sophisticated public administration professionals, though there were some key local politicians and businessmen as well. With this group we raised the questions: "What are your concerns? What are the issues you feel we need to come to grips with in this city? What are the areas of urban action that you find frustrating and think could be enlightened by sharing of current theory and the experiences of noteworthy practice?"

With this list of concerns in hand we then sought out outstanding academics and practitioners who could speak on these issues with rigor and experience. We commissioned them to set their thoughts in writing and come to Kansas City for a series of seminar-discussions with the "action structure." The readings that follow are a selection of those papers and discussions. The anonymous person hiding behind the rubric "Question" in the dialogues is deserving of much of the credit for this work; for as one of the 200 plus urban professionals, academics, and citizens who ultimately participated in these seminars, it is his concerns and his joint commitment to reconceptualization and action that have inspired the effort. If we name one we should name all; so, as is so often the lot of public servants, they will have to know that their contribution was instrumental and appreciated but bear the absence of personal recognition. Although the discussions have been edited to remove the comments that had meaning only in the immediate context, we have attempted to retain the informality and sense of dialogue that characterized the seminar.

Some of the ideas and implications of the discussions were, of course, specific to Kansas City in impact. These have been edited out or taken account of in the chapter on Kansas City by Thomas P. Murphy. What remains is of importance to organized action systems in any United States metropolitan area. Nathan D. Grundstein's chapter on "Future Manpower for Urban Management" has already been influential in the content of the newly adopted goals of ICMA, the national professional association of city managers. This paper helped to provide the rationale for the recent broadening of membership of that association as symbolized in its change of name from International City Manager's Association to International City Management Association. The book should prove of interest to a variety of classes in urban planning, public administration, local government and urban affairs, as well as to professional managers and planners concerned with innovative and successful patterns of action and implementation and to urban politicians and concerned citizens who want to keep abreast of the possibilities of action that technology and administrative theory and experience are opening up to cities in the midst of social ferment and change.

Finally, we would like to express our appreciation to the Missouri Department of Community Affairs and the Department of Health, Education and Welfare, which made possible many of the seminars by partial funding through Title I of the Higher Education Act of 1965. Special appreciation is also due Robert J. Saunders, our colleague who collaborated in many of the seminars, and our assistants, John Tangeman and Richard Heimovics, for their help in editing and rewriting certain of the papers, and to Barbara Gilmore, Erika Hales, Martha Gresham, and the secretarial staff of the School of Administration for their invaluable support and many hours' work on the manuscripts.

F. Gerald Brown
Thomas P. Murphy

**Emerging Patterns
in Urban
Administration**

Introduction

Urban is one of today's magic words. Major contributions are being made almost monthly in such fields as urban planning, urban geography, urban politics. Newspapers are full of articles about housing programs, welfare, employment, civil rights, model cities programs, Office of Economic Opportunity programs. There are exhortations from every side that we must come to grips with the urban crisis. Yet the literature is practically devoid of any consideration of the public administration systems that must be activated and sustained in urban areas in order to address these problems effectively. There is much discussion of substance, a little of form, and almost none of process.

This book attempts to deal with some of the elements that will go into the development of a theory of urban administration. Such a theory must take account of the fact that urban administration takes place within a number of organizations, and outside of organizations, in relationship to formal and informal political, economic and social power structures which may be monolithic or fragmented but are probably plural; with a variety of processes directed toward different but related problems all held together by the fact that they are concentrated in a geographic area know as an urban center.

To deal effectively with the problems of the urban centers we need to identify the goals and values of urban communities and develop more sophisticated understanding of the substantive and process problems and policy areas involved. We must develop programs which are finely tuned to dealing effectively with these problems in terms of the values and goals identified. We must develop understanding and skills relevant to transmitting policies and goals into well-managed problems on a continuing basis in our metropolitan areas. This latter dimension is the field of urban public administration, and it is currently substantially underdeveloped. Available urban theory is not adequate to the dimensions of the urban crisis. There is a great need for better understanding of the ordering of activities of urban public administration and of the roles of individuals involved in these activities.

The papers in this book are part of an attempt to link substantive understanding to administrative implementation at a high level in one metropolitan area. Each contributor is a wise and experienced man in the area of urban public affairs. The focus throughout is on the process for getting things done, the instruments available to assist in doing them and the kind of people needed to administer the public's urban business.

Senator Muskie establishes a philosophical touchstone in the shared commitment to all-around growth of every member of society and the joint, and sometimes dichotomous, task of the improvement of the governmental institutions and the meeting of human needs. From his perspective on the Senate

Subcommittee on Intergovernmental Relations he reviews the all too familiar scene of many governments and many programs at different geographical levels with complex overlapping and lack of coordination. He discusses the evolutionary process whereby instruments have been and are being designed to deal responsibly with urban problems through these governmental structures. He emphasizes the importance of new regional institutions such as the Water Quality Act and the Clean Air Act.

With the added perspective of a former state governor he discusses realistically the added value that states can provide in the formation of urban policies and intergovernmental grant programs. Finally he discusses the kind of federal machinery that might effectively provide the most creative role for the federal government in the urban problem solving process. This framework provides a good view of the ordering that is possible and likely at the federal government level, with some insights into the role of the state in an over-all ordering of federal functions relating to urban areas. The role of the federal level in developing over-all policies and mechanisms of implementation of the relevant over-all value choices is highlighted in his description of the proposed elimination of the fair market value test for the purchase of property involved in relocating people displaced by urban construction programs financed with federal funding. This role is also apparent in his discussion of the requirement that ghetto dwellers be given representation on policy-making boards of federally funded agencies working in the ghetto.

The major jurisdictions in urban areas are state related. Cities and school districts are creatures of state government. Counties are arms of state government. States therefore play a large, if somewhat unpublicized role, in influencing what happens in the urban centers. States have an especially critical role in shaping the basic public organizations in urban areas and in financing, or underfinancing, urban programs. Jesse Unruh argues that state government can and must deal more aggressively with urban problems if the urban crisis is to be resolved and if states and the federal system are to survive.

Our confidence in state governments as they relate to the important problems of urbanization, pollution, poverty, polarization and all the problems attending today's social and economic ills can only be restored when those governments move effectively toward dealing with the problems of today. Unruh traces the atrophy of states' influence in promoting change and suggests mechanisms to revitalize their importance and effectiveness.

The implications of the demise of state government influence spell drastic change for our federal system. Mr. Unruh presents good reason why this prospect is not a meaningful alternative to our form of representative democracy. The former Speaker of the General Assembly of California discusses viable means for strengthening the institutions of state government suitable to the problems of our time. At the minimum he suggests they equip themselves with the capacity to "venture, experiment and set the pace" as well as exert pressure on the federal government to put its house in order.

He finds the success of federal programs for the poor questionable. He urges states to take the initiative and rewrite the rules of the urban game with more responsive rules with which citizens can better identify. He goes on to discuss the changes in state government that can make it possible for states to take creative initiative.

Timothy Costello focuses the reader's attention upon a variety of ways in which change comes about in urban public agencies. Although he touches upon some specific outcomes in his explorations of patterns of change, his emphasis throughout is on ways in which changes occur, upon change processes rather than prescriptions of his preferred outcomes. He begins with an experienced discussion of the nature of a public organization in which he highlights some of the operationally significant differences between local public agencies and private firms. This provides an overview of the parameters within which the urban administrator must function. He then develops a typology of five major ways in which change in urban government can come about, gives examples of each, and discusses ways in which persons close to or involved in the administrative process can effectively utilize each type of process.

Randy Hamilton views the city from the perspective of the consumers of the outputs of urban administration, the citizens. He adds a note of urban optimism as he reviews the substantial success that has been achieved in many aspects of city improvement, both in terms of quality and quantity of output services and in terms of reformed governmental institutions. With this reminder of the strength, capability and innovative capacity of American local government, he turns to the problems that are very much with us today and tries to anticipate some of those that will beset urban areas in the next thirty years.

This leads to a blueprint for the next wave of reform. He identifies six policy areas in which major innovations in urban administration should be sought and can be expected. He urges cities to engage in social planning activities. He suggests that consumer protection and the question of the quality of goods and services is an ancient area of city concern and urges that it become a major area of policy focus and action by cities. Improving mechanisms for the redress of citizens' complaints and grievances is urged as a third major area for urgent innovation. Increased local government executive action is a fourth area. Concerted and rationalized programs of urban government dealing with urban manpower and employment questions is the fifth area. And finally, he urges a new set of civil service reforms.

Against this backdrop, the considerations of the book then move to the level of the metropolitan community. Nathan D. Grundstein is concerned with the actions and the people who take them. He raises issues with respect to the process of social choice in the metropolitan community. Starting with the assertion that big mistakes are made at the top he urges that considerably more attention be given to the general management function and a pattern of tightly linked management in which the generation of better conceived choices of policy and program at the top level is linked to the programs through the general management function. He is rather skeptical of the effectiveness of most public administration teaching programs. As in Muskie's presentation, one of the items that is picked up in the discussion is the way in which changes in the process of social choice will come about, are coming about or can be effectively introduced. Grundstein builds a framework that gives some handles on the social system involved in urban progress, or lack of urban progress, on the division of labor in urban administration and on the kinds of competencies that are needed for effective coping with today's urban problems. He articulates one of the themes which recurs many times through the book in his discussion of the linking of system design, the technology that is currently available to management and the human competences of management. The focus is very strongly on management and the effective role of management in the urban community, another recurring keynote of the book.

Grundstein identifies shortcomings in performance of the general management role as a critical problem facing us in the attempt to solve our urban problems. This becomes apparent in his ordering of the activities in the process of urban governance into entrepreneurial choice, general management, and program operations. Entrepreneurial choice — the generation and selection of fundamental options, problem identification, development of programs and resource allocation at an overall level with the metropolitan community — is conducted in some way or other in every community. Entrepreneurial choices are made by a community process which involves three types of elements: inputs from the community power structure, the level of skills that are available and accessible to the community to apply to the problems that have been identified, and pressures from outside the community. Examples of outside pressures include policies of the federal government and the state government, and broad social trends such as the current pressure from the black power groups. Entrepreneurial choices are obviously made, if all too often only by default. The third level of ordering, the level of program operations, is fairly highly developed. This development is reflected in the number of professional associations concerned with functions carried on in urban government: the Municipal Finance Officers Association, the National Association of Housing and Redevelopment Officials, Building Officials Conference of America, Inc., Federation of Tax Administrators, the National Association of Chiefs of Police, the Fire Association, the Municipal Traffic Engineers Association, Public Personnel Association, to name but a few. This is also apparent in any study, however casual, of the internal organization of governments in metropolitan areas. City government, county government, and school districts are replete with divisions responsible for functional performance. This is our heritage from the rationalization of governments in the first wave of municipal reform.

But there has been almost no recognition of a substantial function of developing public entrepreneurial choice options at a higher level and of linking entrepreneurial choice continuously to on-going and to new program operations in cities or metropolitan areas. As Grundstein so eloquently states, the functions are performed better than ever before but the city has disappeared. This is not a cry for a *position* such as a super city manager of some kind who will make over-all choices about the kinds of program operations that will be included in the city and what and how these will be organized, what resources will be brought to bear in different places, etc. It is not a request for an over-all planning body at the metropolitan level with some kind of program linking authority. It is rather an identification of a function that must be performed if the response to urban problems is to rise above the level of complete reaction to circumstances, pressures, and yesterday's problems. The urban management function is concerned with the identification of probable future areas of concern, the design of programs, and the utilization of analytic techniques for deciding which of different program alternatives would provide the greatest kinds of benefits to the metropolitan area at a given time, and the development of over-all policy frameworks within which it would be possible to decentralize some of the functions and provide in this way for more participation that directly affect them.

Still another theme that first appears in Grundestein's chapter is the concept of area strategies of program operations. This theme is independently picked up and developed by Guy Black in his chapter. Finally, and still without any discussion of organizations per se or of position, Grundstein deals with the question of career paths in the field of urban management. This is somewhat related to the frustrating question of: Who is an "urbanist" and what does he do? The suggestion that is made is that the "urbanologists" with a high level of analytic technology will probably tend to have career paths that move them from one metropolitan area to another and in and out of universities, government and consulting firms.

Robert Williams discusses the role of urban planning and planners in the urban administrative process. He places the planning movement in historical context and outlines the pragmatic contribution of the planning profession. He introduces some of the tools of planning and decision-making that are now being put to urban use. Included in this is the systems approach which Guy Black puts to use later in the book. The concept of community goals which Williams discusses begins to flesh out the public entrepreneurial choice category introduced in the Grundstein paper. Williams also brings in the metropolitan regional area as an important analytical and organizational level. He identifies and highlights the bridging role that planning plays in finding interjurisdictional implications of single jurisdiction actions and in posing regional solutions to regional problems. A positive value is placed on councils of governments, thus foreshadowing and supporting the Mathewson paper.

T. R. Lakshmanan deals with the specific application of very refined planning technology development to some urban related public policy problems. He echoes Grunstein's assertion that the big mistakes are really made at the top, and it is at this level that the technological input should come. It is possible to improve functions, but functions that are operating with the greatest efficiency for wrong or inadequately conceived purposes do not provide an effective response. He represents in his person an example of the high level analytic technology that can be brought to bear on urban problems, if institutions can be

ordered in such a way to bring these technologies to bear. He formalizes some of
the issues that weave through earlier and later chapters in the language of the
economist. He introduces concepts like *complementarities* — the putting together of two different activities which reinforce and support each other in such a
way as to make it cheap and efficient to do both activities whereas the two
activities separately could not necessarily be efficiently conducted;
externalities — the cost and benefits of activities in one area which are incident
on another area, another population group, or another economic group; and
finally *economies of scale* — the benefits that come from a large activity as
opposed to a number of smaller activities of the same type. In elaborating
Dr. Grundstein's scheme of entrepreneurial choice, general management and
program operations as different orders of activity, Lakshmanan indicates that
entrepreneurial choice is concerned perhaps with the total behavioral system in
the community. He sees the general management function as having an analytical
orientation. General management is therefore in his view the appropriate place
for inputs of a developmental, economic planning nature such as his own
expertise represents. Finally he sees program operations as being concerned
primarily with information and with operating on-going kinds of programs
without too many implications for novel modifications.

Another significant observation is that the way in which issues are being
raised flows from the economic and social processes that work in a community.
Therefore it would seem that some understanding of the economic and social
processes is essential to the development of a higher level of entrepreneurial
decision-making. Again the question of the essential importance of the
identification of the problem and the introduction of the concept of *key goals* is
underlined as a theme which resounds throughout the book. In reading the
Lakshmanan chapter one can see the way in which goals rise out of issues
generated in the social and economic development process in Puerto Rico.
Lakshmanan leaves us with a model for ordering the use of analytic technologies
in a community. He suggests that it is not feasible and perhaps not desirable to
attempt to solve everything at once in one big plan. But that it is possible and
desirable to put together an over-all plan for the kinds of information systems,
the kinds of planning models that will be needed eventually and could form part
of a total comprehensive planning effort. Each of the component models would
then be developed only as the need arose in connection with specific
management decisions.

Daniel Grant's contribution moves to the level of the structuring of the
government within the metropolitan area. His concern is with the over-all
structuring of a large unit of government encompassing the total metropolitan
areas, a unit sometimes called metro government. His paper is a case study of
three governments which have adopted metropolitan forms. He reports
particularly on the political stability of these forms of government and the
factors which have affected that political stability or lack of stability. Rather
interestingly he finds that the most important factors here are factors of formal
structure. Also it is enlightening to discover that a single government, rather than

complicating access of individuals to the political system and to participation in the entrepreneurial choice of the metropolitan area, makes access easier. Black people, for example, felt that they had better access to the political structure. This was true because the scale of metropolitan government permitted the introduction of more professionals into the governmental structure, because in fact there was a greater representation, in a proportional sense, of blacks on the council after the adoption of a metropolitan government than there had been before and finally because with metropolitan government, responsibility was more clearly established and it was less possible to "pass the buck." This chapter also highlights a very interesting phenomenon relating to the formal role of chief administrative officers. There is some evidence to suggest that where the formal role is spelled out in detail, the executive will be in a weaker position in accomplishing program objectives and general management objectives. This is because of jealousy and suspicion of other officials, and perhaps more importantly because the executive is then open to attack from all quarters. When the formal role is not stated as precisely, the person in the top general management role is more able to flexibly define his role and carry out a true general management function.

Staying within the metropolitan context, Kent Mathewson develops the idea of councils of governments. This device for ordering metropolitan decision-making is raised in the Robert Williams chapter as well. Councils of governments are the newest and most comprehensive metropolitan form.

Mathewson traces the development of the Councils of Governments (COG) movement and highlights the strengths and problems associated with councils. Councils of governments provide a framework for the implementation of metropolitan planning, especially if a metropolitan planning agency is a subordinate unit of the council. The councils also have the potential of strengthening the grass roots participation that Senator Muskie is concerned about. Mathewson notes three problems which are sometimes present and have proved significant in impeding the growth and effectiveness of councils of governments. These are unwillingness or fear to move ahead, inadequate citizen involvement, and the tendency to restrict the business of a council of governments to physical development. Change is inevitable. Councils of governments is one way of shaping change in metropolitan areas. It is an important locus for the practice of urban administration and a possible focus for much needed urban regional leadership.

Guy Black turns his attention to the question of ways in which urban management might be substantially reorganized with both the newer technologies of analysis and decision-making that are available and the increasingly articulated need for greater participation by people in the programs that directly affect them within metropolitan areas. He develops a very creative application of systems concepts, an approach which he helped develop when he was with the Department of Defense and later with the President's Council of Economic Advisors, to the functions of urban government. His analysis leaves us with some recommendations that bear a striking resemblance to those of Nathan

Grundstein. Area decentralization is shown to be a useful concept with potential application of considerable promise. The methodology developed by Guy Black makes possible pragmatic informed judgments about which functions can be decentralized with efficiency and other key social values protected.

Lawrence Roos and Thomas Kelly contribute a lively exchange on the management of urban counties. This chapter essentially deals with application of urban management competencies in two very different urban areas under different forms of government. The number of parallels is striking. There is agreement, as one would expect from two county administrators, on the pivotal role of urban counties in metropolitan areas. There is also agreement on the value of councils of governments.

Both men comment on specifics in the process of changing forms and functions of county government. Executive leadership is the organizing concept for this chapter. The district election vs. at-large election of councils, appointed vs. elected department heads, home-rule, and the legal and financial practicalities are considered in terms of their effects on executive leadership. The ordering of functions that Kelly uses corresponds to that proposed by Grundstein.

The capstone of the work is the detailed examination of one community, metropolitan Kansas City, against the backdrop of the issues raised throughout the seminar series. Thomas P. Murphy, the author of this piece, was present at all meetings of the seminar and has had extensive involvement in community affairs in Kansas City. He develops a detailed metropolitan study covering the governmental institutions and the public policy issues that are of concern in this area. He reviews the state of development of metropolitan institutions and the expansion of intergrovernmental cooperation. This material is presented in such a manner as to demonstrate the concrete application of several of the concepts developed by each contributing author.

The Urban Polity

1 The Change Process in Municipal Government

Timothy W. Costello

In beginning, I find it helpful to state some very simple but all controlling rules of the political game.

The primary, but not, of course, exclusive, mission of a mayor (or any elected official) is to enhance his likelihood of re-election, while keeping open as many other options as possible. Whether or not this is sound political science theory, I don't know. I do know that anyone interested in effecting change in municipal government should take it as fact. Those proposed changes that are perceived as serving that goal are supported by efforts to implement them; other changes have to fight their own battles, except those that would jeopardize the goal; these, of course, are opposed.

Apart from the selfish interests of the elected official himself, the goal does serve the democratic process in keeping the governing body sensitive to the values and wishes of the electorate. From a management point of view too, it is essential that an elected official maintain his option to gain re-election (or higher office) in order to assure full command of his administration during his term. Lame ducks don't make many changes.

A second proposition, trite and almost redundant, nevertheless needs restatement here. The principal coin in the realm of politics is power. Successful business leaders, we have been told, are high in need achievement.[1] Politics attracts and rewards those high in power needs. Politicians seek power and work hard to maintain it; consequently they respond principally, (sometimes exclusively) to the powerful. Since it is perceived power that is important, politicians assiduously develop all the appearances of power, display them frequently, but use their actual power parsimoniously.

Important proposed change needs the backing of powerful figures; they are more likely to back it if it enhances (or supports) their own power. Unfortunately, in recent years behavioral scientists have written more about the process of power equalization than they have about the acquisition and effective use of power. For that, we have almost to go back to Machiavelli.

A third preliminary consideration has to do with political morality. Reciprocity — among power equals — is the cardinal moral principle in politics. Regular bargaining and exchange is often a prerequisite to change, whether it be in dealings between executive and legislature, or among the Mayor's own staff.

1. Types of Organizational Change

To get me more fully into my topic and to provide an easy way to identify some changes in municipal government, I propose here a simple classification for describing some ways in which an organization (city) can change.

On the input side, there are changes in leadership, in structure, in process, both technical and social, and in resources — fiscal, physical and human. Location could also be added but it is not very meaningful to my topic. Here we can illustrate some input changes that have taken place in New York City municipal government. The Wagner leadership was replaced by the Lindsay leadership. Although in many ways leadership changes are the most significant type of change for any organization. little research has been done on the process through which leadership can be changed. Or on how particular leaders can be substituted for other leaders, in the corporate field and in the public field. We don't know how to get a particular executive chosen as president of a company, nor do we know, in a scientific way, how to elect a Mayor. And maybe it is just as well.

To continue our illustration of input changes in New York City, we can point to the reorganization of some 50 agencies into ten administrations as an example of structural change. I will examine the dynamics of that change in more detail later in the paper. The most complex change in process is the introduction of a new budget planning procedure. Under the leadership of the Budget Director, New York is moving from a non-system of line budgeting to program planning and budgeting. The change has both technical and social aspects. A change in purely technical process, only speculated about now, would be to shift from incinerating garbage to compacting and baling it into building or filling blocks. A change in social process is the cabinet style government introduced by the Mayor, substituting group discussions with the Mayor and concerned principals for one-to-one contacts between the Mayor and his commissioners. On the resource side, the commuter tax, initiated in New York City in 1966 (and soon to be adopted in San Francisco) illustrates a broadening of the fiscal base, comparable to finding a new source of funding for a private enterprise. New techniques of recruiting will soon change the nature of New York City's human resources. Even with regard to physical resources, there is a new attitude toward the land of New York City and its availability for total city planning.

I hope it is clear that I am identifying instances of input changes here, not evaluating them. The only proper evaluation of such change is their impact on changes in output variables.

On the output side, there can be changed goals, greater effectiveness in achieving goals, more efficiency, better personnel morale (as a desirable end in itself) and changed relationships with the market or, in the city, service base.

Here I again merely illustrate output changes in minicipal government, saving for later more detailed discussion of some of the dynamics of change. Largely as a result of the different values brought by the new leadership, a new goal has been established for New York City's capital budget: building human capital. Capital funds are now allocated to training programs to accomplish that. Another example of a new goal (formally recognized) for municipal government is increased community participation in a whole range of municipal decisions — in educational planning and building, park design, site location, expenditure of poverty funds, etc.

Changes in effectiveness (the degree to which stated goals are achieved) can be illustrated — in the police department, where converting police clerks to police duty increased police presence; in the Social Services Department, where emphasis on investigation has been sharply reduced in favor of increased social service, in air pollution control by raising standards of performance for incineration.

Improved efficiency is never easily accomplished in public service; and major examples are hard to find, although not impossible. Dispersing ambulances away from their traditional hospital bases to outposts located nearer the center of demand has reduced ambulance response time appreciably. Careful diagnosis of the nature of fire calls by neighborhood has made it possible for the Rand Corporation team on the New York City project to recommend a more efficient allocation of fire fighting equipment and manpower.

I have listed better morale, by which I mean creating working conditions that are more fully satisfying to the work force, as an output characteristic because it should increasingly become an end in itself for organizational performance and not merely a means to increase productivity (as it is so often described). But here no specific example comes to mind.

Changed relationship to the market or the service base, the remaining output characteristic, is illustrated by the setting up of the Metropolitan Transit Authority, making it possible to plan and provide transit facilities for the larger metropolitan region instead of for the city alone. Enlarging the market (or base) for whom services are provided, in public service better known as regionalism, would be helpful in many other areas — housing, air pollution control, job training and welfare among them.

Nothing of what I have said thus far describes *how* change takes place in municipal government. Some readers may even feel that I am only making out the case for the accomplishments of the Lindsay administration, although that is not my intention in this writing. What I hope to have accomplished thus far is to fit some typical municipal activities into a standard nomenclature used by organizational psychologists to describe change. I hope I have also suggested that change can take place even in as large an organization as the New York City government. Whether that change is good or bad, or as much as somebody else might have accomplished is not relevant to discussion.

2. Public and Private Sectors Compared

I want to talk about how change seems to take place, but before I do I have one more preliminary matter to discuss: the differences between management in the public and private sectors. There are some differences that facilitate change in municipal government, others that add constraints on change, seven in all.

a) **Periodic changes in top leadership** are more drastic and far reaching in municipal government. Except where there is a professional city manager and established high level professional civil servants, a city can experience a complete change in leadership in practically every important decision making position.

This was true in New York City in 1965. A two edged effect results. Because it brings in leaders who are likely to have different values and a mandate for change, it is facilitative; because new management requires time to learn to command an organization, profound and lasting change may be delayed.

b) **It is difficult to quantify** the goals of municipal government — health services, police protection, and the like. Its product — largely services, most of them intangible — is much less measurable than the product of private enterprise. Psychological research abundantly suggests that specificity of goal and specificity of feedback on performance both intensify motivation and facilitate adaptive behavior. The largely unspecifiable nature of urban goals and urban products tends to hamper change or to lead to highly visible but often superficial changes that have little impact on deep set urban problems. Here is one area, as Bauer[2] has recently indicated, in which behavioral scientists can make major contributions to urban management.

c) **The interests and values** of the municipal government's constituency are extremely heterogeneous, much more so than for other organizations that behavioral scientists study. Citizens vary widely in age, education, health, socio-economic status, ethnic background and interest in governmental activities. All of these characteristics are relevant to municipal decisions, because people with different characteristics are affected differently in important ways when decisions are made. This is much less true for stock holders (or even employees) in a private enterprise, for faculty in a university, or the congregants of a religious institution. The impact on the change process, particularly for highly visible changes, is to delay it and dilute change decisions into compromises.

d) **I have just mentioned the matter of visibility.** Here, too, municipal government is different. Many more of its important decisions are highly visible because of the interest of the mass media or of politicians on the other side. This is less true for other organizations. Given high visibility and a constituency with widely heterogeneous goals and values, change becomes difficult. From this point of view it is much easier to change a complex budgeting process (installing program budgeting — a low visibility change) than to change the distribution of police precinct stations across the city.

e) **Many organizations are subject to control** by strong boards of directors, operate within legal constraints, or are regulated industries under governmental supervision; none are as bereft of freedom to make their own decisions as are cities. Cities are creatures of the state and have no powers of government except those explicitly granted them. Where money can be raised, how it is spent, how employees are hired, and what standards are maintained are all matters that can, in some cases, must, be determined by legislative action. In addition to *state* legislative control, municipal administration is also dependent upon Congress and local legislative bodies. Effecting change through legislative action is highly unpredictable and requires tactics totally different from those usually employed in effecting change in other organizations. Nevertheless, there are times when legislative enactment produces quick and radical change, for example, the method of handling narcotics addicts in New York State, or the new arrangements for imprisoning felons. Here, as a result of legislation, on a certain date all arrested addicts and felons were treated in ways that are radically different from previous procedures.

f) **Because of the recurring election process** and the consequent need for early and highly visible gains, changes having *immediate* and politically *visible* effects are preferred to those that work slowly and with less to show right away. Often the former type change is superficial and sometimes meaningless; the latter type is substantial, resulting in important differences on both the input and output side. Walking in the streets of the ghetto is good human relations, good leadership and good politics; its long term impact on urban problems is questionable. Training middle managers of urban governments has little visibility and cannot affect performance except in the long term. Politicians tend to emphasize the former and reject the latter.

g) **Going out of business is an option** not available to city government. This is true not only in the gross sense that the city cannot shut down its services but also in the lesser, but nevertheless important sense, that the city cannot often discontinue a program that has once been established. An absurd example is that for three years running the mayor of New York has eliminated the budget for the Sanitation Band, but each time it has been restored by the City Council. Vested interests are so quickly built up around urban programs, and pressures for their maintenance became so strong that change most often must be the addition of things, not program substitution or the elimination of old programs. As a result the range of change decisions is narrowed.

What I can say in summarizing this section of the paper is that the political dimension, which introduces both facilitating and constraining factors, makes effecting change in municipal government different from other types of organizational change. Not a very profound observation but one that is frequently overlooked when scientists try to help in resolving urban problems.

3. Some Change Decisions and How They Were Made

The meatier part of any discussion of change has to do with its dynamics — how did particular changes take place, and how can the processes of change be conceptualized?

Earlier I mentioned briefly some of the more significant changes in New York City government, dichotomized into input and output changes, and categorized in relation to the general aspect of the organization (city government) that was changed. Here I would like to describe a few changes, selected because they illustrate different processes through which change can take place. Remaining as close to the change process in New York City as I do, I cannot describe them as fully as I would want. Nor can I see them as clearly as I would like. I can only hope that this tentative listing of municipal change processes and some of the details themselves will be incorporated into work that is now being done on organizational change.

Without any suggestion that the list is a complete one, I can list five categories of change, viewed in terms of the factors that led to the change decision.

A. Planned Change

Reorganization of New York City government, so that some fifty independent city agencies were tied together into ten clusters of related activities or administrations and two departments (police and fire), illustrates change planned according to carefully thought out principles and effected largely as it was planned. It is not typical. The original impulse for the change occurred in the 1965 mayoral campaign in the form of a promise to improve and streamline the management of city government. It was a natural issue to raise against an incumbent administration that was widely described as sloppily managed. Soon after the election, a small team of campaigners joined forces with the Institute of Public Administration to convert the generalized promise into specific form. The planned administrations were charted, and in early 1966 a task force was set up by the Mayor to write the plan into a proposed law for submission to the City Council. Sometime in early 1970 the last phase of this planned change will be passed by the City Council. There are very few examples of change in municipal government in which the finished product so closely resembles the original plan. It will have taken four years to establish the plan and this only in terms of the top organization. The internal meshing of sub-units and their successful functioning as elements of a larger whole will take years beyond the original four.

What are the factors that in this case made it possible to move so consistently from plan to accomplishment? There are four I can identify:

1) The change did not directly affect the average citizen so that no very powerful pressure blocs were built up.
2) Careful contact was made to win over what concerned constituencies there were, good government groups and unions of public employees.
3) The Council committee to which the bill was referred was headed by an intelligent and sympathetic chairman.
4) The change had a great deal of face validity as well as intrinsic merit.

B. A Confluence of Force

New York City's program for school decentralization illustrates quite a different process for effecting change. Here the decision to change in a specific area was

crystalized out of the confluence of a variety of forces, no one of which had
been expressed in form very similar to that of the final change decision. Despite
the paralyzing school strike, school decentralization was a fact of life in New
York City in September 1969; by September, 1970 the degree and scope of
decentralization will have been increased. Prior to June of 1967, so far as I
know, no one was planning that this would take place, the plan jelled when
activities in several different areas were brought together by a directive passed
almost accidentally by the state legislature.

The triggering element that brought these forces together was the mayor's
decision, born out of New York City's desperate need for additional state funds,
to ask that the city's school system be funded as five separate school districts
(one for each borough) rather than one. That ploy, which under the state
educational funding system would mean more educational dollars for New York
City, had been tried many times before without avail. In June, 1967 it worked;
in no other way could additional funds be given to the city. To make the
decision honest and almost as an after-thought, without realizing the full import
of what they were doing, the state legislature added to the appropriation bill, a
rider directing the mayor to develop a plan for redistricting (decentralizing) the
school system, perhaps into borough districts, by December 1, 1967. That
legislative quirk provided the impetus to bring together the various other forces
out of which the school decentralization program grew. These other forces were:

1) The mayor's desire to assume more responsibility for educational policy in New York
City and his own deeply set convictions about civil liberties and self-determination.

2) The Ford Foundation had been experimenting with a program that funded local
community groups to increase their influence on local school policy. A Ford funded
mayoral task force was established and directed to respond to the legislature's demand for a
plan to decentralize the schools, that by now was being interpreted much more broadly. The
work done by this task force and its later report played into strong currents flowing
throughout the nation and the communities.

3) The Federal government had demanded "maximum feasible participation" in its
poverty program.

4) The black community was learning to assert itself in many areas and had begun to
demand quality schools, not just integrated schools.

5) Their decision was a realistic acceptance of the failure of New York City to integrate
its school system.

6) And finally, the constituency most strongly opposing decentralization, the United
Federation of Teachers, despite its apparent success in the 1968 spring legislative session,
and the drastic effect of its 1968 strike directed against one aspect of decentralization, has
been hamstrung in any opposition it might feel toward the concept of decentralization by
the awkwardness of it — white middle class teachers seeming to oppose the aspirations of
black and Spanish speaking minorities.

It is hard to know what lesson administrators can learn from this vignette of a
change decision. Perhaps it is only that organizational change must sometimes
wait for a creative combination of supportive forces; or that constructive change
can be forced on an organization by the pressure of circumstances; or, and this is

the lesson I prefer, when things get bad enough, organizations whose continued existence is required by the society will be forced to change and adapt. It may be that in such cases scientists and planners can only minister to demands made by the situation itself.

C. Event Dominated Change

Labor relations generally, and New York City's sanitation strike in particular, illustrate another type of process through which change in municipal government takes place, one for which it is difficult to find an entirely satisfactory encapsulating title. Chain type change is a label that comes to mind. In this type of change the distance between the original problem and the final solution is connected by a chain of events, with each event forging the next decision, which then becomes an event for a subsequent link and so on from beginning problem to completely unanticipated final result. For obvious political reasons it would not be wise for me to describe in detail the sequence of events in the sanitation strike. Here I can only name a string of decisions that were ultimately made, all of them unplanned and largely unanticipated, each of them growing out of an immediately preceding event. In the process, the city's capacity to stand up to its unions was changed and strengthened — something very much desired by the administration but not expected out of the sanitation negotiations.

The problem started with the union demanding a $400 pay increase and the city refusing it; we ultimately agreed to $415 or $425 depending on how it is figured. Along the way, a well-established union leader was repudiated by his membership, a garbage strike occurred, and for the first time in forty-eight years in New York City a request for the National Guard was made to settle a labor dispute. State government was drawn in. Two major political figures offended each other, with impact on their national political careers; and the city's image for standing up to its public employees' unions was considerably enhanced. The sanitation strike is a highly dramatic, well-publicized example of change in the municipal processes. The change process unplanned, unanticipated, sequential and chain-like, in which major change evolves as a series of small but accumulating reactions to previous decisions or events, is characteristic, I believe, of much that takes place in both public and private organizations. March and Cyeart, and others as well, have made the point before.[3] My description adds another case from the public sector.

D. Accidental Innovation

In their book, *Organizations*, March and Simon, in an analysis of innovation in organizations, state that innovation owes much to accident.[4] In any case I am pleased to say that such accidents can also occur in municipal government. The example I have in mind, although it concerns an important city policy on air pollution control, has not received a great deal of public attention. I have selected it because the effect of accident is clear. In the summer of 1967, a major air pollution control bill was passed by the City Council after a long and highly publicized investigation of air pollution in New York City. The law required upgrading or elimination of incinerators and the use of more refined fuels for space heating. It would take effect a year from passage. The bill was passed and, presumably, that was that.

On a completely unrelated front, the mayor had established an Operations Research Council, drawn from universities across the country, that would, in an informal way, advise the administration on useful applications of operations research to city problems. One of that Council's committees was considering the problem of an information system for the mayor. It proposed to develop "issue maps" in each of which an important issue would be analyzed quantitatively, alternatives arrayed, and consequences traced out. In discussions with me it was decided to select for illustrative purposes a closed or dead issue on which abundant data were available, around which a map could be developed. The plan was to use such a map in a presentation to the mayor to suggest to him what could be done. The question of air pollution was taken, since it had already been resolved, and "no damage could be done"; and the analytic work proceeded.

In the meantime, as efforts to implement the air pollution law went forward, an impasse developed between the Sanitation Department, the Air Pollution Control Department and the real estate industry of New York City. The "carefully" developed law was unenforceable. A dead issue was now very much alive, and everyone in city government sought out the opportunity to view the accidentally developed "issue map" on air pollution. Ultimately a major presentation was made to the mayor and his Policy Planning Council. On the basis of that presentation, the original law was drastically modified and its effective date postponed. In addition, top members of the administration learned a creative new way of analyzing issues — an approach that continues to be widely used in central decision making. Something I am afraid would not be true had the so-called dead issue truly been dead.

And here, our conclusion surely must be, how can accidental innovations be more carefully planned.

E. External Intervention: Legislative Fiat

The Model Cities Program — a proposed municipal change that is promising yet hazardous, drastic yet consistent with what urban communities need — illustrates still another process through which change in urban government takes place: external intervention by the most powerful forces present in our society today: Federal law and Federal money. The imposition of change by a force outside the organization itself is, of course, well known in the private sector. It can occur successfully only when the organization on which change is imposed clearly lacks the capability of initiating necessary changes or lacks the resources to support the needed change. Both of these conditions existed in America's cities when the Congress passed the Model Cities Program. That legislation requires across the board municipal change in servicing inner city residents. When fully implemented, the Model Cities Program will have produced change in every one of the categories mentioned earlier in this paper. On the input side new community leadership will be installed, new decentralized structures will be established, more fully participative processes will be used and, of course, additional lump sum resources will be added. The hope is that on the output side, new urban goals, more fully responsive to disadvantaged minority groups will be established, urban performance around these goals will be more effective and efficient, and finally, the spirit of the city dweller will be raised. Despite the great power of the intervening agent here, all of this will long be more dream than reality. The statement is true because not enough money has yet been delivered, but perhaps more importantly because extensive changes within municipal government itself must take place before it can adequately respond to demands for change made from the outside. The rich new resources to be added to city funds through the Model Cities Program will, I am sure, in the long run, constitute a sufficient pressure to cause cities to change and strengthen their internal capacities and processes. Major change will have been effected — through the power of huge sums of money and Federal law specifying how that money will be spent.

Power and the Role of the Behavioral Scientist

In writing of change in political institutions, I find it entirely appropriate that I begin and end with the concept of power. It does not require a very sophisticated reading between the lines to find power or elements of power in each of the change decisions. Behavioral scientists who seek or are asked to play a part in effecting change in municipal government will need to relate themselves to some source of power.

The principal sources of power in municipal affairs are: the legislature, federal, state or local, with its capacity to order things done through the enactment of law; money, always in such short supply that its availability is always a persuasive argument for taking a particular action; powerful community groups who can exert pressure for action; and the men at the head of municipal government and its agencies.

Three principal entry points or roles are available to behavioral scientists to provide suitably powerful backing for the actions they would recommend: 1) political action to work for the election of sympathetic legislators or desired legislation; 2) community action so that the behavioral scientists become related to and accepted by strong community organizations; 3) the proper cultivation or reaching out to men in power to gain understanding and personal acceptance. Of the three, only number two is naturally, although often only theoretically, acceptable to most behavioral scientists. Roles one and three are distasteful.

In my own judgement role three is the most promising, and I base my opinion on routine behavioral theory: strong interpersonal relationships are a prime vehicle for mutual influence. Good friends affect each other's values and courses of action.

In summary, behavioral scientists can make contributions to change in municipal government. They will need the backing of some power base. Friendships developed with politicians and bureaucrats can provide that power base.

Discussion

Question: There is criticism popping up about some of the young mayors like Lindsay, that they really hit the style in rhetoric of change and in giving an image of high energy and so forth, but are really making very little concrete change.

Costello: You're absolutely right. I'm going to be messy now. There is very little concrete change. It's all in the spirit and that's what makes the big difference between the mayors of twenty years ago and the mayors of the present time. We have had all the concrete we need in cities. I'm not kidding. You know you can go into Harlem, and you can knock everything down, put up concrete buildings all over, and you have not changed a thing. You can build sewers and roads — I understand you are building a road right across the city of Kansas City, and maybe it is absolutely necessary but that is not going to help very many people who live in ghettos. What has happened with these high energy, spiritual guys in a nonreligious sense is that they are beginning to delay the concrete accomplishment by asking people whether or not they would like that. And that takes a long time to get done. The Lindsay administration will probably build less and accomplish more in four years than Wagner did in the previous four years.

Question: But I didn't mean concrete buildings. I mean concrete change, real change in terms of power arrangements, social structure, etc. Could you give some examples of those kinds of changes?

Costello: I think what is happening is there has been a shift in the power base in New York. The question of size is always a significant point. It is possible to grow something that is so big that size becomes disfunctional. That may be true in many of the activities carried out in large cities. It may be that you cannot educate people through a board of education that supervises one million students and fifty thousand teachers. It may be that you cannot run a police department with one commissioner. It may be that you cannot run a sanitation department on a city wide basis. So what we have begun to do is to at least relate the services of the city to the communities. We think we will have a better city when there is a closer command over the services at the local level than there has been in the past.

Question: You are talking about decentralization?

Costello: Yes, of schools and services and the decision-making to a considerable extent. One of the reasons why we are held back in our housing program is that we are asking people whether or not they think it should be a high rise or garden type apartment, whether it should be here or there. With a heterogeneous constituency this is a very time consuming proposition. One of the city programs was delayed interminably because we wanted a director to be chosen by the community for each of the three model cities programs that we have. In one community we had a Black, Spanish speaking split. It took a long time for them to agree on who should be the director. That kind of thing I think is responding to the spirit that is expressed in new politics and is very much needed in our society these days.

Question: The answer I think was adequate except that in general — I would like to see if you had an example, some specifics on the kind of structural changes that have been made.

Costello: Well, the success of our decentralized schools is the specific one. There is also an emergency rehabilitation program that is decentralized. We are taking violation records that used to be housed in the buildings department in the municipal building and locating them out in the community. We are allowing contracting with private repairmen to make emergency repairs. We are developing a localized sanitation department building in the model cities area. The City Planning Commission, which in the past was independent of the mayor and busily went on making plans that were then totally disregarded by the mayor, has become a very influential voice in design of buildings. Today you cannot erect a sky-scraper in New York City without getting the design approved. When somebody wanted to put a sky-scraper on top of our beautiful Grand Central Station, which you can do legally, we found a way of stopping them. The chairman just mapped the whole area to be a pedestrian area with no vehicular transport. Maybe they would redesign that building. Those are examples that come to mind.

Question: Do you have any developments of the neighborhood public corporation?

Costello: Yes, we have created a public development corporation through which we are able to receive federal, state and city funds; through which we can also increase black ownership of businesses; through which we can create industrial parks without going through the legal red tape which you have to go through when the city does anything. Whenever the city does anything, it has to go through the question of asking for bids. There must be at least three bids. If you are using city property, it has to go up at auction. When you create a corporation on the outside, you have freedom to act in a much more effective fashion.

Despite the fact that our city council has refused to give us funds we have created five local city halls in ghetto areas with representation from the Mayor's office. There are people in these local city halls who can command service performance. When someone says, "There has been an old mattress on my doorstep for the last three weeks and they, the sanitation department, refuse to collect it," that local citizen can go to a local city hall and really get action. Or there is a lot where air mail delivery of garbage has been taking place. I don't know whether you have it here or not, but in some of our areas the best way to get rid of the garbage is to throw it out the window into the back yard. If that goes on for month after month it piles up and you get rats, it's hard to get a sanitation department truck to clean that out, but through a local city hall you can get it cleaned out.

Question: I am interested in what the change process has been in the field of public employees and the right to strike. I wonder if you have any recommendation based on your experience, whether you are better off under the Condon-Wadlin Law or the Taylor Act or whether you need some other act.

Costello: I am kind of tender in this area. It is an area where the man has thrown me quite a number of hot potatoes, so I changed my own attitudes. I came into municipal service believing that public employees should have the right to strike the same as private employees. I failed to see the significant difference between the two. I wound up by still agreeing that there is not much difference between public and private but concluded that not only should public employees not have the right to strike; but certain private sector employees rendering essential services, like the delivery of fuel oil or the production of electrical power, should not have the right to strike.

I happen to believe that punishment is a totally unpredictable sanction. You never know what is going to happen to somebody when you punish him, whether it is a group of people or individual; therefore, it is not a very useful device for controlling behavior.

Question: And does mediation succeed in replacing the strike?

Costello: No, mediation is not adequate. I think that we are moving toward the identification by legislative act of certain essential services that cannot be disrupted and the resolution of labor disputes in these classes through a legislative court of some sort where the decision has a legislative mandate behind it. I do not mean a legislature should do this. There should be some kind of a labor court that finds in the case, and the legislature puts its imprimatur on that decision so that it has the binding effects of law where a wage agreement is reached, that becomes a law of the land.

The Condon-Wadlin Law punished the individual striker. The Taylor Law does not punish the individual striker. It punishes the Union leader by making it possible for him to go to jail, and it punishes the Union by fining the Union $10,000 a day or some such figure. So the New York teachers union has lost money, and they have lost also their check off privilege. The city of New York collects union dues through withholding payroll. When the teachers struck they lost that; so the Union has had to pay a computer service center to collect dues. They will pay quite a bit for that. The teachers did not lose very much, because we have a funny system in New York which was instituted as an economy measure. When you stay away, you lose the cost of paying for a substitute. But a substitute gets less money than you, so less money is taken out of your salary than when you work. So the striking teachers lost at the rate of single time. Then when they work Christmas vacation and holidays, they get paid at the rate of time and a half. Although they were out over a month, between the time and a half and the make-up time that was offered to them, I think they will get 5 days less pay than they would have if they had not gone on strike at all.

Sanctions just do not work. Now you can point at the John L. Lewis case which is the one case in labor relations of this country where a strike was broken as a result of a federal judge's decision to fine the union one million dollars. That was the end of that. This disproves my case completely.

Question: Don't you have a different situation in the New York teachers case given the dynamics of the Albert Shanker's teachers union tying into all the ethnic problems and all the emotions of the day. I don't think you have got quite the power arrangements that John L. Lewis had.

Costello: I think that is right. I do not think the teachers strike ought to be understood as typical of strikes. Let me illustrate something. We had a teachers strike on economic grounds in 1967. There was one district in the city, Bay Ridge District, a rather conservative district, in which all of the schools were open during the economic strike, and all of the teachers attended. The union was striking because we had not given them as much pay as they wanted. This was a typical strike. Bay Ridge kept all of their schools open; all the teachers there attended every day. In contrast, the one section of the city in which there was not a single school open during the decentralization strike was Bay Ridge. The teachers who refused to picket on economic grounds were the most gallant picketeers on decentralization grounds. So this point you are making is valid. This was not a typical labor relations problem and Shanker made the point that he did not feel his teachers ought to be punished economically. He said he would never ask for this in an economic strike but he felt that they were striking for the good of the schools and therefore should not be punished economically because they were doing something which from their point of view was helping the school system.

Question: What programs are possible in response to the backlash among the lower middle class whites?

Costello: This is a serious concern. The mayor cannot achieve the common goal of all mayors unless he tunes in to backlash of the white lower middle class. He cannot be elected in the city of New York unless he gets the votes of the white lower middle class. This is a little bit more difficult than responding to the black 25% of New York's population, because as a matter of fact the white lower middle class suffers more psychologically than they do economically. I am eating better and I live in better quarters and I have a fuller life and so do most whites who are in the middle class. They are not suffering. And even though taxes have gone up and even though there is inflation they are not suffering in reality. There are some people who are: older people, single people; but most white middle class families are better off today then they have ever been before.

There is not very much you can do to help them out when you compare their problems with the many problems of the people who live in the ghetto. There are severe problems on one side, and anxiety and some sensitive concern over the evaporation of the protestant ethic on the other side.

What you have to do, I think, is to deal with the psyche of the middle class and the stomach of the lower class. That is a very, very difficult thing to do. How do you do this? One thing you can do, which the mayor is doing is walking in middle class areas. I don't mean to be gross here, and I hope I'm not being misunderstood, but today and for the last several weeks the mayor had been visiting, for example, a large number of synagogues. We have held a cabinet meeting on Staten Island, which is a purely middle class section of New York City. In this meeting the mayor had each cabinet member describe programs in the works that will be beneficial to Staten Island. One of the things the elected official has got to do is make a point of talking to middle class people as much as he is talking to poor people. That deals with the psyche a little bit.

Dealing with the psyche is a tough thing to do, because they are going to ask you, "How about more schools for us? How about lower taxes for us? Why do you have to do everything for other people? What about public housing? Are you going to bring public housing?" It is difficult to face up to this, but I think part of the skill of a politician, demonstrated by the fact that he has been elected, is the ability to talk to people in such a way as to get them to understand that you can't give them everything they want without their hating you.

Furthermore, I think there are concrete benefits to the white middle class to be talked about. For example, Staten Island is quite delighted that it is also having a voice in the location of schools, since their schools will also be decentralized. They are also going to get some new projects. An important measure of the game of politics is the degree to which you are able to project an image, to dramatize what it is you are doing for people. We do a lot for white middle class people every day in the week, but we don't project it. Take a most routine thing for example: in an analysis of the police department for the city of New York in terms of the crimes committed, the ratio of protection provided middle class neighborhoods of New York City is twice the ratio provided ghetto neighborhoods. In other words, you can say to your constituency, "you're getting more police protection than any other neighborhood in the city."

Question: Has any thought been given to attracting professional people with higher salaries to live in the ghetto? For example, if you could offset some of the penalties for living in the ghetto, like higher car insurance.

Costello: That is one of the issues that have been issue-mapped as a matter of fact. The issue is stated this way: We have limited resources for public housing. We support middle income housing by tax rebate. Now, should we locate middle income tax rebate housing in ghetto areas and make it so attractive that we attract low income middle class white into it, or should we build it elsewhere where there is more land, it gets higher rents, etc.? We have made at least a policy decision that maximum middle income units will be built in dilapidated housing ghetto areas, so as to attract an integrated population. We haven't been successful though. Harlem has some really magnificent apartments. They are not integrated apartments. They are all black.

Question: We have to offset the penalties that it takes to live in the ghetto.

Costello: Well, some of the penalties are not tangible but psychological, such as the penalty of being the one white resident of an all black apartment. It takes a little doing to stop that process.

Question: I think anybody who would want to live in the ghetto would be aware of those kind of penalties, but the monetary penalties are also very real.

Costello: With our approach they will get lower rent. For example, they would have a beautiful apartment. The suggestion has been made to build air conditioning in moderately priced apartments in Harlem. That would be very attractive because most middle income families can't afford air conditioning. They can't afford nice apartments. But there are still the psychic barriers and also the resentments. Harlem is a black community, and integration is not the goal today.

Question: Could you tell us something more about the use of the task force concept to deal with the problem of decentralization? How has it worked? With what success?

Costello: I think it is a very useful concept. We have identified maybe 19 or 20 areas in the city. They can be labeled in a variety of ways but for our purposes now we can label them as areas of potential trouble. They could be labeled as areas of high social pathology. They could be labeled as high health hazard or poor housing, etc. There are twenty of them. In each of those neighborhoods we have set up a group of people made up of the following types: community leaders, including clergymen and some leaders who are obviously "good guys;" people in city departments that are relevant to the services needed, some in housing, some in health, some in sanitation. This network is in touch with an administrative assistant to the mayor who has been given visibility by the mayor. If during a hot spell in the summer somebody in the community says, "Well, you've got a little problem out here and the people are getting restless about it. They feel that they are entitled to this, that or the other thing." In that neighborhood spot they can get right to the mayors office. We have intelligence service therefore, and the police department is informed. We also have a means of rectifying the conditions that were reported very quickly. We think that this has been a very helpful thing in solving problems and keeping the summer cool. The concept, I think, and the network out there is a good one.

Question: This assistant with whom the neighborhood groups are in contact, does he work above all of the line agencies?

Costello: Well, no. I'm sure the administrator would not describe himself as above them. But you know, power is access to the mayor and not whom you are in the formal hierarchy. The guy that has the most influence is the man the mayor is listening to right now. The more frequently you are with the mayor, the more power and influence you have. So, in an informal sense, because he does have a lot of time with the mayor, he is a powerful person along with the hierarchy. As mayor's assistant, he is way down the salary scale, and in terms of hierarchy. It has to be a low status job to compensate for all the real power he has.

Question: A couple of summers ago when Mayor Lindsay was walking through the streets and going to the area where it looked like there would be potential trouble, this received much national publicity. Could you give us an on the scenes idea of how effective this was? How effective were his visits to these areas in holding down trouble? Was this more or less a gesture or did it make an impact on the situation?

Costello: Yes, it did. I think you have to analyze it very crudely and non-politically, but it stands to reason that any group who feels itself ignored, denied and frustrated, is going to feel better if the major public official comes out, stops, and talks. And Lindsay has charisma. A lot of people blame him because he is such a charismatic guy, but happens to be very useful. He is tall. He is handsome. He is dynamic. He is muscular. And people like to talk to him and see him. They say to the mayor, "Look, would you do something about these streets? Look, would you clean up that lot? Look, we don't like the policemen on the beat," and I think they feel better. They feel that somebody who has power knows they are there, knows how dirty things are, what trouble the people are in. I talked awhile ago about the importance of talking to the middle class. Obviously, its important to talk to people who are suffering real problems even more.

I don't think you solve problems by just talking. Don't misunderstand me, but I do think people feel better if they see a mayor who gets out of city hall and moves around the city. Walter Washington, who is mayor of the District of Columbia, was our chairman of the City Housing Authority. He is black, and he thought well enough of this technique to use it himself in Washington, D. C., where we had similar problems. Other mayors have used the technique. I don't think this is the heart of problem solving, but I think it is very easy to ignore the power of the presence of important people. I think Bobby Kennedy had a tremendous gift for making people feel that the government was interested in their welfare because he was there.

Question: Back in City Hall in New York, how does it work out with a mayor of one party and 36 councilmen of the opposite party? Are there problems that if he comes up with a reasonable program it stands to be defeated on political grounds?

Costello: There are a couple of things that I need to say about that. First of all, we have a charter which was revised in 1963 giving the mayor very, very strong power. He only has to go to the city council to get a budget approved in the first instance. A city councilman has no staff assistance paid for by the city. He is one person. He is not paid a magnificent salary. And the city budget is fifteen inches high. About two weeks before it must be adopted, the city councilman gets this budget, and he's got to approve it. He will shop through it. He will pick out things that he knows he wants to object to.

Most of the budget items the mayor wants have been approved as requested. Beyond that, if the mayor wants a change in the law, if he wants things different in some basic way than where they are now, he has got to go to the city council. But it is astounding how few laws you really need. The operation of the Police Department and Sanitation Department is entirely up to the mayor. Within the budget allocation he can do anything he wants with those departments. There is the principal of reciprocity that I mentioned in the very beginning. A shrewd politician knows how it works.

Question: Why have the council? What is the relationship between the people in New York City and these councilmen? I am not sure what they represent, but if you have such a strong mayor, then why have councilmen?

Costello: Well, the council certainly can stop any expenditure it wants to stop. For example, year after year for three years the mayor has asked for money for local city halls. The council has refused to give him this money, and for a very good reason. They feel that the councilman is the local mayor in his district, and that councilmen ought to be given staff and offices in their districts and be the voice of city hall in their neighborhoods, and the voice of the neighborhoods in city hall.

If we were of the same political faith, maybe it would have happened that way. I am not arguing that councilmen should not be properly staffed or should not be strengthened in community relationships.

Question: How does a district councilman relate to a sub city hall?

Costello: That is a problem. There is no relationship. The local city halls we have created are mayoral instruments and not councilmanic instruments. We like to encourage the councilman to come there and consider that he has a place there, but as a matter of fact, he doesn't feel very comfortable. This is a mayoral operation.

Question: I would like to know your impression of the present level of expectation of a model city resident in New York in terms of citizen participation and the ability of the city to deliver.

Costello: Health services, housing, clean streets, and sanitary facilities are problems in this sense. Expectations have been raised. I have a suspicion that this is probably true of an elite group in the ghetto area who will become sophisticated and knowledgeable and know what the law says. For example, the Model Cities Law says that all construction in the model cities area will make maximum use of local talent. Well now we have a Building Trades Council in the city of New York that has a very jaundiced view of that. They answer it in two ways. "We will build it, and we don't discriminate, and any qualified person can become an apprentice," or "If you want it, you build it, you go ahead. Take your local talent and build it," and then they say, "I don't think you are going to get it built that way. Go ahead and try it." In this example you can see that we have raised expectations, and these expectations are not going to be delivered in the time and fashion envisioned in the Model Cities Program.

Question: Do you see much in the Urban Coalition?

Costello: The Urban Coalition in New York has been successful in some areas and unsuccessful in others. The National Alliance of Businessmen, which provides financial incentives for industry to hire hard core unemployed, has produced more jobs in New York City than the Urban Coalition. The Urban Coalition has provided money for investment in the ghetto businesses, or backing loans or newspaper ads. We have a substantial sum of money that is now being made available through the Urban Coalition. I don't think that kind of a program is going to produce the concrete results, but I do think it has the value of pinning responsibility on the private sector and asking them to become involved. It gives them a lesson in civics. I was astounded to discover that the Chairman of the Board of Union Carbide, which is one of the very big industries in the country headquartered in the city of New York, had no notion about what the City Council of New York City did. He couldn't tell you who was on the Board of Estimate, whether it was a state body or a city body. He did not know anything. He does not live in New York City, but he is a bright, intelligent, very powerful human being. He needed a lesson in civics. I think here is where the Urban Coalition could be very helpful, in helping businessmen understand the way cities work and the difficulties of moving things in the city. You can get things done much faster when you are Chairman of the Board of Union Carbide than when you are the Mayor of the city of New York.

Question: Are you saying NAB is in competition with the Urban Coalition?

Costello: No, I did not say that. NAB works on a different basis. It is a non-voluntary enterprise in which the company gets $3,000 for every hard core unemployed person it puts on its payroll. This turns out to be profitable. I just received a report from Western Electric for example. They have taken on a large number of people. They have been paid for doing this. They held these people, and they are very happy because they have increased their labor force. This is a different program from Urban Coalition. The Coalition is entirely voluntary. The businessman contributes time, money, and talent through the Coalition. That has not been successful in the city of New York in producing jobs. It has been successful in dramatizing the urban problem. About ten million dollars has been collected through the Urban Coalition which we are able to use, as I say, to guarantee loans to black business, for some manpower training programs and things of this sort.

Question: Is it true the idealistic young people, such as the Peace Corps type, who were attracted to work for New York City earlier by Lindsay have had a short stay and passed on to something else?

Costello: No. In the summer of 1968 we had 2,500 students from 100 colleges all over the country spend two months in the city of New York working in a variety of city departments. We received $200,000 from a foundation to set up urban fellowships so that we will be able to select the 20 top undergraduates and college graduates to come work for the city for a small stipend and get credit from the universities.

That is kind of an indirect answer to your question, but I feel that what Washington and Kennedy and the Peace Corps was for the young people in the 60's, cities have become. Let me give you an example. Wall Street law firms have discovered that in order to get graduates of law schools to come to work for them, they have to begin them at $15,000 a year. We can get lawyers, graduates of Yale and Harvard, to come to work for us at salaries at least $3,000 below that with no difficulty at all. Most of the mayoral assistants are young people — most of them are recent law school graduates and so far as I know, all of them are staying.

2

Political Stability in Metro Government

Daniel R. Grant

I am involved in a comparative study of the three metropolitan governments of Toronto, Miami, and Nashville. While one of the major interests is urban executive leadership, my paper is only indirectly related to this problem. This is an exceedingly difficult goal to attain, whether one is referring to large cities or to small ones, whether one is talking about managers, commissioners or chief administrative officers, and whether one is talking about leadership in a segment of the metropolis or in the whole metropolitan area. It is very difficult to attain but it has never been more important than it is right now. In adding up the list of problems that we call "the urban crisis" there are two concerns of contemporary political science that are especially relevant. They are political leadership on the one hand, and metropolitan area government, often called "metropolitics," on the other. But candor requires the admission that political scientists have only begun to scratch the surface in research on these subjects.

By distorting the focus of my research project a bit, it is possible to relate it in part at least to the subject of urban executive leadership. The underlying assumption of the study is that governmental structure does make a difference. In looking at these three metropolitan areas I was asking questions about specific direct effects of adopting an area-wide structure of government in Toronto, Miami, and Nashville. But as I looked at my data and thought of this topic I must admit that the quality of leadership in these three areas shows up as one of the most important variables in appraising them. I would hope that the finding of this particular comparative study would have some relevance to you, perhaps in ways that you would not normally think of a metro government being relevant. So let me simply describe the nature of the study first and then some of the particular findings.

This study grew out of an original effort with a grant from the Ford Foundation to capture and record the experience of Nashville and Davidson County as they moved into a consolidated governmental system from two separate governments; from separate city and separate county to a single area-wide metropolitan government adopted in 1962 and inaugurated in 1963. As a part of this it seemed to be important to provide some comparative basis for assessing Nashville, and this is how Miami and Toronto were brought into it. Toronto adopted their federated metro system in 1953, and Miami adopted a system in 1957 which some call a federation but technically should not be called federal. Each of these, while somewhat different in approach, was working toward basically the same goal of area-wide government for area-wide policy formation and policy execution. In all three cases this new form of government was highly praised by its friends as ushering in the millennium while its opponents frantically viewed it with alarm as opening the doors of all kinds of Pandora's Boxes. Since I did not have sufficient funds for extensive opinion sampling of the population, my method of studying each of the three areas was to select a panel of knowledgeable people of approximately twenty in each of the three areas and to ask each of these the same sets of questions as to what they thought the results were from having adopted metropolitan government. Obviously, a study like this does not permit an appraisal of all of the aspects of metropolitan government. Even if I had wanted to I do not think this would have been possible. It is instead a rather selective effort to study some aspects of metro government. A particular limitation is that the findings are based on the perceptions of supposedly knowledgeable people; not necessarily what actually did happen but their perceptions of the events and forces.

The scope of the study was determined primarily by searching out the major predictions people have made for what would happen if area-wide government should be adopted in the United States generally — predictions by opponents, by proponents, and by presumably neutral social scientists and observers. This produced six major predictions or hypotheses. These may be summarized as predictions that: 1) metropolitan government will facilitate the solution of "area-wide" problems in ways a "fragmented" local government cannot; 2) it will result in efficiency and economy by eliminating the duplication of efforts, cutting down on overhead, and making possible economies of scale; 3) metro will bring about a more equitable distribution of the tax burden by eliminating the "free ride of the suburbs," and by providing services on the basis of need; 4) metro's adoption will be at the price of certain "social costs," such as the loss of small community pride, identity, and participation, and overemphasis on the public works functions to the neglect of the social service functions; 5) metro will weaken or destroy the sense of political access to office holders and political leaders by minority group members and by citizens generally; and 6) metro will be plagued with political instability and unpopularity because it is based on artificial, unfamiliar new boundary lines, and because it constitutes a kind of shotgun wedding of unwilling core city and affluent suburbs.

My emphasis here will be primarily on the last of these six predictions, and on factors related to political stability and instability under metro in Toronto, Miami, and Nashville. But first I would like to summarize the most significant findings about the other five predictions. First of all, strong censensus exists among the interviewees in all three places that the adoption of metro has improved the quality and quantity of governmental services, especially in coping with area-wide problems. There is some agreement that metro is a means of "getting important things done." This is a very common answer — "It helps to get things done that just otherwise would not have been done."

Secondly, concerning the common hypothesis that metro will produce efficiency and economy there are two principal responses. Taxes have gone up but the majority believe that they have gone up at a *lower* rate than otherwise would have been required, that is, that more is being received for the tax dollar. Secondly, expenditures have gone up, not down, and the majority believe it is a *net* increase in expenditures. That is, the actual dollar total is more than it would have otherwise been but also more is received for it. There seems to be a "revolution of rising expectations" related to the adoption of metro, although the word *evolution* is perhaps better. But the enthusiasm in a new governmental structure has the result of building up pressures for new services and new functions. This is very difficult for county and city government to resist. Perceptions of a new increase are strongest in Toronto, next in Miami, and least strong in Nashville, a pattern which correlates with the age of the metro system. Toronto has the oldest system, and so on. Overall, the findings on this hypothesis depend on one's definition of efficiency and economy. But it offers no encouragement to those who support metro solely to reduce taxes and expenditures. It does offer encouragement for those who want economy while getting more things done.

Third, according to a fairly strong consensus metro's adoption results in greater tax equity, that is fairer distribution of the tax burden. This reception is strongest in Nashville, next strongest in Toronto and least strong in Miami. This pattern indicates that the greater the number of functions performed and financed on a centralized area-wide basis, the greater the degree of fiscal equity that will result. In other words, in Nashville with total consolidation more people perceived the greatest financial equity. Toronto is next in degree of centralization and also next in degree of perceived equity. Miami is least centralized. But all three have greater perceived equity.

Fourth, there is no evidence to support the common prediction that the adoption of metro will cause a decrease in small community pride, identity, and participation. Actually, some evidence exists to support a conclusion that such pride, identity, and participation has actually increased. In Miami, for example, it is said that the pride of the 27 cities has actually been stimulated to cause a competitive struggle.

The prediction that metro will give greater emphasis to public work programs to the neglect of social services receives no support at all from the Miami and Nashville experience, but rather strong support from the Toronto experience. Some Toronto knowledgeables claim that metro did respond to their greatest need which was public works improvements; water, sewers, expressways, subways, and so on. Now, however, they say the need is shifting in the direction of social services and that metro is also shifting, beginning to take over welfare and education and some of the functions of this sort. So they agreed with this prediction that it did emphasize public works on the "hardware side" to the neglect of social services and the so-called "software." But it is not supported in Nashville and Miami.

There is fairly strong consensus in Nashville that political access is easier and that the ability to fix responsibility is easier. Toronto and Miami knowledgeables were more divided on these points. But Toronto respondents were more negative than those in Miami. According to a fairly strong consensus the political access of blacks and other ethnic minorities has been made easier rather than harder by the adoption of metro. That is a very interesting result which reverses the prediction that metro will make it harder to get political access.

There is a strong consensus that voters are fairly satisfied with the way metro has worked out. They are more favorable to metro than when it was adopted, and they do not favor a return to the form of government in existence before Metro. Surprisingly there is still considerable sentiment for total consolidation in Miami, and even more in Toronto.

Finally, there is general consensus that Toronto and Nashville have experienced greater political stability with their metro systems than has Miami. To get at this relationship, we asked the knowledgeables in each of the three areas to name the relevant factors relating to formal governmental structure. Most frequently mentioned were situational factors. Factors related to population characteristics ranked third. Toronto interviewees thought the most significant differences explaining their greater stability was the role of the provincial government in determining local governing structures, the personality and influence of Fredrick Gardner, the metro chairman for the first ten years, and the Canadian tradition of deference to formal leadership. Nashville interviewees thought the most significant differences were the elimination by consolidation of the two competing layers of government. They had a smaller number of separately incorporated cities, only six suburban cities, while Miami had twenty-seven. Miami interviewees also agreed that they had experienced greater instability. They had constant warfare with their system in the early years. They named the early hasty action of the lame duck county commissioners as the most important factor.

That is the summary, and it is now in order to consider the instability prediction in more detail. Basically the one viability test of the new metro government is whether it has the ability to achieve political stability. Two questions were asked in the interviews which related to the specific causes of political stability or instability. The first was an open-end query on the extent to which metro has been relatively free from or deeply involved in an abnormal amount of political controversy. What have been the reasons for it? Why has there been more-or/less-than in the other two metropolitan areas? Following this question the interviewees were asked what effect structural factors had on the political stability and acceptance of metro. Such things as form of the executive, personal qualities of the executive, the form of the metropolitan council, its size and selection, metro program priorities, fiscal powers and policies, taxing power, and so on.

I would have to admit to a little methodological problem here, since the interviewees were not asked specifically how stable or unstable they believed the new government could be. I wish now that I had asked that because it was a dangerous assumption to make. However, reviewing all the answers it is clear to me at least that there was a clear assumption on the part of the interviewees that Miami's metro had been relatively unstable and that Toronto's metro had been relatively stable. The Nashville answers indicate a strong belief that its metro had been unusually stable, perhaps even more than Toronto.

Let us look at the instability in Miami first. Explanations for political instability were reduced into three categories which are shown in Table 2—1. Factors relating to formal governmental structure were named by the interviewees more times than any other type of factor. Twenty kinds were named. "Situational factors" such as personality and particular events were named nineteen times. Surprisingly, the factors relating to population characteristics were mentioned only seven times and rank third to the others. It had been intended to use a fourth category relating to the community power structure, since this ranks high in political scientists' lists of explanatory variables in urban politics. But interviewees seemed very little concerned about it and it failed to show up in any of the answers. I think it is significant that formal governmental structure ranked so high. The notion of formal structures being an important variable has been out of favor with many political scientists recently but apparently this has not filtered down to the realities of political life yet.

The fragmentation problem involving the two levels of government was very apparent in Miami. Dade County not only has more separate cities (27), but it has more "full-service" cities already performing the full complement of municipal functions. Nashville has six suburban cities but very few of these do much. Miami has strong suburban cities in contrast. Those who mentioned the two levels of government as a factor related to instability were referring primarily to the vagueness and ambiguity of the charter in Miami. It does not clearly delineate the separate powers of each level and represents a constant source of conflict, confusion, and fear. Others felt that the existence of two levels of government, regardless of how clearly the functions between county metro and city metro are identified, is an inherent cause of instability.

Three interviewees thought the type of executive mattered greatly. When later asked specifically what effects the form of executive had on the political stability and acceptance of metro, a majority of nine said that it had contributed to instability as compared with only two who said it increased stability. We asked it both as an open-end question and more particularly. Only three mentioned the manager plan on the open-end question but when I asked them specifically about it nine said they thought the manager plan caused problems related to political instability. One thought that the manager plan has contributed to instability even though in his opinion it is a better form of government. Another said that a strong mayor plan would have led to greater party or factional loyalty tending toward greater stability. Still another spoke of the inability of the manager to get out before the public on a consistent basis, resulting in a serious political leadership vacuum for a county as large as Dade. One who thought the manager plan was a stabilizing factor didn't see how metro could have worked in Dade County without it. He also maintained the

Table 2-1

Causes of Political Instability
for Metro Government in Miami-
Dade County, as Perceived by
Interviewees

Cause	Number of Times Mentioned	
I. FACTORS RELATED TO FORMAL GOVERNMENTAL STRUCTURE		20
1. Greater number of separate cities	7	
2. Vagueness and confusion in spelling out roles of two levels of government	4	
3. Appointive executive (manager plan) tends to leave a political leadership vacuum	3	
4. Original method of electing Metro Commission	3	
5. Other structural factors	3	
II. SITUATIONAL FACTORS (PERSONALITIES, EVENTS, ETC.)		19
1. Early hasty action by five "lame-duck" commissioners needlessly frightened the 27 cities	11	
2. The closeness of the original vote on Metro encouraged opponents to think they had "lost the battle but not the war"	3	
3. Other situational factors	5	
III. FACTORS RELATED TO POPULATION CHARACTERISTICS		7
1. Unusually rapid urban growth has produced a "frontier instability," a "community in flux," "no established power structure," etc.	5	
2. Other demographic or cultural factors	2	

monumental task of transforming the old county administrative machinery into a more integrated and urban oriented structure than would have been possible otherwise. One who thought it had no effect either way pointed out that the people were already accustomed to the manager plan because of its use by Miami and by some of the suburban cities. Other miscellaneous structural causes of instability included the comparative ease (until recently changed) of initiating charter amendment referendums. Miami has had an abundance of these with one charter fight after another. Also mentioned was lack of action by the state to help settle things, and failure to provide a tax differential like Nashville.

Situational factors that are causes for Miami's instability received almost as many votes as did the factors relating to governmental structure, and the one specific factor mentioned most frequently in this category and mentioned more often than any other factor in all three categories, was the actions of the five lame duck county commissioners. Their actions were described variously as hasty, irresponsible, ill-conceived and threatening to the twenty-seven cities. They gave the strong impression that an immediate takeover of the cities by metro was forthcoming. These are the bad guys with the black hats in Miami. They are looked upon as getting Miami metro off to a bad start. Many of the interviewees saw animosity of the twenty-seven cities lying at the root of metro's involvement in controversy. They felt this might have been avoided if the blunders of the holdover commission could have been erased. In a somewhat different vein three interviewees suggested that the closeness of the original vote for metro and the clear-cut factional line involved caused antimetro officials of the suburban cities to believe that although they had lost the battle the war would yet be won. The closeness of the voting encouraged them to continue to fight and encouraged continued instability. This, of course, is closely related to the ease with which charter amendments could be initiated and doubtless helps explain the large number of contested charter amendment campaigns.

One of the miscellaneous situational factors mentioned by the Miami interviewees might seem to be rather trivial at first glance, but its potency has been confirmed in the experience of metro reform movements elsewhere. This is the nationwide attempt by certain right wing groups to identify metro with communism. For a metro opponent to be strengthened by charges from elsewhere in the nation that metro is a communist plot was considered by one interviewee to be an especially disturbing factor in the early years of metro's life when counterattacks were the heaviest.

Another particular stroke of bad luck for Dade County metro, according to one interviewee, was the decision by the Florida Supreme Court ordering tax reassessment of all property at 100% of value. The interviewee called it a stupid, horrible judicial decision which was further bungled by two county managers so that much of the political onus of reassessment came to be borne by metro in the public mind. Florida has a homestead exemption provision whereby numerous home owners had been paying no property tax at all. A $5000 exemption with a very low assessment meant that nobody was really paying any taxes on his own home. Suddenly when they are pushed up by reassessment over $5000 it is not just a matter of doubling their assessment but rather of going from zero to something which seems to them astronomical. Thus, an event totally unrelated to metro can add considerably to its political woes.

Although structural and institutional factors accounted for about 85% of the causes named, the third ranking reason had to do with population characteristics in the Miami area. Five interviewees expressed the opinion that metropolitan Miami's rapid population influx since the end of World War II had created a community with something akin to a frontier attitude with accompanying political instability. Related to the factor of rapid growth is its status as a tourist town with many part-time legal residents. The influx of Cuban refugees was also mentioned by a few.

The closest any interviewee came to blaming the instability on the community power structure in response to the open-end question was the assertion by one that the unstable population condition made it impossible to develop and establish a viable power structure. A related comment was that there is very little "second- and third-generation money" in Miami. Most of those who made comments like this, however, concluded on a note of optimism expressing the opinion that the city is beginning to move in the direction of more stable community leadership.

Following these open-end questions, the Miami interviewees were asked more specific questions. There seemed to be considerable agreement that the personal qualities of the first two Dade County managers had either contributed to instability or were responsible for the aggravation of unstable situations caused by other sources. The first manager, with a distinguished reputation when he went to Miami from San Diego, was said to have been too weak when vigorous leadership was needed. Conversely, the second manager was said to have attempted to assert too much leadership. Significantly, each one was fired after relatively short tenures as managers go. The third manager, Porter Homer, the incumbent at the time of the interviews, was generally thought to be steering a desirable middle course between the other two extremes. One person described him as a happy compromise who has wooed the cities, but on his own terms. Still another felt that the lessons learned from the experiences of the first two managers "may help in the long run. They both got into bitter fights with the commission and Porter Homer won't make this mistake."

Another factor which probably should be classified as an indirect cause of political instability, according to fourteen of the sixteen who answered, is "metro's program priorities." The strong consensus of Miami interviewees was that metro had suffered in popular support because it did not move quickly to provide some highly visible services or popular "monuments to metro." Toronto did this with water, sewers, subways, and expressways. One of Miami's early ventures was into traffic courts, which is the most irritating type of service you can get into as far as the public is concerned. They took over all the local traffic courts and metro had as its first official function giving people traffic tickets and hauling them into court. This was clearly not the most auspicious beginning for

Dade County metro. Another criticized the failure to provide more visible evidence of metro and felt there had been too much preoccupation with paper reorganization.

Discussion of metro program priorities was followed by the question of the role of metro's fiscal powers and policies in the political stability and acceptance of metro. Many interviewees related this factor to the previous one, pointing out that the chief reason for metro's early inability to provide some outstanding, highly visible service was their restricted fiscal power. While Dade County was given authority to provide both municipal and county type service, the Florida Supreme Court ruled that they had the taxing powers of only a county. This hamstrung them tremendously. In effect, the court excluded municipal taxing powers to a new form of government which has municipal-type responsibility. Most of the blame for metro's fiscal difficulties was placed by these people on the state. I think the voters would not be able to make this distinction but my interviewees did. They also scored the state's failure to give Dade County a fair share of state-collected locally shared taxes. One interviewee ranked lack of fiscal powers as second only to lack of leadership in importance as a factor in political stability.

One factor not mentioned in answers to the open-end question for some reason, but strongly affirmed as a cause of political instability when specifically asked about it, is "newspaper attitudes and behavior." Eleven said newspaper attitudes had caused instability with several adding a strong superlative to their answer. This was the reflection of the depth of their attitude toward the *Miami Herald*. One said that it is not a cause of instability and four gave a qualified "yes-and-no" answer, pointing out that both area-wide newspapers attacked and defended metro alternately. Almost without exception the answers were framed with only the *Miami Herald* in mind because of its large circulation and more active involvement in local political issues. Some explain the *Herald's* contribution to instability in terms of its long-term goal of total consolidation, and an unwillingness to give the two-tier plan a chance to work. As one expressed it, the continual insistence of the *Herald* on consolidation has been an unsettling influence since 1960. Another said the *Herald* has been the largest single factor in metro's instability. Others expressed it more in terms of the *Herald's* giving unnecessary emphasis to controversy. And one metro partisan said they praise it in editorials and murder it in news stories and headlines. When asked specifically about the role of Miami's community leadership and power structure, two interviewees said flatly that "the newspaper *is* the power structure here." The consensus saw a fragmented power structure in which a fairly poor correlation of downtown business interests and the *Miami Herald* constitutes the largest single force. One spoke of the difficulties of uniting business leadership because of a three-way split between the downtown business interests, North Dade industrial interests, and South Dade agricultural interests. Four interviewees spoke of a trend toward more coordinated community leadership with the press taking the lead in urging business and industrial leaders to get together and speak out on more than just narrow business issues. At the time of the Miami interviews, they had just begun to have some luncheon meetings of potentially influential people they thought — *ought* — to be the community power structure.

Interviewing people in Miami with sharply different perceptions of the realities of metropolitics reminds one of the old fable about the blind men feeling the elephant. Some felt the tail and thought the elephant was a rope, and some felt the leg and thought it was a tree trunk and so on. An outsider is soon impressed with a three-way split in views of metro. One group, mainly the suburban city leaders, thought metro was a monster that was about to swallow them. On the other hand, the *Miami Herald* and some chamber of commerce groups wanted total consolidation, first, last and always and they looked upon metro as a temporizing intolerable compromise. Then there was a third group that liked the idea of the two-level approach as a good and permanent compromise. This group was just furious at these other two groups for not letting the metro alone and helping it to work. As a community they were split into almost three equal groups on this kind of perception as to what metro was all about.

As a concluding statement on Miami it is plausible to suggest that stronger, more united community leadership would have produced greater political stability for metro. One is not quite on such firm ground in saying that metro's fragmented power structure was a direct cause of political instability, however. It is a much more complicated thing that that.

Turning from Miami's political instability to Toronto's relative stability it will be noticed in Table 2—2 that the same *category* of factors that rank highest in explaining Miami's instability also rank highest in explaining Toronto's stability. The many factors related to formal governmental structure come to the top. These factors were named twenty times by the Toronto interviewees — the same as for Miami. Most frequently mentioned was the strong power and active role of the provincial government in determining local government structure in Canada. Several went into considerable detail to remind the interviewer that no Canadian municipality has had the tradition of local autonomy of American cities. They have no charters and no home-rule movements. The Ontario municipal board is all powerful, in contrast to Miami. Another added that while there is no Canadian tradition of municipal independence, neither is there a history of excesses in *arbitrary* provincial intervention in local matters as we have in the United States. One interviewee who happened to be a strong proponent of total consolidation made the same point about strong provincial authority over such matters as local zone changing and passage of bylaws, but added that there may be as much discontent here as in Miami. The people simply accept it as a part of the structure. That is probably something of an oversimplification but it is different.

There is one flaw in the erroneous picture of an all-powerful provincial government running roughshod over the wishes of all Toronto citizens. It must be remembered that the party in power at the provincial level depends upon the

Table 2-2

Causes of Political Stability for
Metro Government in Toronto, as
Perceived by Interviewees

Cause	Number of Times Mentioned
I. FACTORS RELATED TO FORMAL GOVERNMENTAL STRUCTURE	22
1. Strong role of the Provincial Government in determining local government structure	8
2. Two-tier system a logical compromise for core city and suburbs	3
3. Municipal officials not excluded from Metro (Mayors *ex officio* on Metro Council)	3
4. Allocation of powers between two tiers made "definite and final — no ifs, and, or buts"	3
5. No opportunity for popular referendums, either for adopting Metro or for borrowing	3
6. Other structural factors	2
II. SITUATIONAL FACTORS (PERSONALITIES, EVENTS, ETC.)	12
1. The personality and influence of Frederick G. Gardner (first Metro Chairman)	5
2. The existence of a clear and demonstrable need, of which the public was aware	3
3. Success in rapidly providing new and improved services	2
4. Other situational factors	2

	Cause	Number of Times Mentioned
III.	FACTORS RELATED TO POPULATION CHARACTERISTICS	10
1.	Canadian (Anglo-Saxon) tradition of deference to formal leadership	5
2.	Fewer core city tensions with suburbs	1
3.	Balance and Diversity in economic base	1
4.	Other demographic or cultural factors	3

votes of the Toronto residents. More than one interviewee made this point. One who was very close to the original designing of metro said that the twelve suburbs were prepared to accept anything except outright amalgamation. They were willing to accept the power of metro but would have never supported a provincial government which forced amalgamation on them. If this is an indication of conditioning factors in provincial decisions that create metro, it seems clear that provincial authorities were concerned about the local votes and pressures and undoubtedly continue to be. It should be added here just as an insert that Toronto's metro was imposed by the provincial government without a vote of the people. This was a decision at the provincial level. There was no vote on it. It came after months and months of arguments and legal hearings, and they finally recommended the compromise. This would be a little bit like the state of Missouri imposing metro government on the Kansas City metropolitan area. Therefore, the provincial government had a stake in making metro work. "They played 'sugar-daddy' to help make it work by providing more generous aid than normal." The Canadian pattern of provincial decisions on local government structures must be listed as a key variable and perhaps the most important one in explaining the greater stability of Toronto's metro system.

Among the other factors related to governmental structure was one very similar to the previous one, but sufficiently different to deserve separate mention. This is the clarity and finality of the delegation of powers between the two groups.

The separate powers of the municipalities and metropolitan government in Toronto was clearcut, unlike Miami. In this connection it is interesting to compare the strategy and tactics of the strong consolidationists in Miami and Toronto, for both groups were pushing for the same ultimate goal. The Toronto move began when the city of Toronto was strongly urging annexation. They called it amalgamation of the total suburban area into the city of Toronto. Miami consolidationists favored calculated vagueness in the delegation of power in hopes that metro would evolve toward consolidation, much as the vagueness in the United States Constitution has permitted the gradual centralization of power at the national level. On the other hand, Toronto consolidationists have been able to accomplish a considerable amount of centralization through formal changes by the provincial parliament. The police power, for instance, was a strictly local function until by parliamentary action it was transferred to metro Toronto.

Three interviewees named as a cause of stability the value of the two-tier system as a logical compromise between the conflicting viewpoints of city and suburb. In view of the failure of a two-tier system to produce political stability in Miami, one cannot avoid wondering whether an equally stable system in Toronto would have resulted from total amalgamation. As long as the province was going to impose it on them, perhaps total consolidation would have been just as successful. In this connection, three other Toronto interviewees said that the key difference in Toronto and Miami is Toronto's inclusion of city mayors as ex-officio members of the metro council. This requirement from the beginning that city officials become involved in decision-making at both levels reduced opposition to metro in the city. Two or three took note of the fact that Winnipeg's metro has a popularly elected metro council and has experienced constant friction which must be arbitrated from time to time by the provincial government. One other structural factor which again contrasts sharply with the Miami picture is the absence of the opportunity for popular referendum. One cannot go around getting petitions signed to amend the charter in Toronto. Undoubtedly, the Miami charter amendment referendums were both the results of political instability and a cause of still greater instability, particularly when margins of victory were close. Nashville's structure would fall somewhere in between Miami and Toronto on this point.

There was one other sense in which the form of the metro council was related both to political stability and to instability. While this was not mentioned in response to the open-end question, several spoke of its importance when asked specifically about it later in the interview. They indicated that the fifty-fifty split in representation between the core city of Toronto and the twelve suburbs as metro got underway was a very important factor in reassuring the suburban officials. Toronto had seven hundred thousand people, the suburbs had only three hundred thousand initially, but the suburbs were given 50% of the representation. This was extremely important in reassuring them and getting their cooperation and support even though it was at the price of underrepresenting the core city of Toronto. But a strange thing happened with the surprisingly rapid growth of the larger suburbs and a slight decline in the core city. This representational interstructure became one of the principal sources of grievance and agitation for change. Toronto soon became overrepresented. There are 1,300,000 persons outside with equal representation while Toronto has a little less than 700,000 inside. So representational structure initially contributed to political stability and later to instability. In a reform which took place in 1967, the so-called Bill 81, they revised this whole structural system and merged Toronto's thirteen-city federation into a six-city federation in order to balance out this representation again.

In naming other causes of instability, Toronto interviewees were divided almost equally between situational factors such as personalities and events, and factors related to population characteristics. Topping the list of situational factors was the personality, influence, and political style of the first metro chairman, Frederick G. Gardner. Several of those who mentioned the power of provincial government as the most important factor also praised his selection of the first metro chairman, and stated that with any lesser man there might not have been the same results. Gardner had very little formal authority as chairman of the metro council, but managed to push through his programs by personal persuasion and practical political bargaining with shifting coalitions of council members. One interviewer quoted Gardner as saying "the secret was that they gave me no formal power and thus I was not vulnerable to attack, whereas in Miami they gave the manager all kinds of power, but this made him highly vulnerable." Gardner and Toronto's city Mayor Lamport worked together initially although they broke later when metro was well on its way. Another interviewee felt that Gardner's strength of leadership was a combination of personal qualities and provincial support and that he terrified the council. They knew he was the provincial premier's man and provincial aid was at stake. One interviewee made an interesting distinction between the role of the formal structure of the executive and that of the personal power of Gardner. He contended that failure to provide for a powerful formal executive in the original structure was initially important in appeasing the fears of municipal officials. Crucial acceptance for metro had to come from the municipal officials and they did not mind Gardner's later power because it was more like that of a strong floor leader at an international conference. When asked specifically about the significance of personal qualities of the executive in achieving political stability, all thirteen who answered stated that this factor had definitely contributed to the stability in Toronto. This was the only factor in which there was no dissent at all. It is difficult to avoid the conclusion that Gardner is personally responsible for a great deal of the political stability of Toronto's metro during its early years. Neither can one avoid speculating on what the effects would have been if someone like this master of political consensus had been the chief executive of Miami's metro during its early years.

Two other situational variables were named by as many as two or three of the interviewees, and apparently neither has been present in Miami, certainly not to the same degree as in Toronto. There was said to be clearly a demonstrable need that was not being met by existing local government of which the people in the Toronto area were well aware before the establishment of metro. Related to this is the statement that metro government in Toronto had unusual success in getting new and improved services provided rapidly and visibly. This latter point was supported by considerably stronger answers when interviewees were asked specifically about the significance of metro program priorities in Toronto. Both of these factors are highly rational in character with the implication that political stability will result when people (a) are in general consensus of a state of need, and (b) are convinced that this need is being met. Several of the interviewees apparently felt that this was the situation in Toronto.

The effect in newspaper attitudes and behavior was not mentioned in response to the open-end question, but when they were asked specifically about it, the newspaper did not come out too well. Five said newspapers tend to hurt stability, only one said they help stability, and the remainder either did not answer or said no effect. Most of them pointed out that all five newspapers are total "amalgamationists" and some felt that this push for amalgamation contributed to instability. One of them said that the people don't have to take the papers as seriously here as in Miami, since there is no chance to get an amendment or referendum. Another said that by assuming that metro is here to stay the papers have helped it. They have criticized many operations but they have never said "metro must go."

A summary of the factors in Miami and Toronto would indicate rather clearly that Toronto had three major things going for it that Miami did not: (1) a strong commitment of the provincial government (which would be our state government) to do whatever is necessary to make metro work; (2) a strong and popular political leader to guide metro through its difficult early years; and (3) a tradition of deference to formal leadership and governmental authorities. In addition, Miami had two primary things going against it that Toronto did not have: (1) a much larger number of separately incorporated cities in the metropolitan area; and (2) weak political leadership and unwise political decisions particularly during its early years. Of these five key factors, two relate to governmental structure, two may be classed as situational, and one as perhaps cultural, relating to population characteristics. It might be argued that one of the situational factors relates equally to governmental structure. So if you are looking at critical variables in making government work, formal governmental structure would seem to be a little more important than we have been saying it is in recent years.

Let us now look at Nashville. From one standpoint it is too early to assess the political stability of metropolitan government in Nashville since the study is based on interviews conducted only four years after its adoption, and only three years after its inauguration. However, these transitional years were among the most difficult and the most turbulent for Miami, and it can be said that the first three years of Nashville metro constitute one important test of its political stability, if not a full and complete test. Nashville interviewees made it clear that they believe metro had been relatively free from an abnormal amount of political controversy. The factors which they felt contributed to the political stability are shown in Table 2—3. The overall pattern of answers included twenty-one factors related to formal governmental structure, eleven situational factors, and only two related to population characteristics. This rank order conforms to the factors in Miami and Toronto, although formal governmental structure was given a considerably greater emphasis in the Nashville answers.

The Nashville interviewees felt that more than any other single factor was the importance of total consolidation as a means of eliminating the continuing rivalry between city and county government. Several made this specific comparison with Miami in saying that "we don't retain the basic elements for a fight." Another said that "we had the advantage of looking at Miami's experience; they didn't get rid of the city and county fights, they didn't cut that poison out." Still another said that "political stability is more inherent in the Nashville plan. Nashville didn't leave a lot of vacuums inviting controversy and opposition." It was clear that those who stressed this particular cause for stability were sold on the logic of total consolidation, and once having accomplished it they viewed Miami's metro as an unstable halfway measure. One interviewee contended, however, that a considerable part of the stability was attributable to the way in which the Nashville consolidation was achieved. He said the plan permitted each of the two major groups, the city faction and the county faction, to think it was taking over the other. Four interviewees mentioned the smaller number of separately incorporated cities as one of the

Table 2-3

Causes of Political Stability for
Metro Government in Nashville,
as Perceived by Interviewees

Cause	Number of Times Mentioned
I. FACTORS RELATED TO FORMAL GOVERNMENTAL STRUCTURE	21
1. Creating a single, unified governemnt (not having the two-tier system)	8
2. Smaller number of separate cities	4
3. Careful attention to drafting charter details	4
4. Elective chief executive (rather than appointive)	3
5. Other structural factors	2
II. SITUATIONAL FACTORS (PERSONALITIES, EVENTS, ETC.)	11
1. Political experience and temperament of the first Metro Mayor	4
2. Newspaper support (sympathetic reporting and editorial support)	2
3. Court support (sympathetic court decisions)	2
4. Other situational factors	3
III. FACTORS RELATED TO POPULATION CHARACTERISTICS	2
1. Homogeneity and relative stability of population	2

principal differences in stability in Nashville and Miami, although all were not aware of the exact number of Miami's suburban cities compared with Nashville's six. As one expressed it, "We were fortunate in adopting metro before we were severely fragmented into many cities." Four interviewees also gave the charter commission credit for much of Nashville's stability by virtue of their careful attention to details, particularly the political details. Eight of the ten charter commission members had served four years earlier when the first effort was defeated, and much of their second effort was devoted to making metro more politically viable. Three of the interviewees named the elective executive or the strong mayor plan as an important difference. This was partly explained in terms of the elected mayor being what the community is accustomed to and not providing a severe break with the past.

It is also believed that stronger political leadership is produced by an elected mayor rather than the appointed manager. I realize that I am getting into a controversy that pervades all the textbooks on city government on the manager system, but I hasten to assure you that I am merely reporting what my interviewees said here. One expressed the strong opinion that the manager plan is poison for the big city. While only one interviewee mentioned the metropolitan council as a factor contributing to stability in response to the open-end question, several others commented favorably on this point when asked specifically about the effect of the form of the council. Nashville's metro council is a forty-member council, thirty-five single member districts plus five councilmen-at-large, and wherever I go around the country people ask me why we created such a big metropolitan council. Most interviewees mentioning it said that while personally they feel it is too big they concede that the larger council had contributed to the stability of the government by helping people to accept bigger government. Another said, "I first thought it was too big, topheavy and unwieldy. I still think it should be smaller but the forty member council has worked remarkably well and has been more effective than I thought it would be." Still another said that he was against big councils in principle, but that its size has probably helped gain political stability and acceptance.

Several said that Nashville's stronger taxing powers were an important factor in political stability. They refer to the absence of legal limits on the amount of property tax levy and the absence of requirements of popular approval of tax increases or bond issues. The one major exception to this was a referendum in 1965 to adopt a one-cent local sales tax predominantly for schools. It was passed by a comfortable majority. A shift in sewer financing from the property tax to a service charge added to the water bill involved considerable controversy but the issue was settled by council decision.

Turning to situational variables, four interviewees spoke of the political experience and temperament of the first metro mayor, Beverly Briley, as a contributing factor to political stability. Neither these four nor others who responded when asked specifically about this factor spoke with the same glowing superlatives as the Toronto interviewees did when referring to metro chairman Frederick Gardner. However, they were moderately complimentary. Briley was previously the County Judge of Davidson County, so it may be said that in the election, the county faction actually won. Some spoke more of the importance of Briley's personal commitment to "making metro work" and to his wealth of experience in local government administration rather than to his particular style of administrative leadership. The interviewees made it clear that they were not describing Briley as a dramatic, vigorous charismatic leader, but were giving him credit for the capacity to absorb a lot of political hard knocks in the process of merging two different governmental structures and political factions. I might add that Briley was reelected in 1966 in a highly contested and close election.

Two people mentioned sympathetic court decisions as an important factor in achieving political stability. They referred to the great amount of litigation during Miami's early years and indicated considerable surprise that Nashville had been able to avoid not only the large number of court cases but also the crippling effects of adverse decisions which Miami felt. Tennessee courts have been very sympathetic with Nashville metro in their decisions, with almost no losses of significant court cases. Two of the interviewees mentioned newspaper support as a cause of political stability. On the open-end question, most of the others believed newspapers had helped. Many made reference to the fact that the *Nashville Banner,* which supported metro in 1958 but opposed it in 1962, had come around to sympathetic reporting of metro affairs. Several mentioned the warm support of the *Banner's* city hall reporter, Dick Battle. The *Nashville Tennesseean,* whose crusading support in both 1958 and 1962 had been a real factor in the adoption of metro, continued to provide sympathetic treatment of the news. Although the *Tennesseean* came to a political break with Mayor Briley in late 1966 and 1967, they sought to make it clear they were not criticizing the metro structure. A few interviewees indicated the feeling that the *Tennesseean* was too aggressive, with too much of a polarized "all or nothing" attitude in reporting metro news, and that this contributed in some ways to instability in the long run.

In summary, the Nashville interviewees placed great stress on the significance of formal structure factors in explaining the difference in political stability in Nashville and Miami's metro systems. The fact of total consolidation rather than creation of a two-tier system, the elected mayor rather than the appointed manager, the large council, and the detailed charter provisions concerning transition were the structural factors most stressed. Situational factors such as personal qualities of the mayor, newspaper support, and favorable court decisions were mentioned to a lesser extent. Population characteristics and community power structure received very little mention but on specific questions they were given an indirect role for *not causing* instability and they seemed to consider this as somewhat different from *causing* stability.

In each of the three areas I asked the people whether they thought the whole metropolitan area was a single community, or whether this was just Chamber of Commerce propaganda or "image building." We got some interesting comments that are shown in Table 2—4. You will notice that Toronto and Nashville generally agreed that not only they, but other people, thought it was a single community. In Miami it is an exact split with half agreeing and half disagreeing. You can argue it either of two ways: (1) That this disagreement contributed to instability, or (2) that because of their instability they feel that it is not a single community. So it is a little difficult to know which came first.

Table 2-4

Recognition of Existence of a
"Single Metropolitan Community"
by Area Residents, as Perceived
by Interviewees

	Toronto	Miami	Nashville	Total
A single community	12	8	17	37
To a certain extent — a "type" of community	2	1	——	3
Not a single community	2	8	2	12
Total answering	16	17	19	52

Let me just make this concluding statement. I think you would be the first to point out, there is considerable risk in attempting to draw simple conclusions from these three very complex situations. But with caution I believe one can learn some lessons in the critical role of urban executive leadership. In Toronto the strong personality and influence of Frederick Gardner undoubtedly was one of the two or three dominant factors in the early success of metro. This was in spite of his weak formal power. In Miami, it would be unfair to blame the manager plan of government for their problems of political instability, but it seems clear that both the formal structure of the manager plan and the leadership style of the first two managers were ill adapted to cope with many of the problems once they arose. Nashville's experienced elective political leadership is ranked high among factors contributing to political stability during the very difficult time of merging these two major governments previously controlled by opposing political factions. With that, let me throw it open to questions.

Discussion

Question: Do you think that the success in these three situations in part was due to the fact that you were dealing with either one county in the metropolitan area or no counties? At any rate, not more than one county.

Grant: Yes, I think this is very important. I don't think it matters particularly in Toronto because the key there was the provincial government's willingness to take a strong stand. So even if it had been the equivalent of five counties, I don't think it would have mattered. But in Miami and Nashville the fact of one county was crucial. We now could also add Jacksonville, Florida. In August, 1967, Jacksonville and Duval County consolidated in a plan very similar to the Nashville and Davidson County approach. But all of these were single county metropolitan areas. Given the American tradition of political jurisdictions with their many hurdles, I think a multi-county situation makes metro very difficult to obtain. I'm not willing to give up the possibility that some state may take a strong stand and decide that our structure of government in metropolitan areas is so important that we'll just start carving this thing all over again. I would be the first to say that this won't happen soon, however, and it probably won't happen ever in many states.

Question: You mentioned that when the Toronto metro was first formed the representation was split evenly, but since then the suburbs have grown to a disproprotionate population. Other than this demographic difference, has it developed that the suburbs and the city representatives demand different services?

Grant: They have now reapportioned so that they're back on a one-man, one-vote basis. I think a considerable part of the split was difference in goals but it wasn't in its simplest form, the suburbs versus the central city. Toronto and two or three of the largest suburbs were unhappy with the very small suburbs because they had equal representation. Four of the suburbs had no more than 13,000 people, whereas most of the four largest ranged from 130,000 to 340,000 people. So the big suburb began to talk like Toronto on the importance of one-man, one-vote. There is one study of voting behavior in that council which found with rare exceptions that they never really broke down on the basis of suburbs versus the center city. Part of this is attributable to Gardner, who got his support from either Toronto plus a few key suburbs, or a majority of the suburbs as opposed to the central city. Generally speaking, he was shrewd enough to avoid the simple dichotomy of city versus suburbs.

They're pretty sensitive on this point of suburbs being more interested in the hardware, and the center city being more interested in the social services. They claim they're having to correct this now. This is a real test as to whether Toronto metro can make the shift. Gardner was very sensitive about people coming to the metro council meeting and protesting. He said this was not the place. Rather, you're supposed to go to these cities at the lower level and let their representatives come up and vote. Delegations to the metro council meetings were not welcome. Toronto metro has added the welfare function for the first time at the metropolitan level.

There's no question now that Toronto is outvoted by the suburbs. Toronto no longer has half of the votes, but they have their share of the votes. They have only 650,000 people of a total of nearly 2,000,000 for the whole area, so I didn't find anyone who felt there was anything they could do about this. But some were a little apprehensive about an area-wide government being given the responsibility for welfare which has traditionally been a purely local function. This holds true even for more housing and public schools. In the original plan metro was responsible for financing capital outlays for schools but the thirteen municipalities were responsible for the operating judgments. But under the new reorganization, as of 1967, they added even more of the financial responsibility for schools at the metro level. A minimum level of operation is also a part of metro's obligation and if these five boroughs and Toronto want more they can add it on.

Question: You mentioned the problem of the elected executives versus the city manager. Could you elaborate?

Grant: My feeling is that manager cities have less visible corruption and generally have a better image, at least with the community power structure and the opinion leaders in the community. They have fewer crises of political corruption. I have a theory that no one will adopt metro at the local level without a highly visible public crisis of some sort. In Nashville it was sewers, and everybody agreed that 150,000 people with septic tanks was undesirable. This was public problem number one, on which everybody agreed. Here was the crisis, and the only question was what to do about it. Metro got a strong push because everybody agreed something had to be done. In Jacksonville the crisis was crime and corruption and grand jury indictment of both city and county officials. This, I think, would be less likely to occur in a city manager city. So you might argue that if Jacksonville had the manager, they might never have gotten metro. I don't think it makes a whole lot of difference politically in terms of the opposition of the people of the area whether they've got a manager or mayor.

Question: If you had your choice would you construct some form other than the manager plan to effectively integrate both the political and the management problem? Is there some other system that could better serve the cause of metro?

Grant: In recent years I have been increasingly reluctant to endorse any particular plan as inherently better. My early training in public administration tended to give me a strong pro-city manager bias. In the profession we began to have doubts as the cities grew larger and we began to see this leadership problem. But I have not reached the stage to say categorically that an elective mayor is better for large cities and that the manager is better for the smaller cities. I just think you have to look at each city and its traditions.

Question: Do you see some sort of merger? I'm sure you are familiar with the growing feeling that a strong mayor plan tempered by some kind of professional chief administrative officer built into the system with legal responsibilities may combine the best of the two plans. It looks good on paper and I am interested in cities attempting to do this. Have your elective mayor for the leadership purposes, but also have a strong number two kind of permanent undersecretary for the managerial-technical-professional competency. I'm not sure we have enough experience yet to know whether it works out that way. So much depends on whether the mayor really will let this professional chief administrative officer handle purchasing and personnel management, budgeting and some of these things. These are awfully important political pay-off functions and there is just this real question — whether it will ever work out this way in practice? Maybe the answer is an elected manager?

Grant: Have an elected manager? This is even harder to conceive of; I think it would be very difficult. After you have had a manager for five to ten years he may get so popular that he could be elected, but I don't know whether this has ever happened.

Question: What has been the effect of metropolitan government on relations with the state?

Grant: One question I asked my three separate panels of knowledgeables was in this area. What effect has this had on intergovernmental relations and in particular relations with the state and relations with the nation. The answers were rather unimaginative. I don't know whether it was because it was the end of the interview and we were all pretty well tired out but no one said that it had hurt relations with the state. One of the charges had been that the state will be far more suspicious of this consolidated mass of power. Here you have combined a city and a county. No one said this had been the effect in either Miami or Nashville or Toronto. A few did say they thought it had improved relations with the state since it had given them more bargaining power and they were able to make a stronger case for the things that they wanted. All of them said metro brought in more professional people in the various functional departments and that generally the state respected this professional expertise more. From this standpoint they got more of what they wanted, particularly in dealing with administrative agencies. So in this sense the limited amount of evidence was favorable.

Question: Do you feel that the new concept of an area council of governments can provide an alternative method for regional cooperation to metro? Not necessarily as an end in itself, but as a stepping stone to area government?

Grant: The council of governments approach is a step toward greater cooperation of the many fragmented elements of government in metropolitan areas, and I am for any more cooperation any way we can get it. I think this is on the plus side. For this reason I think they have to be supported. There are, however, some reasons to oppose them, but in general it is like being against motherhood and the home. You have to be for more cooperation. I strongly suspect that we are guilty of doing an overselling job on what the councils of governments can accomplish. The federal government in providing some financial incentive for them undoubtedly meant well, but I hear all kinds of overly optimistic statements of what these councils of government are going to do. Their major contribution may be area-wide planning in regions where they have not had it, but in most other respects, if it ever gets to the matter of attacking a problem which requires regulation or enforcement, the councils of government approach is just impossible. It's voluntary and the people are going to drop out if they don't want to comply with it. It may be the old question of getting half a loaf. Are councils of governments stepping stones in the direction of ultimate metropolitan government, or by taking the pressure off do they actually slow down the progress toward area-wide government? The same question could have been asked in Nashville. Our major problem was sewering the whole basin area. There was no question at all in the minds of many of the people in the early stages that we could have solved that problem with an area-wide district — one new unit of government for the function of sewers. But if we had done this, we would have taken the heat off and solved that number one problem, and there would have been very little impetus for going the whole way toward what we feel is a much more comprehensive approach.

Now you can't always say this. Many years earlier we consolidated a staff from the city planning commission and the county planning commission. This was a modest kind of consolidation and cooperation, and undoubtedly their area-wide vision and influence on city and county officials and others helped keep alive the spark of area-wide government. It was that fact which eventually spearheaded the study of governmental structure which proposed a plan of metropolitan government. There it did result in keeping area-wide collaboration alive, and maybe the council of governments idea can do this too. It can bring people together to talk about common problems. My hope would be that the answer would be yes, but I'm afraid it's fifty years down the road rather than five or ten, unless we have some real crisis that makes people act with some sense of urgency.

Question: With regard to crisis as a unifying force, have there been any instances of a traffic-control crisis bringing about pressure for metro?

Grant: If you just look at the areas which have adopted some kind of metro in the United States or Canada, it may well be that Toronto comes closer to this than any other. I can't think of any place where it was traffic by itself. In Toronto one of the real pre-metro problems that people were so frustrated about was that streets didn't connect. They had roads and avenues from one section of Toronto going over to another that came to a ravine and just never connected, and for years nobody could get agreement by voluntary arrangements to build the connecting roads. Only when they finally got metro did they get these streets connected up.

Question: What are the alternatives open to bi-state metropolitan areas like Kansas City?

Grant: Maybe I should urge you to be the first city in the United States or the world to go for a municipal corporation by interstate compact, and get the states of Kansas and Missouri together to govern this metropolitan area in some rather dramatic way. We used this in Davidson County as one of the selling points in securing the adoption of metro. It was argued, "If you adopt metro here the national floodlight of public concern and attention will be placed on Nashville and written up in the national magazines and delegations will come to Mecca every year to see how Nashville is making her system work." If you think this was an overselling job you ought to see the mayor's office with delegations from various places to see what it's all about. They don't always buy what they see, and maybe they just came to see the Grand Ole Opry but the mayor has had to have a person almost full time to handle the people who come to look over this new form of government. I think it has been helpful on the whole in terms of public relations for Nashville. But if you were able to do something in a dramatic and unusual way to get at least certain of the area-wide problems handled on this interstate basis, it will have to be done by interstate compact. Perhaps, while we are dreaming, the Supreme Court will rule that all these people are in interstate commerce and Congress will pass a law incorporating an interstate metropolis as a part of regulating interstate commerce. It will be a few weeks yet before this happens!

Part of it depends on how serious you think the problem is — whether you need a formal bi-state structure or not. At one time I thought perhaps civil defense in the wake of the possibility of nuclear attack might be the factor that would bring areas together on some kind of coordination. Civil defense has fallen into the evil days of public apathy, so the national defense power has not been brought to bear on this problem of metropolitan coordination. At least this is a possibility and someone may come up with some answer. I have always thought the Washington, D. C., metropolitan area might be used as a classic case of national action to achieve area-wide coordination. If we run a serious enough risk of burning down our national capital in the wake of riots and other things, Congress just might grab the bull by the horns and require the whole national capital area to get together under some interstate compact to provide area-wide government. Don't misquote me on that. I think it will not happen, but it is at least interesting to think about.

Question: Don't you feel that with the federal grant-in-aid mechanism there is really some kind of coordinating structure at the central level of government? Very clumsy, admittedly, but at least enforcing some area cooperation.

Grant: There's no question that that's a real problem. The fragmentation of the federal government is almost as bad at the top level as metropolitan fragmentation is at the lower level. You just can't bring all federal agencies together that have anything to do with urban programs, and the analogy was recently given of the Department of Agriculture and the Department of Urbi-culture. At least agriculture was a distinct function related to farming but urbi-culture does not relate to a specific occupation in this sense and every agency of the federal government has something to do with it. I don't know what the answer is to this, but they are doing a bit better in some respects. In Nashville and Davidson County some years back, the federal government gave a planning grant to a suburban area to plan a sewer system. Engineers were hired and the sewer system proposed for this suburban area was a beautifully designed plant which would take the sewage over and dump it in the Cumberland River just above the City of Nashville's municipal water intake. Here was a case of one federal agency indirectly encouraging not only fragmentation, but rather curious disregard for other governments concerned. We've had escalation of the number of federal programs so I think it's a losing battle . . . three steps forward and two back. All the great society legislation has so expanded the number of federal programs that we need to pause long enough to catch our breath and coordinate them.

Question: I wonder if the method of selecting the respondents isolated those who were attuned to metro?

Grant: The method of selecting the panel is subject to some honest and proper criticism, and I have a footnote there which I didn't read in my remarks. The biggest criticism I've heard used is that you will tend to get a pro-metro bias in that kind of panel. Almost by definition knowledgeable people are high income people and high education people and they tend to have the power structure's point of view. I tried to structure it into categories of people who had opposed metro originally and people who were critical of metro today, a category of labor leader, of black leader and some others. But even with this, there's something of a bias for metro. In Miami this shouldn't really matter since almost everyone was for it originally. It was said that they didn't know what they were buying. Everybody thought it was just county home rule and they voted for it rather innocently. The opponents now claim that they didn't know, or the people generally didn't know, what they were buying. In the case of Toronto, the proponents and opponents were split in a variety of ways and I felt the rather unusual thing there was the criticism rather than the support for it. They were very honest in their comments on metro not being as responsive to the people and not giving as much political access as previously. In Nashville I got about seventeen out of my twenty as being pro-metro. It's hard to justify but I would think that's roughly the way the people feel right now. Only one of the twenty said that they would want to go back to the previous form of government.

Question: There have been quite a few questions raised here with regard to the limitations of your research design. Could you comment more fully on it?

Grant: We've had so many individual case studies that go in depth in one situation, but you can't say they have meaning for all cities and all situations. This is one of the problems of social science generally. We have great difficulty generalizing. This is why I was unwilling just to study Nashville. I wanted to give it at least a very modest comparative background and I went to the other two areas. The ideal would have been to have a systematic sample of the total population, or perhaps of the registered voters in each area. But I didn't have this money, so I just felt the next best thing was to talk to a structured group of knowledgeable people. At least if I made mistakes in hearing them they would be the same mistakes in each of the three areas. So my mistakes are comparable, I certainly would not contend that twenty people can be counted on as a reliable reflection of public opinion. I would defend it however as the most valid knowledge we have to date on these three areas. There are several things that encourage me. I was able in the Nashville-Davidson County area to do some systematic sampling of opinion and attitudes of the whole county. Almost without exception these results support the results I got from my sample interviewees. This encourages me to believe that these twenty in most respects will reflect the opinions and the perceptions of the people as a whole. Some polls have been taken in Miami, and the people that I interviewed were reflecting those poll results.

I have been troubled by the methodological problems here myself. I would argue that it's at least better than a lot of research that goes on where someone just barges into a city and interviews the reporter for the newspaper and a few others who are available at the time. I have seen a lot of people come into Nashville and do this. I spoke of the metro mayor's having to have a full time person to meet the people from outside. I have just about had to have a full time person for the people who come out to Vanderbilt and want to talk to me about metro. When they can catch me, one of my frustrations is that they ask the wrong questions and I keep wondering if I should tell them. You can embarrass us a lot more if you ask this question, but no, they ask you easier questions. When I see what is written by some who go away, you can hardly recognize the area. So I would merely say that I defend that approach as a little bit better than what is frequently being done in the name of research.

I'm strongly committed to comparative studies and comparative urban studies in particular. The growth of urban areas and their problems are at the key of development of any new young nation. I think the cross-cultural or cross-nation aspect of comparative studies presents a barrier. It's very difficult to do. I tried to do a little bit of comparative study during a year I spent in Bangkok. I was fortunate enough to get some interviews with people in the Bangkok areas on how they looked at their local government. I came back to Nashville and did a summary study of the Nashville area. I learned a lot about how not to do it, and how I ought to do it the next time, but I don't think we'll make progress in this until we begin to do something.

Question: You indicated at one point that blacks had very good political access under the metro form. Could you tell us why?

Grant: My interviewees said that they had better political access. This included black interviewees in each case. So it was rather surprising a result. In Miami-Dade both the black and the white interviewees said they did have better political access after metro's adoption for two or three reasons. One was that metro had made the government more professional. It had replaced the old red-neck Southerners with some professionals who are more open on the race question. Discrimination was not a characteristic of professionalism as much as it was in the old political type. So they were comparing Dade County metro with the old, highly politicized county government. In Nashville-Davidson County, the black and the white interviewees stopped and counted on their fingers how many black councilmen they had previously. There were three black councilmen out of a thirty man city council prior to metro, and no black county squires, as they're called, out of fifty-five members of the county governing body. So out of 85, they had three in city and county government. Under the metro council they had five out of thirty-five single members. None of the five at-large were black. So actually, they didn't lose and they slightly gained in this respect. Some also said that a good deal of buck passing was stopped. Cities pass the buck to the county, and the county back to the city on top political issues such as race. But now the buck stops at the metro mayor's office and the metro council. This at least has fixed responsibility and they know where to go and where to put the pressure. Of course, the other argument is that you have diluted black voting power. Prior to metro, approximately 38% of Nashville's total population was black. After the consolidation of county it dropped to about 20%, so statistically it can be argued that they lost political strength.

Political access is a little different from political power, and I defined it in terms of whether they felt that metro has affected their ability to get attention when faced with a problem. Access is the open door concept rather than actually getting what you want. Many had said that people are opposed to metro because they will lose their esteemed sense of access. This is what I was testing, whether people really feel they've lost their access. In Nashville another study of the population at large indicated they had more confidence in the ability to get a hearing from their present metro councilman than they previously had from either their city councilman or county squire. So there was a vote of confidence in that kind of access in Nashville. In Toronto they felt it had hurt political access. Gardner didn't want the delegation coming down to the metro council. So they were very clear in saying metro in Toronto had hurt political access, but they don't have a significant black minority in Toronto. I had a category "black or other ethnic minority," and it turned out to be Italians in Toronto. Everyone said that while we have 200,000 Italians here, they never vote as a block. They have never been to the council to ask for something as a group of Italians, so apparently they will have to wait until they have children or grandchildren before they get a sense of ethnic identity.

Question: In Toronto you are dealing with a situation dating back to 1953. This is a much older experience than Dade County, and I wonder whether this discrepancy hurt your research design or helped it?

Grant: They had thirteen years of experience whereas Miami had nine years and Nashville only three or four. It did hurt in the sense of memory. I'm sure this failed them to some extent, but it also helped in giving them more perspective. I felt more insecure about asking the effect of metro in Nashville after such a short time then I felt in Toronto after a much longer time. On the whole, the perspectives had more advantages than the time lapse had disadvantages. But I would have to admit that this was a problem including the fact that two or three of my interviewees were not even living in Toronto at the time it was adopted. I had a category of metro officials, and one of them was a present department head. He was not even living in Toronto when the plan was adopted so some of his response was just going on his memory of what other people had said. One reason I conducted the research as I did is because there has been quite a bit done already on what happens *before* metro is adopted or rejected. There have been "rejection studies" one after another, and then there are pre-metro studies of the two or three cases where metro has been adopted. I felt the greatest need was to go in after it was adopted and study the changes that have occurred because of its adoption. So my emphasis was on post-adoption politics and post-adoption changes.

Question: Are we asking the questions you wanted to hear?

Grant: Yes, I think you've asked some very interesting questions, but I feel like apologizing in one sense. I certainly do not want to imply that I think that area-wide government in the sense of consolidation is realistic for this area. I have come to talk about my experience and you people have to make of it what you will. I am inclined to believe that it's not very realistic politically to talk in terms of this experience as exportable wholesale to the Kansas City area, but I would defend it as having certain elements that are exportable or at least of value to Kansas City. But I don't want to suggest to you that I am trying to sell something either here to this area or to this country.

Question: What kind of aids are available with regard to structural changes for the promotion of the metro idea in the Kansas City area in particular? Is there anything we ought to be talking about or doing over a period of time?

Grant: I personally think that the idea in the abstract should not leave you cold, in the sense that I would defend very strongly the idea that you have a reasonably single metropolitan community here. I think it is important for the total community to be able to get together and make some decisions for the total area, in the best interest of the total area. It is most unfortunate that white suburbanites don't have to confront practically the problem of the blight and slums and racial ghettos in the city. So there are many reasons I could argue in the abstract for some kind of area-wide government. But if you're talking about what is realistic politically, realistic legally, realistic from any kind of human relations standpoint, and when you add this interstate wall between your areas plus the multi-county situation, then you have virtually insurmountable barriers to actual metro government.

But I would also ask whether it troubles you that throughout virtually all of our 231 metropolitan areas in the United States, the higher-income predominantly white suburbanites are politically segregated from the lower income, largely black, and non Anglo-Saxon city residents. It seems to me that this problem is going to be increasingly critical in the future. This disturbs me terribly. There are various ways of getting at this, and one is simply to go to Washington to compel the suburbanites to participate in the solutions of inner city problems. If you ask me what I think is coming, I think that is probably the way we're headed, but it disturbs me that we can't do it at a local level.

I partially agree that right now metropolitan government is politically unfeasible. However, I would say that in the process of making various plans and arrangements, perhaps it would be timely to plot out those kinds of arrangements that can eventually lead to something bigger and better. In reaching toward the bigger and better mark, I think we must do more than respond to crises. By mistakenly concentrating only on crises we ignore the root causes and eventually allow them to overwhelm us — like a cancer. What I'd rather see is that we work in fields, step by step bringing together the government to meet structural and functional problems. For instance, the Missouri Constitution provides that the county lines be set by statutes, as well as consolidation procedures. I can see the feasibility of the consolidation of a number of county governments.

Question: You talked about the relationship between structure and stability. Is there also a relationship between structure and leadership?

Grant: I think I would have to say yes. I'll have to add, though, my surprise that the answer came out so strongly on the importance of the structural factors. I was surprised although it supports my own bias. I have committed part of my life to tinkering with structure, and it helps your ego to find out that it is a little more important than many people have been thinking. Yet, I'm just a little skeptical that it's quite as important as these people indicated. Political scientists for years have been talking about how important it is to adopt a master plan, and now there has been a backlash in saying that all that matters is the people who run it. There may be a middle ground here. Let's try to understand that structure is more important than we had suspected, although it's not everything. Structure does influence even the capacity of community leaders to rally people to causes. Structure will tend to attract certain community's leaders into action and certain other kinds of structure will repel community leaders. It has been argued, and I think I agree, that the new structure has caused more civic interest and civic action particularly among young professional people. Again, though, it brought in the suburbanites who had previously been considered carpetbaggers outside the border of the old city government. For the first time, the mayor could appoint suburban people to certain key commissions, boards, and agencies. Structure in Nashville provided an open door to getting a new group of people involved.

3

Bridging the Gap Between Citizens and City Government

Randy H. Hamilton

Cardinal Montini, the Archbishop of Milan, later Pope Paul VI, said that in his opinion it was the role of cities to establish programs which would tend to make them the institutions where men are working for the union of the people, for social peace, for the welfare of the poor, for progress, justice, and liberty. And that is the view of the city that I am going to use in this paper, an institution working for those things.

We have in America a unique device for solving our social problems and that is the local nature of cities. We do not have to wait for directives from a Ministry of the Interior, or from a Ministry of Home Affairs, or whatever the title may be, as is frequently the case in European countries. Given this advantage, our problem is to learn how to administer cities for all their citizens and not just some of them. The stakes are fairly simple. If we do not learn how to do that, then our American cities are in fact in danger of becoming irrelevant to the major domestic problems of our country today. If they become irrelevant, then they may in fact become vestigial organs of government. Inevitably the national government will respond if the cities do not.

It is useless for city officials to hide behind the often repeated lament that they do not have the responsibility, the financial resources, the organization, that they do not have the mechanisms to cope with the problems. The lament may make administrators feel better at night when they go home to sleep after a long and weary day, but it is a useless lament and will produce nothing. I recognize, of course, that cities come in different size horsepowers. Some of them are in need of drastic overhaul in terms of their engine. Some of them react quite slowly. Some of them have power steering, others have power brakes. Some have just had major tune-ups. Some rely on the bull-horn. Some have experienced men in the driver's seat, others do not. Some cities are under the control of hot-headed hotrodders, others are indeed driven by quiet, elderly people who expect the machine to function only as it goes from home to school to church. As city councilmen know, or are learning rapidly, cities also come out with new models every two years. It is a fact that the councilmanic turnover in American cities runs around 25% every two years.[1] And it is quite difficult for city administrators to deal with these changes in councilmanic makeup.

Nevertheless, cities are beyond doubt the most innovative level of government in America today. The problem is the glass half full of water conundrum. Is it half empty or half full? I take the view that it is half full. We are using city departments for social change and learning how to relate between our citizens and the government structure in such a multitudinous variety of ways that it is quite literally impossible to keep up with what's happening.

Even such a stuffy city department as a treasury can be utilized as an instrument for social change and as an instrument for relation with its community. Some cities, for example, have begun to spread their deposits in neighborhood banks rather than in the central bank downtown, thereby guaranteeing neighborhood banks an annual float of city funds, which increases their public holdings and consequently their lendability. By guaranteeing a minimum annual float of deposits and thus creating lendability in those banks, the cities extract a *quid pro quo* from the bank and say, "We will not only see that you comply with normal F.E.P.C. requirements but we will also demand that you utilize a portion of this increased lendability for socially desirable programs in your neighborhood, such as loans to small businesses, loans to home owners and renters who ordinarily would not qualify for typical bank loans, loans to minority controlled business and industries, and loans for neighborhood improvement projects." Banks that serve as depositories for city funds are now being required by some cities to certify not just that their hiring practices are not discriminatory but that in fact they have a program to move up into the executive ranks of the banks those people who would not formerly have held executive positions.

City courts are rapidly becoming instruments for social change. Policies of bail on one's own recognition are becoming increasingly numerous. If I were arrested tonight, for example, it would not be very difficult for me to provide bail. If I were arrested for a motor vehicle problem, I have an A A A card which gives me a bail. Otherwise I could get bail from a bail bondsman, or perhaps I could even post a certified check. A person not in my social and economic class, on the other hand, has a great deal of difficulty in posting bail. But there is now good social research in several cities that indicates that determining whether a person is in fact a good risk is just as good a guarantee of appearance in court as a money bond. The loss rate is about 4.2% either way you go, by money or on one's own recognition.

Police departments can be used as instruments for social change. Such simple mechanisms as issuing summonses for the usual Saturday night family argument is a good example. A great deal of police work is concerned with extended family arguments — the guy who beats his wife on Saturday night because he had too much at the saloon, or maybe at the country club. These become a police matter and are reported as crimes, assault with a deadly weapon. The issuance of a summons for crimes of that nature, if they are in fact crimes, can have a tremendous effect on the relationship of the local government through its police department and its citizens.

Recreation departments can be utilized to bridge the gap between the citizen and his community. All over the country we see signs reading "Keep off the grass." One wonders what a park is for. Why not suggest that using public parks for a "love-in" is in fact a legitimate purpose of government?

Even a purchasing department can be innovative and creatively utilized to bridge the gap between citizens and the community. Many cities are now requiring, as a precedent condition for the award of a contract, not only that the contractor but all unions and subcontractors as well certify that they have fair employment practices and that they are not lily white unions. There is really nothing startling here. Why should public funds be utilized for construction purposes through unions and contractors that are lily white? If public funds are being used, why should some members of the public be excluded from participating in that work? Public construction programs at the municipal level in the United States now total over twelve billion dollars a year. That is a billion dollars a month — a sizeable portion of the construction in this country.

Personnel departments are beginning to reorganize the delivery mechanisms for human service. We have not even scratched the surface in developing new sources of manpower for the public service at the local level. And yet we know from very reliable statistics that, excluding school teachers, local governments in America are looking for one thousand new employees per day. The whole concept of "new careers" is just beginning to percolate into personnel departments in cities.

I am weary of policy prescriptions that tell us that we must do such and such within X years, or that unless we do thus and such by a week from next Tuesday the whole system is going to explode. That is simply not going to happen in this country. We stand on the shoulders of giants, and our descendants will look upon our times of turbulence with precisely the admiration that we look upon our forebears. We have the courage equal to the task, as they had; and we are discussing our problems openly and frankly, as they did. I am an urbanist optimist, optimistic because we have never stopped redesigning our administrative structure to bridge the gap between the citizen and the community. Any notion that we have slowed that process down is simply wrong. We'll look back in the year 2000 at the structures of local government we have now and consider them just as quaint as we now consider the structures of local government we had in America fifty years ago. Why shouldn't the people of the year 2000 consider our structures and administrative organizations quaint by their standards? As others have pointed out, there is a striking disparity between the literature of protest and the fact that a clear majority of Americans who live in our urban areas look upon their lifetime experience as one of progress and improvement and not one of retrogression. The clear majority of Americans see their lot as being better than that of their parents and confidently expect that their children will do a little better still. Let me use some examples and illustrations to explain why I am an urban optimist.

Take the question of housing. In the mid-nineteenth century the teeming slums and conditions of life in nearly all of our cities were incredibly shocking even by the middle class standards of that time. By contrast the contemporary slum areas of East St. Louis would look benign. We have dramatically improved housing conditions and reduced the stock of substandard housing in this country most markedly since 1950. The best available census data we have indicates that the number of substandard units declined from 14.8 million in 1950 to about 8.4 million in 1960 — 25% improvement. And while 15% of our population still lives in substandard housing, only two thirds of that percentage live in the urban areas. The impressive decrease of substandard housing has occurred despite the fact that almost one million metropolitan housing units went from white to non-white in that same period of time. Almost 30% of all black families living in metropolitan areas occupy housing that ten years ago was occupied by whites. The number of black families living in substandard housing decreased 20% from 1950 to 1960, from 2.8 million to 2.3 million.[2] I do not for one moment suggest that we stop; I do suggest that we look at what we have done. From that point of view we may be somewhat more optimistic.

Another example is transportation. Evidence indicates that the transportation problems of our cities forty, fifty, and sixty years ago were infinitely worse than they are today. A century ago New York's downtown area was a jumble of brewery drays, horse trolleys, hackney coaches and steam locomotives. The situation was so acute that the cities in those days built pedestrian overpasses over streets because you could not walk across them.

Or take the broad field of public services. No reasonably well informed person can doubt that our public urban services are incomparably better today than they were forty years ago. To illustrate this, let me quote to you from a chap by the name of Lincoln Steffens who wrote *The Shame of the Cities* around the turn of the century.

The visitor is told of the wealth of the residents, of the financial strength of the banks and of the growing importance of the industry yet he sees poorly paved, refuse burdened streets and dusty or mud covered alleys. He passes a ramshackle firetrap crowded with the sick and discovers that it is the city hospital. He calls at the new city hall and finds that half the entrance is boarded up with pine planks to cover an unfinished interior. Finally he turns a tap in the hotel to see liquid mud flow into the wash basin or wash tub.[3]

Mr. Steffens wrote those words in St. Louis, Missouri. I will not take up any more time to illustrate my view as an urban optimist. The fact that I am an optimist however, should not blind me and should not blind any of us to the kinds of problems to which I alluded. In addition to the kinds of problems that beset us now, we must realize that we are going to have a hundred million more people by the turn of the century. Ninety percent of the additional hundred million will be living in the cities.

Let's turn to the minority of our population. Here I refer to the heart and core of our cities. This heart tends to be both old and black. New institutions are needed if we are to bridge the gap between the heart of our cities and the city hall. New kinds of involvement are required. New reforms are necessary. I suggest that we are about to embark on the second wave of municipal reform within a century. We embarked upon the first wave about fifty years ago, shortly after the turn of the century. By and large we have accomplished the goals of that reform movement. My father viewed those goals as beyond the realm of possibility, just as we here today think about the second wave of reform and say, "Impossible!" Who would have thought fifty years ago that most local government employees in the United States would be under a merit system? Who would have thought fifty years ago that the majority of cities in the United States over 10,000 in population would be governed by a council-manager form of government? Who would have thought fifty years ago that retirement systems would cover most government employees? Who would have thought fifty years ago that most of the reforms, which frankly came out of the midwestern America, would have been achieved in so short a time? What now remains for us to do is to contemplate the second wave of reform.

The quest for a higher quality of human existence in the city should be reinforced with new ideas, new approaches, new actions. Where existing programs fail to meet targeted needs they should be revised and reconstituted. We are about to reach the point where we get *hardening of the categories.* Some of the approaches that we tried in the post-Watts era are failing quite obviously, but they too have become institutionalized. We lack the guts in many cases to realize that these initial reactions and these initial experiments have failed.

Let me lay out for you some of the things which are today uncommon in the adiministrative structure of local government but which I think will be common outcomes of the second wave of reform. First of all, cities should engage in social planning activities. There is a department of city planning in just about every city hall in the United States over 25,000 in population. For the most part these departments have forgotten people and emphasize things. Urban planners have failed to collaborate with their clients — the citizens. The present approach in many cities smacks of the Renaissance. Only the patron has changed. The modern patron is usually the director of planning or redevelopment. He concentrates on urban design as did the patrons in Florence in Italy a couple of hundred years ago. The amount of contact between the designer and the user of the environment by and large is minimal. The conventional model of the city planner is still the city of things. Professor Bertram Gross of Syracuse has pointed out those good old hard techniques of budgeting, zoning, building regulation, subdivision control and capital budgeting, all of which are simply insufficient to cope with the nature of city planning as it must be performed today.[4] The pressing urban problems of post industrial America in the emerging world society, with its ideas of city planning as physical planning alone, has been riddled with bullets on the streets of Watts and Harlem. The body stinks. Let's bury it quickly.

Most city planning today fails to come to grips with the most pressing issues of social organization and interaction, while nevertheless appearing to deal with these matters through segmental treatments of components of life in the cities.

Certain phenomena in our cities can be treated in a variety of ways, but they are never, or seldom, looked upon by city planners as social problems. For example, mental retardation is seldom regarded as a social problem, nor is prostitution, nor juvenile delinquency, nor alcoholism. I have yet to see a city plan that treats the alienation of youth in cities; there is little treatment of the aged in terms of the social and psychological factors in the lives of people over sixty-five. There is very infrequent treatment of the common skid row problems in America. When they are treated at all, they are treated as a redevelopment project. There ought to be some realization by our city planners that there are enough skid rows in our societies to consider them as social problems, not just physical problems. Cities should, and will I am convinced, engage in social planning activities. There are about six cities in the country now which have such a department; but even they do not mention the vicious cycle of welfare subsistence as having any relation whatsoever to a city plan.

City plans which treat employment issues assume somehow that if we offer low income blacks the same incentives that we offer middle income whites, the black employment problem would be solved. But jobs alone are not enough; the culture of many in the core city is heavily influenced by anti-employment incentives. The hero is not the guy who gets up in time to get to work at 8:30 in the morning and punches a time clock and comes home with a pay check. The heroes are the bookie, and the pimp, and the gambler — the guys who make it the easy way. Unless we understand a culture with such values and understand such hero worship, unless we learn how to deal with it, we are never going to solve its employment problems. Telling a black man he should get up at 6:00 o'clock in the morning to work for $1.65 an hour when he sees a guy riding around in a flashy Cadillac, with a "stable of lace," (that is, several ladies working for him in various professions) will not be very effective.

If city planners turn to social planning, they will be able to build their plans into something more meaningful politically. They would then not have to be frustrated, as all of my planning friends are, by the political processes in cities.

I suggest that it we want city planning to have a minimal impact on the lives of people, then we ought to put this introduction on the first page of present city plans: "This plan is not designed to affect the lives of people of the communities of this city, just their physical environment." That's the way it is. If, on the other hand, city planning explicitly tried to affect the lives of the people then we ought to do it as explicitly as possible. I know of no way in which our city laws can bridge that communications gap any faster than beginning to think about social planning.

A second direction for reform is the involvement of cities in consumer activities. With few exceptions, notably the city of New York, cities in the United States do not engage in consumer services, consumer education, or very much consumer protection. Yet there are few functions, if any, which have a longer lineage than consumer services protection and education. Lewis Munford tells us that people first came together to live in cities for three basic purposes: water, protection, and the provision of a market place. In the provision of a market place what was necessary was consumer activities; so that trade could take place in the coin of the realm based upon an agreed upon standard; so that the trader and the tradee came out even. That is a consumer activity. Brand new? Maybe by the year 2000 our cities will get interested in it. Maybe we ought to take a lesson from the ancient Mesopotamian cities.

It is possible to administer cities with consumer affairs in mind. If a city is going to improve its relationships with the citizens of the many communities within it, it must develop methods and administrations suited to their needs. The citizen expects his city to protect him from unscrupulous operators and merchants. Each unscrupulous operator and merchant has on his wall a business license tax from the city. You would be amazed at how many times he points to that license and says, "If I wasn't a good businessman, and I was going to cheat, do you think the city would give me a license?" In our sophisticated knowledge, we understand that it is not really a license, but actually a business privilege tax. But, we must either acknowledge that it is only a tax, or else, if it *is* a license, we must look up the word in Webster's and find out what it means. The existence of a license implies that there is a sanction imposeable for violating the terms of that license, and as long as that license hangs on a wall, it is fruitless to tell an unsophisticated person that you have no enforcement powers. We need positive administration to utilize that license so citizens of our community who are forced to deal with unscrupulous merchants are not cheated.

The practices which offend citizens and against which they expect their city to protect them are as infinite and as varied as the mind of man. The city must function as a place for suitable human existence, for the support and the maintenance of life, for the enchancement of civilization. The citizen of one of our cities is both a producer and a consumer of goods. While he produces goods, he is protected by labor laws, workmen's compensation laws, union contracts. What protection do we provide him as a consumer of goods? We are living, as Eisenhower once said, "In an economy oriented towards consumption, not toward the consumer." I believe it to be a legitimate function of a city to initiate policies and programs that affect the commercial activities within it, so that they are consumer directed. For example, food prices tend to rise seven to ten per cent in certain communities of every major city when the welfare checks are due. These checks represent the expenditure of tax dollars. It does not seem illogical to assume that the city should take positive steps to prevent the dissipation of these hard earned tax dollars.

I am well aware that most city administrations are not involved in welfare administration; and, of course, this is a very convenient excuse for not becoming involved in consumer activities. But it will not solve the problem. It should come as no surprise to some officials that citizens in many of the communities within the city conclude that, because of some vague jurisdictional conflict which they do not understand, their city, their city officials, and their city hall are unconcerned with their problems.

By 1980 more than half the average city's inhabitants will be in their twenties or younger, with only 30% in the thirty to fifty-five group, and 17% over fifty-five years of age.[5] We know from sociological research that one of the major sources of trouble for young families is money management, particularly the use of credit. When a family is burdened through mistakes in borrowing, other social problems often are attendant upon them. The low income consumer not only has no budget cushion to absorb small errors in buying, but is also particularly susceptible to making errors.

In Watts, Harlem, and in Detroit — and wherever else one may look — the poor city resident is explosively critical, if I may use those words, of poor quality goods and services. He complains of exploitation at the hands of money lenders, merchants, and salesmen; and he wonders if anybody is listening to him because he sees no improvement. I believe it to be the responsibility of the city to listen. The merchants are in our cities. What prevents us, for example, from simply requiring that the full and true price of any article displayed for sale visible from a public street must be disclosed on the article? There isn't a city in the country that has such an ordinance. Consequently the youths on our city streets seeing the goodies behind the store window, take the first step toward going into hock for the rest of their lives. Any city could, if it wanted to, adopt a consumer protection, consumer education, consumer services program.

Let us look at some of the other things that go on. I will quote from a recent Federal Trade Commission letter to Senator Magnusson cataloging what the commissioners termed a number of practices commonly used to victimize poor and aged persons. They include "bait advertising," or the advertising of an attractive offer not in good faith for the purpose of obtaining leads; "referral selling," or the promise of commissions on sales made to friends, relatives, or neighbors; false claims that the prospect has been specially selected as part of an advertising or introductory promotional program; selling used or reconditioned products as new; false claims about safety or health benefits, quality or performance of products.[6] I suggest that cities are peculiarly well suited to control these practices, much more so than any other level of government.

Why should it not be possible for a city to require a cooling off period of twenty-four to thirty-six hours before a doorstep contract becomes valid? A doorstep contract is a contract signed on the spot with a door to door salesman. There are all sorts of practices of which white, middle class people are simply unaware, but which are victimizing people in our cities. I know that in Richmond, California there was some selective burning during our last unpleasantness. The Institute for Local Self Government had the opportunity to ask some of those involved why they picked those particular stores to burn, since there was obviously not much merchandise within them. What they were burning was the credit records and the burden of their fantastic interest rates. I could go on and on about some of the consumer practices rife in our cities about which our cities have done absolutely nothing.

I have talked about social planning; I have talked about consumer services. I also believe that cities are in dire need of improving their mechanisms for the redress of citizens' grievances. Folklore has it that "you can't fight city hall." In a democracy this is intolerable, yet it is so. Most urban administrations are not sufficiently aware of the problem, let alone being structured to provide simple, orderly, inexpensive, widely-known processes for the redress of citizens' grievances with both justice and equity. We tend to improvise when the panic button is pushed. We need planned, phased administrative restructuring that would make our cities better able to handle citizens' grievances. I have a lot of fun talking to city managers about this particular subject, because city managers view themselves as grievance handlers. I have two or three questions I ask them when I get into such a discussion. The first is, "What is the percentage of population in your city that works by the hour?" This is important because if I work by the hour and I want to complain, and if I have to take three to four hours off from my work to come to the city hall, assuming I find the manager, assuming I find his assistant, or assuming I find the department head, I am still out three of four hours pay. And that complaint may represent my weekly payment on that television set. Quite frankly I'd much rather pay for the television set.

"Oh, that's all right Randy, anybody can call me." One city manager told me that he received twenty telephone calls every weekend. I believed him. I said, "I believe that you get a thousand calls a year at home in which you handle the redress of citizens' grievances, but how many people in your town don't have telephones?" His answer, "Well, everybody's got a telephone," was interesting. This was in California where there are nineteen million people and twelve million telephone instruments. Two of them are on my desk, so somebody in that manager's town must not have a telephone. His concept of a grievance handler as a city manager, either by someone coming down to see him or by telephoning him, indicated to me that he did not know the nature of his community. He saw a mirror image of himself in his community. This was not true. He was not handling very many of the grievances of those who did not fit the mirror image. About two hundred years ago our forefathers dramatized their refusal to accept a condition in which they could not have their grievances redressed. You will recall some of the statements in our great American documents concerning that subject.

I do not plug for a particular institution to handle citizens' grievances. There is a great deal of current fascination with the subject of the ombudsman. We have given some study to the position at the Institute for Local Self Government. We are not at all convinced that the ombudsman, per se, is a transferable administrative device. But we are convinced that ombudsmanic concepts can be instituted throughout a city hall. Some cities are playing with what they call little city halls. If this concept will work in a particular city, then that city should go with it. Anyone who claims that a city should have an ombudsman or should have X or Y, I think, makes a mistake. All that is needed is an understanding of the fact that there are many, many citizens' grievances concerning the administration of our cities for which people have no outlet and no legitimate way to redress the grievance.

Many administrative processes which we have developed over the years have become oppressive and inflexible. There are many daily incidents of unfortunate experiences in contacts between city officials and the public giving rise to the feeling that city officials are either unfeeling, or indifferent, or arrogant. Many complaints about the lack of city services really have no way at the present time of being satisfactorily redressed, unless of course you are a member of the Rotary Club and you see the city manager or the mayor at the Rotary Club meeting and you can suggest to him that we ought to fill the chuck hole over there on country club drive. And there are in fact, in terms of application or in terms of administration, many laws and ordinances which seem reasonable but which in their actual application cause grievances for which there is scant, if any, redress.

Another area ripe for further reform is city administrative activities. As a case in point, city halls should increase their activities to improve housing conditions. Professor Dan Dodson of New York University made this statement, "A major part of the blame for social unrest in recent years lies in poor housing conditions. We must take steps at the community level to correct those situations which lead to expressions of dissatisfaction and perhaps eventual rebellion." He made that statement to an audience which may at first blush seem to have been a very peculiar one to which to address such a statement. It was the 13th Annual Institute of Police and Community Relations at Michigan State University in 1967. Many in attendance thought it was irrelevant to the police service, yet within ninety days police officers from six different police departments represented at that meeting were faced with the tragic experience of riots, to which poor housing conditions were an important contributing factor.

If you live in substandard housing and you inform the public authorities that the house you live in is not up to code, the landlord evicts you. Then he tries to go down and make a deal with the city hall. Isn't that a heck of a way to reward a good citizen? Is it not possible for our cities to say that a landlord may not evict solely for the reason of reporting a housing code violation? That would encourage good citizenship. At the present time the reward system encourages bad citizenship, because if you report the housing code violation, the odds are you are not going to have a place to live. Lodging a complaint, according to the best social research we have, will in most cases result in eviction. So you don't complain.

Both cities and the federal government subsidize slums. Because the bulk of our real estate tax incidence falls not on the land but on the improvement of it, improving a property or bringing it up to code results in higher taxes. Therefore it doesn't pay to improve a property. That is subsidizing slums. And while I'm kicking everybody in the teeth, I'll kick Uncle. He does the same thing. He subsidizes slums by allowing a five year depreciation on slum property. I buy a slum apartment building and then I sell it to my wife after five years; by which time my son will be twenty-one and she will sell it to him; then my daughter will be twenty-one and he will sell it to my daughter; and then she will sell it back to me. Around we go, writing the property off every five years. That is where the profit is.

Wouldn't it be an interesting experiment in American intergovernmental relations if the Federal government said, "We are not going to reward illegal activity." I'm kind of a patriotic American, and I don't think that my government should reward illegal activity, but it does. Keeping a house occupied in violation of the law is an illegal activity. A Housing Code is law. If a tenement or multi-family unit is occupied in violation of a housing code, it is an illegally occupied dwelling. The owner is engaged in an illegal activity, yet he can write it off. Uncle Sam rewards him. Wouldn't it be an interesting experiment in intergovernmental relations, if the Internal Revenue Service, by a simple administrative regulation requiring no laws by the mighty Congress, said, "We will not allow depreciation on a multi-family unit unless the claim for depreciation is accompanied by a certificate from the unit of local government in which the housing is located, attesting that the unit is occupied in full compliance with all local ordinances, regulations and codes." It might do something to improve the housing stock.

Very few cities, if any, give concerted continuous policy attention to maintaining the economic health of the city. Generally, what they do is give a thousand dollars or so to the Chamber of Commerce Economic Development Committee. Sometimes they have to hide it in various ways because they are not supposed to make contributions from public funds. They then say we are helping the economic development of the city. There isn't a city in our country that has a gross community product. All of us are familiar with the gross national product. How in the world can we understand anything about the economic health of our cities unless we begin to think in terms of gross community product.

We at the Institute for Local Self Government read minutes of something like four hundred city council meetings. We have a built-in library and we can do that. When we got to the number of four hundred, we quit, because it was getting pretty boring. We found that councils and planners were zoning and designing the city beautiful, but all the time they were doing this, neighborhoods were deteriorating. We found not one single discussion recorded in the minutes — I don't say that the discussions did not take place — but we found not one single notation in four hundred council meetings of a concerted, continuous policy discussion concerned with the economic development of the city. It is almost sophomoric to point out that the result of this is unrest, social disorder. I believe it to be an essential administrative task in bridging the gap between some citizens and the city for the city to become involved in manpower and employment service activities, to coordinate them, to create innovations in the field. I think city administrators have the imagination if they would only have the will.

I would suggest that if social democracy is the goal of the nation, and if political democracy is the goal of the nation, cities might take a small piece of the action by carving out for themselves the goal of economic democracy. Cities should play an active role in placing potential employees, scouting job markets, soliciting employment offices, counseling, testing, training, working with the National Alliance of Business Men, cranking in important segments of an Urban

Coalition that have to do with employment. No other aspect of the urban problem is as chaotic as manpower and employment. It is as if segments of railroad track, many of high quality, were nailed down haphazardly all over the landscape. Some are longer; some shorter; some approach a station; but most end somewhere in the countryside. A good many run parallel to each other, leaving wide areas without any service. If all these chunks of tracks could be placed end to end with a clear direction, they would undoubtedly go far toward meeting existing needs. Many would have to be upgraded and some new pieces would have to be added. But, the big job is to design a sound pattern for using the available hardware. This is the heart of the problem. I believe the job of designing that sound pattern is a city job. At the very least, we could put a municipal manpower coordinator to work in the city hall and see what he stirs up.

Finally, I believe that cities should again reform their civil service systems. You will recall I talked about the first great wave of municipal reform. In that wave, of course, we took employment out of politics and politics out of government. I don't know how we did it, but that was the goal. It is time for another look at our municipal civil service regulations. It is time to question the mandating by state legislatures of civil service regulations. It is time to question merit system procedures which are frozen into city charters. It is time to take a good hard look at those crusty old independent (and they sure are) commissioners on the civil service commission. I was talking in Oakland, California, which happens to be my home city, to the civil service commission about some reforms which could be done even though most of the regulations are in the charter. A civil service commissioner who had served some thirty-five years on the commission was on the podium. (It is one of the nice things about independent civil service commissions that they always meet on a dais, and the petitioner has to look up to them). He looked down, and he said to me, "Young man, I don't understand what you are talking about." I said, "Sir, fifty feet from where we are sitting, there hangs on the bulletin board of your city an announcement: 'Animal Control Officer' (that is what we Californians call a dog catcher), Continuing examination (that translates out in civil service terms to mean perpetual shortage). Line I 'Qualifications: High School graduate.'," I suggested to the Civil Service Commissioner that an examination of a dog catcher's job would indicate that a dog catcher had to do roughly these things: Drive a quarter-ton or half-ton pickup truck; be able to tell time; be able to write a simple report that he picked up something that looked like a collie on the corner of 3rd and Main at 2:45 and delivered him to the pound master at 3:15; know the streets of the city; have some physical agility; and maybe love animals. None of these had anything to do with the qualifications on the bulletin board, which consisted of one: High School graduate. A New Yorker, whom we all hate, but who was a high school graduate and who did not know the streets of Oakland, and who hated animals, could qualify to come to work today in the city of Oakland. That is all I am talking about.

I am suggesting that it is time to look at our job descriptions and our civil service requirements in terms of analyzing the task of the job and then to make the punishment fit the crime: have the description and the job suit the task.

As I go around I read city hall bulletin boards. I like to read the junior level things. They always say the junior level planner assists the planner, aids the planner, helps the planner. The junior engineer works with and assists the engineer with the preparation of . . . . Then if one goes and talks with a planner, junior grade, or an engineer, junior grade, and says, "What in the world do you do?" he tells you what he does. He does not view his job as assisting, helping, etc. He has a real job. What happens is that because the head of the department, the senior person, writes the job description it comes out in the announcement as assisting the . . . The poor guy looking at the announcement says, "Gee, I can't assist an engineer. I can't assist a planner." But if you go into the planning office you will find he *can* run a Xerox machine, run a blue print machine, put Zip-a-tone on a land use map, go down to the building permit department and find out what permits were issued during the week or month and come back to the master land-use plan and begin to color it yellow where it was green. He can even go out and tack up on a telephone pole an announcement there is going to be a public hearing about a variance. Believe it or not, you do not have to have a master's degree to do these things. In fact, you do not even need a master's degree in city planning to make a windshield survey. I never made my first windshield survey until I had my master's degree in city planning and was working for the Cleveland City Planning Commission. Twenty-five years later I figured out that I really did not have to know very much to ride around with a lap board and a census tract map. All I did was check our land-use map against what was actually on the ground. Where I found a difference, I simply had to make the notation on the bottom that Block H, Parcel 23, Lot K, which we had shown as yellow, has now been converted into a store, so we ought to change it to red back at the city hall. You really do not need a master's degree to do that.

I could go on and on and on and on with similar illustrations. All they imply is that we are living in a credentialed society. If we examine the job — the task that is done — and find that there is a guy in city hall who really does these things: he runs the Xerox, he runs the blue print machine, he tacks up notices on telephone poles for variances, he goes down to the building permit department, he does filing work, he collates the annual report, etc., etc; and that he really doesn't have to have an MA to be a junior planner and perform those functions; if we really examine all these things, then we might make some progress in the reformation of city hall. In the process, we could open mobility and professional advancement to large segments of citizens whom we are trying to reach, who have heretofore been locked out of the mainstream of professional American life in city halls.

Discussion

Question: Why have cities been so slow in incorporating social planning departments into their administrations?

Hamilton: I suggest that there should be some summary review of the reasons for the lack of social planning in our cities. I can understand why planners don't want to tackle it. It is pretty tough. Of course, there is the magnitude of the responsibility for engaging in social planning. Community behavior is extraordinarily difficult to analyze, let alone to plan for, and of course, we have the threat of totalitarian approaches to planning if we suggest social planning, because isn't that what they do in Russia? The cost of social planning is not going to be low, either. However, I suggest that if city planners continue to talk about physical resources, physical planning, and continue to make reference to planning for the people, and yet fail to deal with the basic facts of community existence, there is every reason for people to pay little attention to the planners' recommendations. Planners can talk about amenities or benefits. They can talk about the need of controlling the use of space so that we can all enjoy a fuller life, but we will still have to come to grips with the fact that millions of Americans live below the poverty line and are concentrated in the hearts of our cities.

Question: In bridging the gap, what role should city halls play in the manpower activities?

Hamilton: Another reform that might help to bridge the gap between many of our citizens and city halls would be for cities to become engaged in manpower and employment service activities, functions which are today almost as unspoken for by cities as consumer activities. Cities hide behind the defense that the county or the state employment service is responsible for these functions. Nobody ever burned down a state employment service building, and marches on state capitals are still rare. But they sure march on city halls. Unemployment has a deadening effect. Economic development is held back in cities where there is unemployment. The cities where unpleasantness has occurred are all cities with high unemployment. I fail to see why we cannot make the connection between cause and effect.

Question: Don't you agree that we must make significant inroads to understanding the attitudes and the perceptions of those particular groups of people we public administrators are trying to reach?

Hamilton: Of course — I suggest that if you are looking for bridges between the city hall and the citizen, and if you understand what the citizen is faced with, you will then know how to build the bridge. It is purely an engineering problem. If you are building a bridge physically, you know that if you want to go from here to there, the first thing you must do is examine the substrata and the soil and its bearing content. You learn a great deal about that little hunk of ground on which you're going to build a bridge tower. When you learn all rhere is to know about it and still wish you knew some more. So you spend a year or two boring, testing, devising, designing, redesigning. If we are going to build bridges between the city hall and its citizens, I suggest that we had better find out what those citizens' lives are like. We'd better bore, and test, and design, and redesign for their substrata — substrata of culture if you will.

Question: Would you comment upon bridging the gap as it relates to the problem of political access, which in turn relates to political accountability?

Hamilton: I sometimes suggest to city councils that when they have a city meeting or an official meeting of the city council, to go outside of city hall. Have it in a high school or elsewhere. You'd be surprised how quickly that communications gap disappears.

I would suggest that the cities should pay councilmen to have offices in their districts. Cities should pay for full-time administrative assistants for councilmen in their district offices.

I am now not so skeptical of ward elections as I once was when I studied public administration. There was strict accountability in those days. All the books tell kids today that ward elections were bad. When we threw them out in the reform movement, we may have lost something. This is a subject I would like to rethink for a while. May be could look back and capture some of the good things from ward politics, such as "access" which you suggest.

Question: The one group of public officials in constant touch with the community are police officers. They are as much public administrators as anyone. Would you comment briefly on their role?

Hamilton: A relevant question to ask is: "What are the requirements for police officers?" Some of my research has indicated that there are only two universal requirements in the United States for police officers: age and citizenship. There are no other universal requirements. We have also done research that indicated the average police force in the United States, and particularly in California, has a turnover rate of 12% in the first two years. No business could operate seeing 12% of its most highly trained professionals leave in two years. We asked what aspects of an applicant's background do you study? The answer is often three things: booze, credit, and women. This is the so-called background investigation that every police force makes before it hires a man. We examined 14,000 folders of discharged police officers who had been discharged "for the good of the service" or were asked to resign before they got fired. Do you know what the greatest causes for separation from the police service are? Booze, credit, and women. With that we went to the Ford Foundation and asked if there is any way in the world that we can screen out the kooks. If you examine the Kerner Commission Report, you will find that "almost invariably" the riots occurred as a result of a police activity, legitimate or otherwise.[7] It was the primary causitive factor in some 64 riots the Commission studied. We then asked a second question that the Commission did not ask. That is: "how long had that individual officer who was involved in the initial stages of the riot been on the force?" Strangely enough, he tended to be on the force less than 2 years. We are now going back and examining these folders, trying to extract from them the commonalities in these officers. Fortunately the computer makes this type of research possible. We have run thousands upon thousands of life history cycles of discharged officers covering everything from the sibling relationship on up. We are now down to some 65 items which seem to have a bearing on a guy who is psychologically unsuited to be a police officer. This does not mean that he is psychologically unsuited to be a city manager or president of the United States, but that he is psychologically unsuited to be a police officer. If you hire a policeman who has a tatoo and has been a defendant in a divorce proceeding and has two moving violations within three years of applying for the police department, the odds are two to one that he will not be on your police force two years after you hire him. We never thought of these things in police service in the United States before. You hire a guy who can stand up and see lightning and hear thunder and that is about it. Now, hopefully, with a little bit of luck and some more work, we will be able for the first time to give to the police departments of this country a list of 65 things to look for in hiring a police officer and some good sound data on which to base their recommendation. The need to examine our police recruiting practices is one starting point for improving the relationship between citizen and government.

Question: What role do the media have in bridging the gap, particularly on the local level?

Hamilton: Problems usually generate from misinformation or no information. Furthermore, people often do not want to hear what is right. They have a deep-rooted mistrust of city hall. The average Joe calls city hall to complain about the chuckholes in his street. He is given an answer, very likely an honest answer, even though it is not very exciting just to believe it. He calls the press and gives a blown up story about how city hall duped him. He wants to believe that city hall is misleading him and is not giving him the truth.

There are ways to tackle the problem. Very little about local government is taught in public schools in order to make the citizen more knowledgeable about his city government. The news media and the free press demand an educated audience and unfortunately few elected officials are fully cognizant of the unlimited potential of television. I would bet coverage of some city council meetings might be exciting enough to win an Emmy.

Urbanization and the
Federal System

4

Urban Administration and Creative Federalism

Senator Edmund S. Muskie

Inasmuch as I have served in government at all three levels, and in both legislative and executive branches, I suppose I am an object of uncreative federalism, but my interest in the problems associated with this federal system has grown the longer I have been exposed to it. I would like to begin with two quotations, one of which is from the early part of this century, and the other is very recent. Both are pertinent to our current problems and taken together they illustrate our dilemma in dealing with the crisis in urban America. The first is an observation by Martin Lomasney, an early twentieth-century Boston political leader. He said, "There has got to be in every ward somebody that any bloke can come to and get help. Help, you understand, none of your law and justice, but help." In a recent speech at Cornell, John Gardner said this, "Men must be discriminating appraisers of their society, knowing coolly and precisely what it is about society that thwarts or limits them and therefore needs modification, and so must they be discriminating protectors of their institutions, preserving those features that nourish and strengthen them and make them more free. To fit themselves for such tasks they must be sufficiently serious to study their institutions, and sufficiently dedicated to become expert in the art of modifying them."

There in a nutshell are the conflicting drives which plague urban administration and the concept of creative federalism. On one side, we are confronted with the rising tide of demands for help against poverty, discrimination, and an unhealthy environment, and on the other side are the suggestions for improving the structures and techniques of government. The one is founded on the elemental needs of people and the other is rooted in the rational approach to problem solving. These two views are not mutually exclusive and they are both necessary to an understanding of a democratic society in a changing world. To accede to the demands for help, without giving attention to the system which must provide the help, is an exercise in futility. To become absorbed in the improvement of our public and private institutions on the other hand without giving attention to pressing human needs is an invitation to disaster.

Urban administration and creative federalism in its broadest sense is a question which has been gnawing at many of us for the past few years. In a country of 200 million heterogeneous people, pressured by external events and internal strains, are we capable of realizing the promise of America for every American? Through the years, we have been committed to an ideal of a democratic society, where institutions guarantee each individual an opportunity for normal development and to participate in the forces that shape his life. As Professor John Dewey said, "Democracy has many meanings, but if it has any moral meaning it is found in resolving that the supreme test of all political institutions and industrial arrangements shall be the contribution to all-round growth of every member of society." So we conclude again as the founders did that government in a democracy must be based on civic cooperation and citizen participation and that its concern is the people's health, homes, jobs, rights as citizens, and their security as free men.

Your studies here match the central concern of the Senate Subcommittee on Intergovernmental Relations. The aim of all of our activities is the progressive adaptation of the forms and procedures of government to the present and foreseeable needs of the country. Since 1962, the subcommittee has been engaged in continuous study of the interacting functions of government at the federal, state, and local levels. It has provided a forum of some value in which governmental processes have been examined and criticized, and in which new and innovative ideas have been advanced. It would be misleading to focus exclusively on the needs and prospects of any one of the component parts of our governmental system. Governments can no more exist in isolation than can individuals. We are an indivisible whole, whose strength is derived from the strength that each part lends to the other parts, and it is only in this perspective that the urban areas can understand their own problems and can realize their full potential for service to their people. We must press forward with reforms and innovations in each sphere of government in order to strengthen the whole federal system.

One of the most alarming manifestations of our times, revealed in many pages of testimony before our committee, is the helter-skelter growth of bureaucracy at every level which tends to fragment policy making, executive direction, and resources. We have some ninety thousand local units of government, most with their own taxing, planning and operating authorities. We have fifty states with thousands of relatively autonomous agencies, departments and authorities, carrying on additional operating and planning responsibilities, and at the federal level we have over twenty-one federal agencies and hundreds of regional and subregional offices, administering more than five hundred separate grant-in-aid authorizations.

Our challenge in this concept of creative federalism is to convert all this into a partnership of federal, state, and local governments with goals understood, responsibilities clearly placed, authorities adequately provided, and fiscal resources available for each member of the system to function effectively in its own proper sphere. The importance of this challenge cannot be overestimated, for we are confronted with a crisis in confidence in our society which I think is almost as serious, if not as serious, as that which confronted the country as it emerged from the period of the Articles of Confederation and to the period of nationhood under the Constitution. What is at stake is the question of whether or not the society we have created here is a society in which its individual members can be confident. Max Ways put it this way in a recent *Fortune* magazine article — "Few of us, white or black, really trust the communities in which we live. We have no reason to suppose that they will keep the air and the rivers clean, or that they can effectively protect our lives or our property. All this is no secret — the whole world knows the condition of United States cities and has known it for decades. The billions we have poured out for foreign aid and propaganda, the more numerous billions we spend for military support of our foreign policy are half cancelled by the damage that is done to United States prestige by our long-standing inability to deal effectively with gangsterism, slums, high infant death rates among our poor, traffic jams, junk yards, billboards, and all the rest of the noxious mess. Much of the world asks what is the point of being the richest, most powerful nation, if such problems can't be handled better? What is the point of capitalism and of democracy?"[1]

Is this the promise of America for which we organized ourselves explicitly under the Constitution in 1787? We have believed that when man is free to grow he will enlarge his intellectual and spiritual powers, he will achieve a more satisfactory life for himself, he will become a better neighbor to others, and he will make possible a more enlightened and more civilized society. We have believed this but today as we see on every hand evidence of our weaknesses, failures, and shortcomings, we begin to wonder whether it can work. Unfortunately, we have not given it a full trial and that failure is the basis of today's uncertainties. Our forefathers enslaved the Negro, freed him reluctantly, and neither they nor we have yet done what is necessary to give him his full and equal chance. Our development as a complex industrial society, with its accompanying technological explosion, has created other disadvantaged groups as the product of forces they cannot control.

These Americans, too, seek improvement in their lives. They know that is America's promise, and they are aware of America's resources. Their hunger is a force which cannot be chained, it cannot be drugged to sleep, and it cannot be stamped out. It is a force which will not be easy to deal with because it is already partially unleashed. It is impatient with the political processes which have fallen short in the past and it lacks confidence in our good will and intentions.

What are our intentions now? Are we ready to do what is necessary to give every American his chance or are we inhibited by fear, by prejudice, and by reluctance to change the status quo, to make sacrifices, to accept burdens, and to share our affluence? Ours is not an easy kind of society to build or to maintain; it means learning to live with, to work with, to understand and respect. Many different human beings of different colors, different races, different national origins, different cultural levels, different tastes and intellectual capacities, different educational attainments, different social backgrounds and personalities and dispositions make up the country. It means learning to trust them, to mingle with them, to think of them all as neighbors. It means making our lives part of their lives, taking them into our lives. It means diminishing our prerogatives by as much as is necessary to respect their prerogatives. It means granting them all equal opportunities to participate in community life and the policy making processes of our society.

There are risks, of course, in all of this. There are bad people as well as good. There are mean people as well as generous, dishonest as well as honest, violent as well as peaceful but such risks are part of life and part of a free society. So we must take the risk of misplaced confidence, undeserved injury of friendship and generosity rebuffed. But if we are willing to try to build such a society, it will survive such risks, by stimulating and making possible the growth of each citizen in knowledge, understanding and capacity. It will gradually raise the level of individual attainment in the quality of our life together.

I have framed our urban problem in these philosophic terms because I believe it is only in this context that we can successfully improve our intergovernmental relations and the federal system. Intergovernmental relations and the federal system are something more than organization charts, procedures and parliamentary rules. It is a system designed to create a climate in which man can grow, and in the process of growing cannot only enrich himself but also his society. As we examine the problem of reorganizing our efforts we must approach it in such a way as to focus them more meaningfully upon this objective; our forefathers enshrined slavery in the Constitution, that is gone now; we are in a position to enshrine freedom in the new federal system which we must create out of the old. I think it is true that many of our institutional problems result from our failure to adapt them to changing conditions. Problems have outgrown the traditional institutional frameworks and their jurisdictions, in part because of the fact of population growth, in part because of the complexities which have been created by the technological explosion.

But there are some signs of hope. For example, there is the emerging recognition that regional institutions capable of assuming some of the responsibilities heretofore left to local, state, and federal governments are a necessity if we are to preserve the substance as well as the form of democracy. We are seeing the need to use it in controlling the uses of and enhancing the quality of our water supply, and we are in the process of implementing just such national policy under the Water Quality Act of 1965. We have seen the need to use the concept of regionalism in controlling emissions into the ambient air and we are on the threshold of implementing that national policy under the Clean Air Act of 1967, now Public Law 90—148. The great difficulty as we move from the traditional forms of local government is first of all that the Constitution does not envision the kind of regional institutions we need, and we have difficulty in the light of parochialism and the vested interests in present forms of local government in identifying or creating regional institutions which are politically acceptable and viable. The attempt currently used is to stimulate the development of evolutionary processes which could emerge in different kinds of regional institutions depending upon the areas of the country and their traditions and the kinds of problems involved. The regional approach is mandatory if we are to find solutions for one of the most serious and pervasive problems of metropolitan America, which is the growing imbalance between central cities and their suburbs. This imbalance has been accentuated by the creation of a multitude of independent governmental units within metropolitan areas. With their separate taxing, financing, and operating powers they hold to the illusion of a certain immunity to the problems of the core cities. This illusion, in my judgment, must vanish as the urban fabric thickens and they find themselves incapable of solving their problems in isolation from their neighbors. In too many cases today, the core cities carry the burden of furnishing many services for the surrounding communities, and for the industrial and commercial interests, which are more and more relocating in the fringe areas. They must provide increasing costly services to the poor such as education, health, welfare, housing, and job training. They must wrestle with the problems of the ghetto. As they face these demands, their fiscal resources are declining from an eroding tax base and also from discrimination at the hands of state governments, which demonstratively favor the suburbs in their allocation of state and federal assistance.

If the states are in earnest in seeking a more significant role in the federal system they must accept a greater responsibility in providing assistance to their central cities. Over and over again I've heard governors testify either before the Subcommittee on Intergovernmental Relations or before the Subcommittee on Air and Water Pollution that we ought to eliminate direct local federal programs. My answer is that each of them has a way of getting a piece of the action if he really wants it. All he has to do is to buy in. In my state, when I was governor, I was concerned that the 701 planning program was a direct federal-local program. We solved that very simply. I asked the legislature to provide matching state funds which the communities were eager to pick up and we had a piece of the action. The same thing happened in 1956 when the first water pollution grant program was enacted into law by the Congress. Again, this provided for direct federal-local programs and again I recommended that we buy in a piece of the action. Ever since the state has been in a position to guide the development of its water quality program. It would be tragic in my judgment if the hard won victory of reapportionment resulted in a coalition between the rural areas and the ever-more populous suburbs leaving the core cities to fend for themselves. Nothing could be more damaging to the future of state government, or, ultimately, more damaging to our federal system itself. The reapportionment decisions were a great advantage but they do not automatically provide the kind of equality of treatment and broad gauge perspective of state and nation unless there is a deliberate and conscious effort on the part of citizens and leaders alike to put that kind of narrow parochialism behind. If the states fail to act the federal government will have to act on a scale commensurate to the scope and depth of the needs of the least fortunate of our people.

What can the states do? Among other things, they should join with the federal government in fostering and encouraging intergovernmental arrangements for dealing with the problems of whole metropolitan areas. Local government, after all, is the creature of the states. They are in a position to direct this kind of evolutionary development. One such arrangement is the council of local governments. Your own Mid-America Council of Governments is an example of this new and useful instrument of government. It is a coordinating device that embraces city and suburbs alike, and acts on the principle that they share a common destiny. State legislatures should grant such bodies all the power they need to do the job they have set for themselves. The political units that make up the metropolitan regions should use the councils to the fullest extent in region-wide planning and in the development of common services. Federal agencies should look to them more and more for the coordination of development programs. Region-wide planning and actual experience in coordination is a way to begin the evolutionary process.

The possibilities of comprehensive planning and the coordination of development programs have been greatly enhanced by two recent pieces of federal legislation. One is the Comprehensive Health Planning and Public Health Service Amendments of 1966, which combined a dozen or more separate categorical health grants into a single program, enlarging the area of discretion open to states. The other is the Demonstration Cities and Metropolitan Development Act of 1966 which contains two innovations of great significance. Title I provides that cities participating in the model cities program may receive supplemental grants for a whole range of locally determined needs related to the objectives of the demonstration. Title II looks outward to the whole metropolitan area. It provides that applications for federal assistance for planning and development within a metropolitan area shall be reviewed by a regional planning body. And it provides a strong incentive to planning by making supplemental grants available for projects which conform to a coordinated regional development program. Despite the road blocks that have been put in the path, I understand that these provisions, as simple as they seem, have already resulted in moves to establish the machinery of regional planning and coordination in many parts of the country where they have been lacking.

I recall when these provisions were first introduced and the resistance to them from within the local units of government. That resistance was reflected in the House of Representatives, where the so-called Kramer amendment to an appropriations act last year prohibited HUD from spending any money to implement that section of the law. I can't recall any similar step taken in an appropriations act to foil legislation that had been approved by the Congress. Fortunately, the executive branch at times displays a little ingenuity as well. And the Bureau of the Budget undertook to assume the responsibilities assigned to HUD under the act. Area-wide agencies qualified to perform the required reviews now exist in 206 out of 230 metropolitan areas of the country. Of these, eleven extend into two states and five into three states. In general, the area-wide agencies reported to the Bureau of the Budget that the requirement had stimulated considerable interest in interlocal cooperation and facilitated coordination of metropolitan planning.

I think it would be a mistake to try to create a blueprint for metropolitan government that we try to apply to every metropolitan area in the country. But an evolutionary process involving at the minimum comprehensive planning and the practice of developing common services and coordination will result in more effective government of metropolitan areas in many different and varying forms. That kind of development, of course, is the very essence of the federal system.

In some places it may result in a formal structure of metropolitan government. In other areas it may not go beyond the level of interlocal cooperation of planning. The test is whether it works. The form is simply a means.

With respect to the federal level much remains to be done. There has been a steady enlargement, as you know, of federal aid to state and local governments to deal with problems of national concern. In this fiscal year, the federal contribution to joint endeavors with state and local units of government under existing and proposed programs will total more than 20 billion dollars. The level of federal aid will have more than tripled since 1959. During the same decade expenditures of state and local funds to match federal funds will have more than doubled. Federal aids for metropolitan or urban areas have risen from four billion dollars in 1961 to an estimated twelve billion in 1969, nearly tripling in less than a decade. Unfortunately, the arts of management have not kept pace with this growth of program activity. The result has been a serious overlapping, duplication, and conflict of purposes among the more than five hundred separate program authorizations for federal aid.

As I suggested at the outset, what we've done by using this categorical grant-in-aid approach is to fragment our resources, our policy making, and our executive direction. At the federal level I've urged for some time legislation requiring that the executive office of the President must be strengthened to coordinate the activities of the departments and agencies in support of national goals. In keeping consistent policy, President Johnson recognized the need and initiated a study which we hope will lead to constructive changes in the machinery available to the President for management of the executive branch. It could be a separate office as I have recommended, or it could be a function of the Bureau of the Budget, or it could be outside the executive office of the President entirely. Personally, I think it should be there so it is tied in with a coordinating office in every department and agency which is involved in federal, state, and local grant-in-aid programs.

We also need an overhaul of the federal aid system itself. There must be a reduction in the number of separate programs through the elimination of those that have accomplished their purpose, and coordination wherever possible of those with closely related purposes. In the case of water pollution control, with which I have a special concern, there are five separate departments and agencies involved with different congressional authorities, with different formulas for assistance, with different constituencies and overlapping constituencies.

The federal government must also develop better methods of communicating with the states and cities on the availability of federal assistance for various purposes and the terms and conditions on which it is offered. Increasingly, the largest cities and states are employing men in Washington to do this kind of fishing or hunting, depending upon which label you prefer. I hate to see someone displacing me in exercising that function. Several measures sent to Congress would, in my judgment, greatly enhance the ability of the national government, the states, and the local governments to work together. One of them is the Intergovernmental Personnel Act. The administration introduced a comparable piece of legislation called the Intergovernmental Manpower Act. The two were combined with the best features of both in one bill. The act provides for federal grants to state and local governments to improve their systems of personnel administration using merit principles as a basis of performance. It makes federal aid available to support training programs undertaken on the initiative of state and local governments and it provides for the interchange of personnel between the federal government and state and local governments for limited periods of service.

The Intergovernmental Cooperation Act was a complex bill on which we had long hearings. It does things such as provide the ground rules for improved administration of federal grants-in-aid to the states, and permit federal departments and agencies to provide special or technical services to state or local units of government on a reimbursible basis. This is now done in a limited way on separate authorizations. The legislation would authorize all agencies designated by the President to provide such services. The bill would further authorize the President to coordinate the administration of federal grants for urban development. It would provide for periodic Congressional review of federal grant-in-aid programs and it would provide that all future grant-in-aid programs would terminate at the end of five years unless expressly exempted from that provision or renewed by the Congress. There has been great objection to this provision of the bill from the liberals who are afraid of losing their programs. In my judgment, and I've been described as a liberal, this is a form of status quoism which is usually identified with conservatism. We need to realize that even in this well-endowed country there are limitations to what we can do. Our objective in providing this title is to redirect, reshape, and terminate programs in the interest of a more efficient use of resources and by focusing them on real needs as they develop and change.

Another title of the act authorizes the use of the Reorganization Act technique for the consolidation of federal grant-in-aid programs. I think this deserves special comment. You are familiar with the Reorganization Act and that it authorizes the President to reorganize the executive agencies of government by plans which he submits to Congress. The Congress can do only two things with respect to it. Le it go into effect at the end of sixty days, or one House by passing a resolution of disapproval within sixty days can kill the plan. As originally written into the Intergovernmental Cooperation Act this would have given the president the same authority to consolidate grant-in-aid programs which operate in related fields. Everybody opposed it, including the President and the Congress, so the staff developed what I think is a most ingenious modification of it. Under this form the President must submit a consolidation plan at an early time in a Congressional session, conceivably by February 15 or March 1. The Congress could then disapprove the plan within ninety days as contrasted to the sixty, or it could enact legislation to amend or otherwise modify the proposal. If the legislation passes in that session of the Congress the original plan is then voided and the new legislation takes effect. If no legislation is enacted in that session then the plan takes effect thirty days after the end of the session. This is an interesting mixture of executive initiative and the preservation of Congressional prerogatives. It may be so good that conservatives in the Congress may try to modify the reorganization powers of the President to dilute them in this way.

The next provision in the act would require that land transactions by federal agencies in urban areas shall to the greatest practicable extent conform to land use programs of the local governments effected. Our intent in writing this title was the obvious one to make the federal government and its agencies good citizens in communities in which they live by making them subject to the planning processes of the community. Architects came to us and said we ought to do the reverse and so frame this that the national government could dictate sound planning at the local level. We haven't quite bought that.

The provision of the act that has the greatest appeal is Title 8 which would establish a system of uniform relocation assistance for all federally assisted programs that displace people from their homes or places of business. The concept is that no public program is justified if it relies for its economic rationale upon the displacement of people and forcing of them to bear part of the cost. If you can't make people whole when you displace them to make way for public improvement then the public improvement isn't justified in most cases. There are instances involving national security when you may have a close question, but in general I think that's a sound concept.

In order to move completely you'd have to eliminate the fair market value test in the taking of property. An illustration of what the bill provides in the event a home is taken, the federal government can pay not only the fair market value but up to $5000 additional to make up the difference in costs for acquiring a reasonably comparable home as a substitute. To those displaced, that may not seem generous enough, but I think it still is quite a radical departure from current policy. The other major issue involved is whether or not the bill ought to be fully funded by the federal government, or whether the costs ought to be shared in accordance with the sharing formula of the particular grant-in-aid program. I felt it ought to be full federal funding because we ought not to wait until the fifty states decide to adopt such a policy. Again we compromised and for three years it is going to be full federal funding if we have our way. After that the costs will be shared in accordance with the formula.

Finally the act establishes uniform policies governing land acquisition in federally aided programs. The aim of this title is to move in the direction of greater equity and justice for those whose land is taken. We don't think this ought to be considered an arms length transaction with equal bargainers on each side. The weight of government does an injustice to the bargaining process when we are dealing with people in this kind of situation, and we have undertaken to require that those whose land is taken shall in no case receive only the fair market value.[2]

If I may sum up here again with a bit of philosophy; there are a great many questions asked these days about the effectiveness of the political process and the system of government under which we live. It's unfortunately true that a great deal of the dissent among disadvantaged groups and on the campuses among young people is directed less to the effectiveness of the current leadership of our country so much as it is to the system itself. And I am afraid that this fact is pushing the country quite rapidly toward the right. Tom Wicker, Washington Bureau Chief of the *New York Times,* has just written an excellent book in which he made this observation that is both reassuring and cause for concern — "What the public wants, the public gets more often than not, and the real problems of American politics are that the public so often wants unworthy things and is so seldom set straight by anyone who will be listened to."[3] In my judgment in the light of the problems that I have discussed this afternoon, the real danger which faces us is not so much institutional inadequacy as the evidence that public sentiment is moving to the right, in the direction of less involvement in each other's problems — toward less inclination for the reform of institutions and of policies in the directions of human needs, toward less patience with each other's shortcomings and weaknesses, and with less generosity in their impulses toward each other. As I consider this which seems to me to be the real danger in the times in which we live, I'm reminded of a bit of wisdom of President Kennedy on which I will close: "Those who make peaceful revolutions impossible, make violent revolutions inevitable."

Discussion

Question: The Senator mentioned the fact that Section 205 of the Housing Act of 1966 had been approved, but as you know, it was never funded. This is the section that would have provided bonus grants for projects which are within a metropolitan area plan. The only way to get a grant is to start through your legislative delegation in Washington and it ends up as sort of pressure game. We have a little application in right now through the Metropolitan Planning Commission for a hundred and fifty thousand dollars to do sub-area planning for four of our seven counties. It has been seven months in the process and there is nothing wrong with the application. They told us this, but it is just that it is related to the shortages of money. Could you comment on this?

Muskie: I am not particularly troubled that you can't do the whole job at once. I don't think that it is futile to be using the time that you have got to reshape your policy and your objectives, and to get the directions clear, and to develop the political support so that when the fiscal situation eases you are in a position to move. It took a long time to get these programs on the books — they were the product of the frustrations of fourteen, fifteen, sixteen years. Look at the long time it took to get the federal aid to education programs with the constitutional problems, the race problem, the church-state problem. But we got it on the books and it is funded — not as fully as it needs to be, not as fully as we would like, but would we be better off if it were not on the books at all? The same thing is true with the water pollution programs. The administration has taken the initiative and the cities have pulled back. Why? The administration proposed that they contract authority which would result in the issue of bonds to cover the federal share of the sewage treatment projects with contract agreement on the part of the federal government, to pick up the principal and interest each year for the life of the bonds. Here was a way to fund projects to the full amount anticipated by the amendments of 1966 which set up the 3.4 million authorization. What is holding it up? The Treasury wants to make these bonds taxable and municipalities are sensitive about their tax-exempt prerogatives. We are willing to work out a compromise in the agreement that bonds would cover only the federal share. The federal bonds are taxable, so if local bonds are to substitute for federal bonds I don't really see why the community should object. As far as I can see it, and I took the last reading yesterday, the League of Cities are adamantly opposed to anything, even though this means coming to a screeching halt on water pollution projects.

This is a little bit of a diversion but my view is that you keep getting your organization and your policy in order, ready for the funding. As far as this bill is concerned, there is only one title that involves a great deal of money. And that involves in some part a shifting of resources that are now spent in this field. I think that you ought to get it passed. If worst comes to worst you could pass the policy and make the states assume the burden. Whatever you have to do, get your policy written.

Question: Senator, you are working very hard on this problem of overlapping federal grant agencies. What I am wondering is how much of this gets back to

Congress itself? Congressmen have pet agencies and even if the President is given the power, he may not want to use if for political purposes because he doesn't want to offend legislation and their pet agencies.

Muskie: I don't think that it is a question of whom to blame. We are not blaming the President. We suggest that he ought to have this authority — we are not blaming the Congress, actually. I think that this is the way the grant-in-aid device has grown in the hundred years since it was started back in the Civil War. The grant-in-aid device started in the midst of that war. You take the Railroad Grant Act, The Homestead Act, the Morrill Land Grant College Act were all passed in 1862. They didn't have the resources and were just as plagued by the cost of the war but they enacted it. We didn't have to worry about proliferation of programs then or a good deal later. When I first went to the Senate suddenly we had the political muscle to recognize a lot of problems and we used the same device. You remember how legislation poured out of that Congress. Almost nobody knew what the total result of our efforts was and so before we knew it we had a proliferation problem. So it isn't a question of going back and assigning blame. We have got a situation that has grown quite logically, and now we have to find a solution to it.

In trying to come up with a solution, you have the problem that local government is not as viable as it ought to be. Then you have regional-areal problems that are not governed at all and state governments that have been used to obstruct government rather than to advance it over the years. To get them to shift gears is another problem. This proliferation problem within the governmental structure is not quite at the point where you can see a solution. Ideally you should move in the direction of giving state governments a greater share of federal resources and greater discretion to use it with fewer grant programs. But they are not ready to accept that kind of responsibility. If they were, you would like to assume that they in turn would give similar discretion to local governments, to exercise initiative and responsibility and authority. We are trying to find ways to move all three levels of government in the direction of that kind of relationship to each other. I think that you ought to do it, not because of any states rights philosophy, but because in a country of this size and of this complexity you are going to get better programs, better administered and participated in to a greater degree by the people if you have it operating at the local, state and federal levels. I think that you need, increasingly, the national government to set national goals. What I am talking about is implementing those goals at those two lower levels, not simply as administrative outposts of the federal government but as viable, political agencies of the people who are their constituents. I think that it can be developed but it is going to take a lot of hard work. It is this new approach that I describe as creative federalism.

Question: But don't you feel that there are certain kinds of programs that should be implemented at the national level? I will give you one example. I see where Secretary Freeman is going around the country making talks on how to keep them down on the farm. He is saying that many industries should be encouraged to locate in these small rural communities. Now we know perfectly well that the national trend at the present time indicates that by 1980 over 80% of the people will be living in larger urban areas. It seems to me that the federal government could carry out a program of deciding what should be the apportionment of population throughout the United States. Even during Roosevelt's time we had the National Resources Planning Board. I think we need a national planning board of a similar nature. The Department of Defense, for instance, could allocate contracts on such a basis. Boeing went out to Wichita during World War II and the place has grown ever since. Couldn't this be a way of apportioning the wealth and the resources and the jobs? Perhaps incentives are needed like relocation stipends to families to move to the jobs wherever the industries are. It seems to me no one else can do this except at the federal level.

Muskie: I am not suggesting that the federal government simply be the fund-raising agency for other governments. There is obviously a national role too. Whether it should take the particular form with respect to that particular problem you raised, I think that I am not quite ready to commit myself. But we can assert ourselves in our subcommittee on this business of the impact of federal contracts, and we have an interesting statistical report on that. The national government's policies both with respect to grants-in-aid and the distribution of defense and other contracts, and the distribution of research support has a tremendous impact upon the growth of the country and the distribution of its growth and the potential of different areas of the county. I think that we must give more attention to that and initiate integrated policies with respect to all of these different inputs to the system. I couldn't agree with you more. There is a role here for the federal government. However, you are not going to be able to do it without giving a voice to the state and local governments too.

Question: I see a great need for governmental cooperation, but it seems to me that there has been a crucial element left out in that we are not franchising the ghetto dwellers. We are still not putting them in places where they can have a say in the decisions; I am thinking of the panels that met after the many riots. It seems to me that they went ahead and planned for people who were not present. If we really believe that they should be represented, shouldn't we find a way to do it?

Muskie: Sure, I think that we should contrive ways to do it. These methods might eventually fade out but not until they generate confidence in the regular political system.

Question: Do you think that might also be a way of building a constituency which would become more sophisticated and demand and expect more intergovernmental cooperation?

Muskie: I think so. A lot of cities do that now, and I think that it should be cranked into every conceivable program. The reason why you have to operate outside the regular governmental structure is obvious to all of us. I guess that we should do it at the federal level as a requirement. You can't yet just turn federal money over to the state because they are not going to necessarily use it equitably or wisely.

Question: Are there any provisions in any federal programs for training ghetto dwellers to obtain the sophistication necessary to meet with planning boards and other such groups?

Muskie: *Interaction,* I think, has some of that. I think that is something we have to try. There has been difficulty in some model cities in getting them to come in. They are suspicious and not sure that they are welcome and so you have to supply some training. You can't just take people who have never had any experience at all in the political process, off the street cold, whether they are white or black and expect that they are going to feel at home, or are going to be able to make a meaningful contribution.

Question: How do you feel about the usefulness of integrated information systems in assisting in intergovernmental cooperation?

Muskie: It is very important. There was another provision in the Demonstration Cities Act, which hasn't been funded, for setting up information offices in cities, SMSA's, and states. In the Intergovernmental Cooperation Act we have a provision to require that governors should, upon their request, be given all information on federal grant-in-aid programs that are going into the state government. There is some discussion on the part of the subcommittee to enlarge that, to require that all public officials be given information on all federal grant-in-aid programs going into the state. The federal agencies say that this is not readily available and that it would be a cumbersome job. Cumbersome or not, I think that it ought to be done. This whole business of penetrating the system to get the resources that are held out is a tough one. Take this question of regional offices. It is more of a problem out in the West than it is in the East, but even there you will have different regional offices in different cities for agencies having related programs. This may not be so bad for a large city which departmentalizes its operations, but for cities of up to thirty thousand where you have to have generalists operating your bureaucracy it presents a real problem. You have to have one man going down to New York from my home town of twenty thousand people to personally run from one department to another in that regional office. It is a ridiculous performance. We need somebody there who is sensitive to this kind of problem of small towns, and the only way you can do it is to first give state government the information and get them in the habit of taking into account the federal resources that are available. As governor, I always presented budgets in terms of what the state was going to appropriate. I am ashamed to say that I didn't know how much federal money was going to be involved in the same programs. It never occurred to me to ask. You have to develop that habit in the states. You have to arrange for the information to move and secondly you have got to follow through on what is proposed.

Another bill before our committee, the Joint Fund Simplification Act, would authorize the President to have federal agencies with related programs work together on setting up joint funds to support these programs. This would simplify forms and develop single forms or single entries in these fields although multiple agencies are involved. It would not change substance — but just simplify the process procedurally and mechanically and make it easier to penetrate the structure. I think that is a minimal first step. If you go beyond that you may give them some authority to change formulas and eliminate overlapping eligible citizens or groups. Finally, you have got to have at the federal level a day to day coordinating function. The Bureau of the Budget has accepted this duty now and it has done it by centralizing policy making with respect to budgeting. It does it even though you have all these agencies, with their own budgeting concepts and budgeting guidelines. Nevertheless, the budgeting office has been pulling it all together so that there is some meaning to it. We can do the same thing with coordination. John Gardner set it up in HEW, and Robert Weaver has done something of the same sort in HUD. I think it is a revolutionary thing that is beginning to move.

Question: What is the current status of the tax sharing proposals vis-à-vis the states and the federal government?

Muskie: I think that they are just proposals. I am cool to tax sharing as such at this point, but I am very warm on what I think those proposals are going to lead to. What we are going to finally get is something that has been described as block grants. In the broad functional areas you are going to have single federal grants, as education or health. These broad block grants will carry with them wide discretion to the states as to how to use them. There may be some conditions for quite some time related to civil rights and to a fair share for metropolitan areas and cities. Tax sharing proposals need equalization formulas now, to equalize the capacities of the different states. When they get these, I see a bright future for them.

Question: Senator, I just want to make a comment. I am a localist. About eight years ago, before President Truman appeared at one of the subcommittees on intergovernmental relations in Kansas City, he made a statement which I think we should keep in mind. He stated that he had enough experience in tax sharing to scare him. The first thing that would happen, as soon as we shared the tax locally, he predicted, would be that some demagogue would get elected on a platform of reducing taxes locally, which he would do. Then he would go on to Washington with his black bag and introduce a program to solve the local problem. The reason I point this out is that I wonder in all the tax sharing proposals, is there some consideration as to how to resolve this kind of situation?

Muskie: The amusing thing is that the most vocal opponents of tax sharing are the very people that say that the federal handouts to people make them worthless. Eliminate their incentives and reduce their sense of responsibility seems to be their rationale.

Question: You spoke favorably of block grants to states. Could you elaborate?

Muskie: I don't have any fixed view, but I am not ready to give up the direct federal local programs until I am sure that either the states have developed a sense of responsibility which will generate its own head of steam, or that there are conditions attached to block grants to states that assure a fair share of the proceeds to local governments.

Question: On the intergovernmental exchange of employees, I presume that you also intend exchanges between the elective and the appointive offices. To make all of this viable, has anybody given much thought to a joint and common pension plan, so that this one real bugaboo problem of exchange would be settled? Maybe all governmental employees would have some sort of common pooling arrangement. This is one of the real problems. The other, of course, is the old one about elective and appointive people. Has any thought been given to these sorts of mechanics?

Muskie: Yes, the bill doesn't spell out the solution to them but it creates the authority to deal with them. Nobody had a solution, but perhaps what you are going to have to start with is *ad hoc* arrangements. If particular exchanges work out all right, you can finally develop something that is sound.

Question: What about a uniform funding plan for pensions for all governmental employees?

Muskie: Well, it is an answer. I can give you some reactions to it. In my state, for example, there has been a reluctance to leave the state retirement system and go to Social Security. Certainly this ought to be the minimal objective in any exchange plan. We ought to make sure that people do not lose any part of their pension rights on any time that they spend in another level of government. Their continuing contributions ought to be in some way arranged so that they wouldn't lose by reason of loss of time, but whether they should actually participate in a better pension system in the level of government to which they may be temporarily assigned is a broader question than that. A single pension plan would simplify the problem with respect to exchanges. But then you have sickness rights, sick pay, vacation rights, and so on. I think that those are details that could be worked out. The bill creates the authority.

5

State Government and the Urban Challenge

Jesse M. Unruh

There is no need to impress upon anyone that the urban crisis is extremely complicated. Historically, I suppose it could be described as a convergence of this nation's long term failure in racial relations plus its frenzied urbanization, largely unplanned and never fully anticipated. The urban crisis includes the metropolitan sprawl of the fringes as well as the decay and human despair in the interior. It also includes the problems of rural poverty and displacement. This country today is suffering acute digestion pains resulting from malnutrition of brotherly love and an overdose of automobile induced metropolitanitis. This produces severe convulsions in the political system as well as intergenerational strains, burning of the soul and blotching of our international image.

There are many diagnosticians of this condition. Some take the view that we live today in a sick society; I do not agree. I think the organism is basically healthy. In fact we have the strongest and most vigorous system the world has ever known. But even so strong and vigorous a system seems unable to fight a small enemy with its left hand while it suffers such painful indigestion. And although the organism is strong, no diagnostician really knows what the treatment is; and, furthermore, there is no assurance that the patient will follow the prescription. Moreover, the patient is confronted with so many diagnosticians that he doesn't know which to believe.

At the minimum we know many deep-rooted habit patterns will have to be broken and the treatment will be so costly the patient will have to forego many of his other cherished expenditures. The savings account at Fort Knox is already in danger of collapsing. What concerns me most is that the political system may be permanently damaged, if indeed not destroyed, in the process of treating the urban crisis. Most of those who prescribe for the urban crisis are suggesting larger and larger doses of federal programs with little or no analysis of how the federal drugs administered through diverse programs and bureaus blend with one another. Furthermore, no prognosis is made of the effect of such drugs on local issues or on the other parts of the body politic. I am seriously concerned that the cities and local school districts will become so permanently addicted to massive federal aid that the states will atrophy.

In terms of current trends we can predict the atrophy of the states and the subservience of the cities with far greater accuracy than we can predict the cure of the urban crisis. The consequences of the ultimate decline of the states and of total federal dependency in cities, school districts and universities ought to be very carefully examined now, before the process proceeds much further. There are grave consequences throughout the political system. Representative democracy reasonably close to the people will have collapsed. The United States

Congress will be left as the only effective organ of representative government in the entire country. The only restraint on federal executive power will rest with the United States Supreme Court. Now how will the federal government and political parties function if the states do not perform a checks and balances function? What are the implications for the future of democratic government if we cannot make it work at the state level? For the most part the growth of the federal system — of the federal government — is not due to presidents, bureaucrats and congressmen sitting on the Potomac and planning ways to sieze more power. On the contrary, they seem to be under pressure to accommodate the increased needs and demands to give system and effectiveness to the diverse muddle of programs which they have already established. As a consequence, there is little long-range overall thinking in planning about where the country is or where it should be headed and certainly very little thought about the future of our system of government.

In discussing the future of the states we are severely handicapped by the traditions of the recent past. Tragically, states rights have become identified with the rights of some states to maintain two classes of citizenship. Moreover, in recent history, states' rights have been identified with the notion that government at all levels should do nothing or very little. These notions of course have not disappeared. They certainly have not disappeared in my state. We need to, in fact we have to, rise above the kind of thinking which identifies the rights of states with the right to do nothing. I am of the conviction that states have declined in considerable part largely because of their own failures. I feel that state government can and must deal more aggressively with urban problems if the urban crisis is to be resolved and if the states in the federal system are to survive. As I mentioned previously, no one has a full and adequate prescription for what it will take to resolve the urban crisis. It is reasonably clear however that it will take much. In considering this we should think in terms of coordination, cooperation and initiative among the governments. We should think primarily in terms of people and their problems.

When we approach a problem associated with the urban crisis from the standpoint of the people in the ghetto, we have reason to question whether or not, quite apart from the future consequences for our system of government, the urban crisis in fact can be resolved through federal action. Even if we assume the tenfold increase in federal aid, experience in the past cannot give us very much confidence that effective results can be obtained while the initiative and the structuring of the welfare, rehabilitation and job placement programs derive primarily from Washington.

The undereducated, unemployed black or Mexican-American who finally summons up the nerve to approach one of our government programs or agencies is really beginning an obstacle course. There are literally dozens of reasons for rejecting him at dozens of places along the process, or dozens of reasons for referring him to other government programs or agencies to start the process all over again. There is little wonder the people we want most to help are the least inclined to accept help. We found in California that an intensive study of our hard core unemployment showed some people have gone through training cycles at least four times and never wound up on a job. Many, if not most, of the programs thus far which have derived from federal initiative have contributed further to the alienation of the hard-pressed poor.

Thus far the federal government seems most successful with programs such as social security and programs which eventually benefit middle class or main-stream citizens in their time of personal crisis. The strength of these programs rests in a clean, bureaucratic system with forums and systems and clients that know something about forums and systems. For a hundred years the federal government has had the primary responsibility for the American Indians and has failed tragically to assist them toward self sufficiency. This is a tragedy not only on the part of the federal government but also on the part of the state and local regions who have failed to assume any responsibility whatsoever. Further there is a recent well publicized report on poverty which points out that the Department of Agriculture has been highly successful in developing agricultural technology and in providing basic support during periods of low prices, drought or other contingencies for essentially self sufficient, self supporting farmers.

But that department has failed totally to assume any responsibility whatsoever for the rural poor. As a consequence, the rural poor leave the country, go to the city slums, with no preparation for the city environment. So long as the federal government conducts or sets the rules for programs there can be no greater coordination or system on the state and local level than there is in Washington. There is very likely to be less. And we are engaged in problems as complicated as those of the poor, the rural and the urban, the black and the Mexican American, the Puerto Rican and all the rest. We are confronted with such a problem that we need an approach which will enable and encourage and reward their feeling of identification with their local communities.

The federal bureaucracy can never produce this needed sense of community. We need a system which will give the down and out in our society an identification with our system of government. Despite the scandals and swindles connected with the old city political machines, they did provide the European immigrant the feeling that government officials, someone important, cared about them and their families, was ready to help them with their needs and their welfare. For a long time the labor unions in this country provided some of this also. But city government has become, as some say, extremely well run but totally ungoverned. Neither the city governments nor the labor unions have been serving this purpose in the last thirty years, partly because many of the old cities have become predominantly ghettos and partly because city governments and labor unions have become middle-classed and professionalized. And to this we must add the observation that the urban public school system went through a period of ignoring their primary mission of providing equal educational opportunities for all children. They, like most other institutions in this country, did a far better job for the European immigrant than they have done for the blacks and our other contemporary minorities.

Now that everyone recognizes the urban crisis is upon us, it is relatively easy to diagnose what has gone wrong with our system and the various institutions within that system. Except for a very few of the larger states, state government has been almost totally unresponsive to the needs associated with the urban crisis and rural poverty. The states have declined in considerable part because of their failures in these areas. State governments must deal more aggressively with these problems, if the crisis is to be resolved, and if the states and the federal system are to survive. State government within the present structure of government still has the power to assume an effective initiative. It has obvious powers and opportunities which cities and counties do not have. It has the power to encourage and guide and prod local government to do more, do it more effectively, and to do it in keeping with the conditions of the local regions. In considering the need for initiative and leadership of state government, we ought to keep in mind that we still have a federal system. Many programs, even those initiated by Congress are administered or implemented or sometimes interfered with by the state, although, as I stressed before, the states may be finally buried by the urban crisis. They will not die easily; certainly not rapidly enough to allow close ties between the city and the federal government to solve the urban crisis, if indeed it can be solved. At the very least, if we do not make instrumentalities of progress out of the states, they are going to survive as impediments, short of major constitutional revision. This is a fact of life, and I do not think that it is viable politically to assume that we are going to have that kind of constitutional revision. The states are going to be there; and if they are not helpful, they are going to be roadblocks. If the state government, especially legislatures, will face up to the needs of the people; a great deal more initiative can come from state and local governments. This of course depends in part on the people. Are the people able and willing to permit the state and local governments the revenues that are needed? Do governors and legislatures have the courage to ask for them? These are the issues which confront governors and legislatures and voters.

The interest of the cities in solving their problems is directly associated with the more effective operation of state legislatures. This is not just a matter of why can't those bums up there understand what we need, but a matter of understanding that the legislature itself in far too many cases is poorly equipped, if not totally unequipped, to deal effectively with today's problems of the cities. Legislatures have to go against many difficult pressures with very little information and very few decision making tools, with the consequence that they are in large part an obstruction. Legislatures also have the right and the obligation to ask whether or not the programs supported by state revenues are effective. If they are not, and there is a vital job to be done, it is the obligation of the legislatures to suggest constructive alternatives. If representative democracy has any meaning, it is that legislators and city councilmen ane even congressmen ought to be closer to the people than executives and administrators. The alternatives which are initiated by a legislature are likely to be closer to the people and more meaningful to the people.

Pouring additional revenues into the state and local government is not sufficient — maybe highly desirable and certainly necessary, but not sufficient. Our institutions in themselves need to be strengthened. We need to develop a system of state government which is suitable to the problems of the urban areas. To broaden the powers and opportunities of cities to deal with the problems associated with the urban crisis depends upon state action, especially upon legislative action. The legislature which prevents the city from raising its own revenues to meet current problems can certainly expect the city to step up its efforts to get federal revenue. This kind of activity also has the effect of lowering the stature of that city's legislative delegation. I think a legislature that consistently refuses to give local government the financial independence it needs to solve its problems ought to be told flatly and completely by the people that they are in fact encouraging further encroachment for the federal government. Obviously cities and other units of local government must be given the autonomy they need to cope with their problems and conduct their own programs. More positively, state governments should reward and encourage and promote such an issue. At the same time we need to keep in mind that many cities and counties are not meaningful units of government.

Since all such units are created by state statutes, or in some cases by state constitutions, meaningful organization and consolidation of local units of government depends on state action. But it also depends upon some give on the part of the local people. If a state legislature is to be asked to help all local units of government, and clearly many of those are incapable of helping themselves even with such aid, then the legislature in its efforts to consolidate and update and make more meaningful local government ought to have the support of the meaningful units of local government in that drive. Unfortunately, I know of no study in any state, including my own, that has thought through in any systematic way the range of action which a state government can take concerning the problems associated with the urban crisis.

Obviously state statutes need to be reviewed to determine whether and how, and I suppose more the latter, the poor are penalized. And I think it is demonstrable that the poor are penalized in diverse and devious ways: interest rates permitted on short-term, high-risk loans; tax systems including the loopholes permitted for people who have the ability or the resources to crawl through, that used to protect the seller but fail to provide any protection for the consumer; welfare assistance that discourages the poor from seeking any forms of gainful employment; and juvenile and penal codes which can reasonably protect those who can afford legal services, but penalize those who get into courts with no legal representation. We still consider it exceptional when a middle-class boy gets into serious trouble, but our social subconscious also recognizes that a black kid in the slums has to be alienated from his own environment not to get into serious trouble. Penal institutions, including our so-called juvenile correction institutions, in most cases operate primarily as schools of crime. Those who take the course come out better schooled in how to become criminals and even more alienated from the orthodox society.

This complex issue has no ready solution, but it is clearly a responsibility of state government to operate the lion's share of the penal systems in our country. Although I am not optimistic that the primary initiative for solving the current crisis will come from state government, I think there is a possibility, and certainly there is the hope, that it will participate considerably more than it has in the past. The reapportionment of state legislatures combined with the impact of the crisis is pushing some state governments toward a realistic consultation with urban problems. We all try to start out in our own little sphere — recognizing that if we face the kind of momentous decisions we need today and the kind of complicated problems that confront us and feel that we are solely responsible for their final solution, that we will be frozen into total inaction — we all try to do our best in whatever little corner we operate from. And this has meant to me, principally, attempting to upgrade the status and functioning of the state governments. The master movement has gathered some steam across the nation. The Citizens Conference on State Legislatures which has its headquarters in Kansas City is a very important part of that movement. There are a great many more groups doing something to attempt to give to legislatures the independence, the extra teeth to make it possible for them to begin to understand these problems and eventually to cope more meaningfully with them.

If the states are to act meaningfully in this crisis, they must rapidly reverse the trend of the last fifty years. The governors and agency administrators must change their traditional habits of thinking small. Legislatures and governors must force state programs to coordinate effectively at the local level and to relate meaningfully to the people. If the states are to become a viable force again, they must think beyond minimal federal standards. Some states, in fact many states, have the capacity, if they will but give themselves the ability, to venture, experiment and set the pace. The states should also exert counterpressure on the federal government to get its messy uncoordinated house in order. And to accomplish this the first thing that will have to be done is to revitalize state legislatures and do it rapidly.

It is difficult to say for certain how one gets an active, creative legislature; but certain things are clear. Any large state with sizeable urban problems requires regular annual sessions and the machinery for legislature to call itself into session in response to crises. Legislatures must be willing to spend time in studying complex issues, and they must be equipped with the research and staff services needed. If they cannot understand the problems themselves, and there are many legislators who can't, then they need to have the expertise on a full-time basis that can and will do that kind of job for them. If legislators are to get closer to the problems of their constituents, they should be equipped with offices not only in the state capitals but also in their home districts so the people can make their views known in a better fashion than they now do. The role of the state legislatures in resolving the problems associated with the urban crisis should be accepted, recognized and supported first by the legislatures themselves, from whom the principle initiative must come, by civic leadership, the mass media, the general public, and the executive branches of state governments.

A governor who will not support strengthening a legislature does not deserve to have his own powers strengthened or perhaps even continued. The governor who thinks that a supine legislature, over which he can walk at will, is a great thing to have around should remember than governors come, and governors go, but the lobbyists stay on forever. And if he can walk over the legislature occasionally, the third house can do it all the time.

I think essentially what is now going on in our society is the struggle to see whether in this era of radical change, when the physical limitations on our life have been so drastically altered, when we can see solutions for most of the physical problems that man has faced all of his life, our social institutions can accommodate that rapid change. That is essentially what the students on our campuses are questioning. It is in fact what the people on the streets are questioning, and it is demonstrably true that up to this point institutions have not been able to accommodate that change. Our social institutions which should be the most susceptible are in fact the most resistant. We know that in this connection state legislatures have not in the past served as effectively as they should as forums for airing the problems of blacks and other minorities. Largely we have swept this problem under the rug, if indeed we recognize that it was there at all. The role our large cities once served in the sociopolitical assimilation for the various groups within our society is becoming less and less the case, largely because of the altered composition of the population within the boundaries of the old cities.

Thus it seems to me that state legislatures should be developed and recognized as a sort of a meeting place; as a place of negotiation and as a place for developing understanding among suburbanites, city dwellers and various socioeconomic classes and among racial and ethnic groups. If this does not happen in state legislatures, then I don't know where it will happen in our society; and I suggest that our society will not be the same as we have known. The current crisis demonstrates the loss of public confidence in almost all of our established public institutions — political institutions. Many have remarked in recent years that we are beginning to behave more and more like a Latin American republic.

I do not believe that the public is likely to have any more confidence in our political system than they presently do if it continues to be ever more remotely centralized in Washington. This gigantic insoluable bureaucratic block between public and program, between public and policy makers, must be hewn down. As things stand, public confidence in government depends upon confidence in

Washington. It is very likely to center on a very transitional confidence in the personality of one man — the President. At times that is fine, but the events of 1968 demonstrate, if nothing else, that we ought never again to settle for such a system. The alternative then, it seems to me, is to try to restore confidence in the state and local governments; to try to impress upon the people and the politicians who deal with these instrumentalities the necessity for giving to them the tools that will bring their decisional capacity into this century and allow them to cope with the problems of today. Confidence in state governments can only be restored when those governments have moved effectively, by themselves and with the support of the people, to bring themselves into this century so that they can cope with this century's problems.

Discussion

Question: How much political action should local units of government take with respect to state legislative bodies? Should they actively lobby their state legislatures? Should they lobby their state legislators just when the legislature is in session? What are other means of motivating the legislature from both the legislature's point of view and the local government officials point of view in our democratic system?

Unruh: That is a long and involved question. I think of a very crass reply that I heard someone give once to a rather high powered operator who came to Sacramento and asked how much it would cost to get a major bill passed. Someone told him that you can buy the legislature but you got to do it on the installment plan. That is a little bit too callous but has a great deal of truth in it. The fact of the matter is that if you go only to them in your moments of crisis, you are likely to find them relatively unresponsive. If, however, you are involved with them on a long term, on-going basis, they are more responsive.

I think legislators are mostly impressed and influenced by people with on-going contacts in whom they have confidence. I had my big school superintendent from the state come in last week on a crash basis. They had to have seventy million dollars this year or their major school districts were going down the drain. Well, I am not terribly impressed with that, because we have been in session for four and one-half months; and this is the first time they have bothered to say their need was so desperate. Similarly I am not much impressed with people from the business world who come up and tell me that all of a sudden they need this or that. But I am impressed with people I know on an on-going basis who have bothered to call me and to talk to me even when I have a problem and they don't have.

I think if local groups were involved in trying to help a legislator who has some desire to help himself obtain some of the tools that are necessary to enlightened decision-making, they might find the legislator more responsive when they came to him with their problems. I think lobbying is a year-round activity. Our major cities and counties, and certainly the cities associations in the League of California Cities and the County Supervisors Association, work diligently all year round and they are awfully effective.

If you turn loose the County Supervisors Association and the League of Cities on the California Legislature, you are pretty lucky if you can beat that combination. They don't always get what they want on a positive basis, but nobody runs over their combined efforts. If you are going to expect the legislatures to work all year round, even if they are not in session, you are going to have to keep on lobbying them. I'm not sure I have answered the other part of your question but it's an on-going effort that's impressive to politicians. You need to be with them sometime when they need you and not just when you need them.

Question: What is the best way to improve the quality of our legislatures?

Unruh: Well, there are many ways. I think the one single thing that a legislature needs in order to enable it to cope somewhat realistically with the problems that of a state this size, is a decent staff operation. That means staffing it at least up to the level of what is available to the executive branch and probably considerably beyond that. I would not be surprised if the executive branch also needs some strengthening in the state. I think that beyond that you have got to give the legislator a place to do business. You can't conduct any other business without a place of business, and I don't know how you can expect the legislator to operate if he doesn't have an office too.

Beyond that there are a good many things that a legislator ought to have, but if the legislature can first feel that it really can have an effect on these major problems then the rest of it will come, such as salary increases and other things. I think quite clearly that your legislature of Missouri is far too big. [House of Representatives 163, Senate 25.] We have a House of eighty members and Senate of forty members in California, which enables us to do some really meaningful things for our individual legislators. For example, we give each one of our legislators two thousand dollars a month to run his district office. That means he can have an administrative assistant to keep the office open full-time with a full-time secretary, people who can handle the case load — the complaints that come into his office — so he can devote his time to studying his legislation. In addition to that we give them a full-time secretary in the Sacramento office, each one has not only an office for himself in Sacramento and at home, but adequate office space for his staff assistant. But you can't do that if you have such a big House.

Missouri should have about fifty representatives and a senate of about thirty, or thirty and sixty, or something like that. That not only gives the advantage of being able to do more things for the members but in addition, gives the legislator more visibility. It makes him a bigger guy around and puts him in a position where more people are watching him, which is good for a lot of reasons. It gets rid of a lot of the shenanigans. The more people who get involved in the process, the more people who are watching, the less likely you are to have the kind of things that go on in state legislatures now. Many legislatures or individual legislators get by because nobody is watching. You can't possibly keep your eye on one hundred and eighty-seven people. Even the *Kansas City Star* can't do that.

Question: Could legislative reapportionment improve the quality of the state legislature? We have often heard that the city would be much better represented in the state legislature and more inclined toward solving some of the urban problems of the country if reapportionment gives the urban areas a larger vote. **Unruh:** No, it is not true at all in California. It varies from state to state. I believe that it has been true, for example, in the state of Maryland which was able last year after reapportionment to move rather dramatically in the field of taxation and enacted what I think probably is the most progressive tax system in the nation. In California the folklore of liberalism indicated that reapportionment of our senate (our house has always been on a population basis) would result in liberalizing that body. The fact of the matter is that our senate this year, I think, is the most conservative it has been in the last thirty years.

Reapportionment resulted in bringing the liberal-conservative issue to a focus, pitting the suburban and the core cities eyeball to eyeball.

Previously when we had senators from rural areas it was possible to deal with them because, by and large, they were not sitting with a bunch of scared suburban whites surrounding and encircling the black core of the city. As a consequence you could deal with them on some things that were of help to the core cities. You can't do that with the suburbanites, you know. They sit right there, and they represent the guy that lives down the block from them, scared to death that he is going to get a black neighbor, or that his kids are going to have to go to school in an integrated neighborhood, or that someone is going to change the school financing formula in order to put more money into the problem areas of the city. Suburbia has already done a pretty good job of protecting itself by writing most of the state-wide financing formulas. So reapportionment, I would say, has aggravated our problems and particularly the problems of the core cities in California.

Question: Do we have representative government in the United States? If your answer is yes, why is major legislation usually reaction against crises which would imply you are not representing the situation. If your answer is no, what would you propose that we do about it?

Unruh: I think it quite clearly representative government, as I said during the course of my main speech, but it is not functioning well. It is not responding quickly enough to problems we have and we are reacting to crisis — we have to kill John Kennedy to get a civil rights bill, we have to kill Martin Luther King in order to get an open housing bill. The crisis is that we are in a time of crisis politics, when apparently the only way our systems do react is to pressure. That is the reason the people are on the street instead of at the ballot box. That is the reason the kids at school are protesting — because the institutions are not responding. I think there is an explanation. I am not at all sure what to do about it.

John Kennedy once told me, when he was having trouble with a very reluctant Congress in passing his legislative program — this was the last time he was in California in June of 1963, about the time that Lassiter and various and sundry other commissions were excoriating Congress (largely on the mistaken thesis that Congress was out of step with the majority of opinions of the people) the President said he felt quite clearly that this was not true. He said that Congress was reflecting the opinion of the majority of the people.

We are today in a situation where in the short run, it seems to me, a majority of the people feel that they have more to lose then they have to gain by significant action to deal with these very tough problems. Conversely, the people who have something to gain in the short run are a distinct minority — a big minority but a distinct minority. This is a very difficult situation to resolve, so what is that poeple will not respond, will not move to give up some of the short run advantages for the long run advantages to save the system, until there is a crisis. That is why there was no action in the war on poverty until after the riots in Los Angeles or Cleveland or Detroit or other places.

It is the reason you don't get action at the universities. We just don't respond; and I don't know — really don't know — how we face it. I've come to conclude that at least the beginning is to do whatever we can from wherever we sit. That to me means being a state legislator, giving the state legislature tools to understand at least some of these things. That doesn't mean we are going to respond, but it certainly means that we are going to be a little bit better than before. The legislatures won't like it. Change will be forced on the members, and many times the legislatures themselves will be the biggest impediment to change. They have a nice little fraternity with leadership having dinner with the lobbyists every night, not wanting to change anything. You have to force that change. But this is the great question of our time — whether we can make our institutions respond rapidly enough so they will not be destroyed. If they can't respond, they are going to be destroyed. I think it is that simple.

6 ## Executive Leadership in the Urban County

Lawrence K. Roos and Thomas C. Kelly

Lawrence K. Roos, Supervisor, St. Louis County, Missouri: As chief executive officer of a large urban county I know the importance of serving our citizens efficiently and effectively. I am convinced that, unless we find the means to improve the ability of our local governments to meet local problems, there will be an increasing trend toward greater involvement of the federal government in local affairs — a trend which I would not welcome.

County government has traditionally occupied a middle posture between state and city government. It was once fashionable to poke fun at county government as the "dark continent of American politics," a governmental "no-man's land" which no one knew or cared much about. To some extent this criticism was justified, for the administration of county business was largely inefficient and archaic. Today the situation is changing; county government is improving. Counties are in an ideal position to perform certain area-wide functions which fragmented smaller units with limited jurisdictional authority cannot. Well-run counties which provide area-wide functions to all citizens of the region, whether in cities or in rural sections, may provide the true salvation of local government as we know it. Serious obstacles constrain the full potential of county government; archaic constitutional restrictions, impossible state laws, crude and chaotic administrative organizations, primitive tax structures, and unbelievably prohibitive operating procedures act as barriers to effective government. These impediments must be eliminated if our counties are to perform their best function. Counties must modernize their organizational structures, adopt modern procedures for the conduct of public business, institute modern personnel practices, and meet the area-wide service needs of the citizens they serve to fulfill their potential.

I occupy the office of Supervisor, or chief executive, of St. Louis County which has a population of 900,000 people and covers an area of 500 square miles. It is a county whose population has increased threefold in twenty years and which is destined to continue to grow to an estimated 1,500,000 by the year 1980. We operate under a limited home-rule charter originally adopted in 1950; limited, because we still have been unable to obtain from the Missouri legislature the full home rule authority essential for the best operation of our government. Under our charter, we have a chief executive, elected at large, and a seven-member county council, each member representing a particular district within the county. Both the supervisor and the members of the council are popularly elected at partisan elections. Unfortunately, our 1950 charter did not go far enough toward streamlining our government, leaving intact numerous independently elected administrative positions such as treasurer, coroner, sheriff, recorder of deeds, county clerk, and circuit clerk. Only gradually, through a series of charter amendments, have most of these positions been made appointive.

There are four essential ingredients for effective government in today's urban counties: (1) a strong elected executive; (2) an elected legislative body, small enough to be workable, with members elected from districts of equal population; (3) appointed, rather than elected, administrative heads of departments and divisions within the government; and (4) full home rule authority to enable the citizens of the county by majority vote, to design their government so as best to meet local needs.

It has been suggested that the county chief executive be a professional manager, appointed by the county council, instead of an elected official. Certainly there is much to be said for the council-manager form of government. More than 1800 city and county governments have adopted this system in the past fifty years. Professional administrators bring skills of formal training and education to bear on solving governmental problems. In my opinion, the disadvantages of the council-manager system outweigh the advantages. Such an arrangement defies the traditional separation of powers principle embodied in our Constitution and American tradition. All other levels of American government traditionally encompass separate branches of executive, legislative, and judicial functions as a means of providing checks and balances. The professional manager system concentrates virtually all power in the legislative council, which can hire and fire the executive. I believe this can make the administrator more concerned with pleasing the council than serving the interests of the citizens. The appointed manager cannot be as sensitive to the needs and desires of the people whom he serves; he is not in a position to be as reflective of citizen opinion as is an elected executive. Frequently managers are recruited from outside the community, and have no native loyalty to it.

An elected chief executive is more "visible" to the public than an appointed official. It is easier to fix the responsibility for the functioning of government on an elected executive than on a multi-member council which appoints the administrator. If the elected chief executive fails to function effectively, he can be removed at the polls. There is nothing to prevent him from having professional talent on his executive staff, while at the same time bearing the decision-making responsibility. In my opinion the chief executive of a large urban county should be elected at large in partisan elections held preferably at times other than presidential elections.

To perform the legislative function, I recommend a county council, elected on a partisan basis with members chosen from districts of equal size. There is justifiable difference of opinion concerning the optimum size of such a legislative body. St. Louis County, with 900,000 people, operates satisfactorily with a seven-man council. Los Angeles County, with a population of eight million people, has a legislative body consisting of only five members. Whether the council consists of five, seven, or thirteen members is of little concern as long as its size is not so great that members become overly responsive to local pressures rather than to the welfare of the whole community.

As one who has experienced the consequences of a charter with an unnecessarily large number of elective administrative positions, I strongly recommend that all administrative officials, except the executive, the county council, and the prosecuting attorney, be made appointive rather than elective. The existence of many independently elected officials diffuses the executive responsibility, and severely limits the power of the executive to coordinate the functions and programs of his government. It permits "buck-passing" between the executive and elected department heads and it lends itself to potential disunity between the executive and heads of important departments if they are of different political persuasions. Look what happened when Ford tried to operate with a General Motors Executive . . . or imagine if the members of the President's cabinet at the national level were elected officials. Just think of the chaos we would have if the Secretary of Defense or other cabinet rank officials were elected and were members of the opposite political party of the chief executive. Yet this frequently happens in local governments with a multitude of elected administrative officials.

The successful operation of modern government requires the highest caliber of professionally trained and qualified employees. Government can no longer function effectively on the basis of "to the victor belongs the spoils." Employees must be recruited for what they know, not whom they know. While the chief executive should retain the authority for appointing his key department heads, other employees must be given the job security and professional status of a modern merit system. In 1966, St. Louis County extended the merit system to all 2500 of its employees with the exception of principal department heads, their immediate assistants and the staffs of the executive and legislative officials. The new system removed the pressures of partisan politics and, as a result, upgraded the status of employment in county government. The merit system has already proved its value as a recruitment aid and represents an essential element in efficient county government.

A final ingredient for urban county government is full home rule. By home rule I mean the right of the citizens of our urban counties to determine by majority vote the form of government best suited to solve their particular local needs. Without home rule, counties must go hat in hand to state capitals for permission to function in the ways they know are best suited to solve their own problems. Unfortunately, our requests for home rule have consistently fallen on deaf ears, and the legislatures have continued to refuse to permit the citizens of our largest urban areas to solve their own problems in their own way.

As I said at the outset, I believe that local government is best suited to meet local needs. Yet for local government to meet its responsibilities it must be structured to do the job. Strong, streamlined counties are an important part of effective local government. I earnestly believe that county government today, particularly in urban areas, has an unprecedented opportunity to prove its worth as the keystone of a durable nationwide local government structure geared to an everexpanding urban society. If we cooperate in strengthening our counties and succeed in prevailing upon the state legislature to give us the tools to do the job, then and only then will we succeed in strengthening our local governments and thereby assure the survival of a system of free democracy.

Dr. Thomas C. Kelly, Administrative Assistant, Prince George's County, Maryland: County government is moving in the United States. We see it in increased levels of expenditures, by the quality of people attracted to county government and by the type of services counties are rendering. Two factors have contributed to these changes. First, the federal government requires a streamlining and professionalization of local government to qualify for federal money. Second, the National Association of County Officials has brought effective administrative changes to county government by attracting professionals from various walks of life, and by bringing mutually interested parties together.

Formerly, in Prince George's County, the judge or the commissioner who spent the least anount of money was considered the best elected official. The courthouse was staffed with people who were effective in the precincts but who were not fully qualified for their professional tasks. The county government did not have many problems because it did not do much. However, today, eight hundred people a week are moving to Prince George's County. The county's population has increased from 119,000 in 1951 to about 650,000 in 1968 and Prince George's is still growing at a rapid rate. This growth has created many problems. Many former counties are now urban centers providing a full range of municipal services. Today's politician is caught between the new citizens' demand for services and the old timers' desire to hold down taxes.

Two levels of county organization can be considered: the first and most important is the policy-making level of the elected official who must choose from among alternatives, the most equitable expenditure and taxation levels. All too often there are no alternatives, there isn't enough information.

The second level of county organization is the technical layer of local government including officials such as the personnel director, the central purchasing director, and the public works engineer. The specialization of these technicians is probably more pronounced in agencies such as welfare and health where the first loyalties of the public health nurse or the social worker is to her profession and not to her organization. Quite often the most resounding criticism of welfare policies comes from within and not outside the welfare department. The directors of these agencies are often not concerned with the larger problems of the county. This is a particular problem when budget requests are being presented. The generalist manager is responsible for evaluating these requests, for knowing the goals of the policy makers and for reconciling the two.

There must be a good relationship between the manager and the policy body if the manager is to function adequately as a "buffer" in resolving conflicts.

Let us look at the three different forms of local government most prevelant in the United States and evaluate their strengths and weaknesses. First is the commission form of government generally consisting of from three to seven members each of whom has a portfolio of departments for which he is administratively responsible. The big disadvantage is that there is no central leadership and if the commission is politically split, it can cause continual struggle. Another problem results from the liaison responsibility imposed on the commissioners. For example, one commissioner may be in charge of health, welfare, and the library and is to keep the other commissioners informed. In practice, the department head can use his liason commissioner as a lobbyist for that particular agency, with the result that the craftiest department head ends up with the biggest budget. This is not good government. The major advantage of the commission form of government, especially with an elected chairman, is that it spreads the work.

The second form is the so-called "county manager" structure which provides for a professional administrator in the local charter. The manager is usually prepared by education and experience for his position and is often recruited from outside the county. Such a county manager lacks a political base. However, since the nature of his job *is* political, this is one of the paradoxes of the system. The manager must combine a knowledge of the needs and values of the citizens as well as of the elected officials. The manager form has the advantage of bringing professionalism to government. It is an excellent way to move from a rural to an urban county because it puts a man in charge who knows the most important administrative changes needed. A county commission which meets only once or twice a month needs a county manager.

The third form of local government is based on an elected executive with a county council which introduces the possibility of executive-legislative conflict. For example, in Baltimore County the elected executive refused to talk to the council for a whole year, resulting in much "buck-passing" and little action. There is an assumption that separation of powers is an intrinsic part of our heritage. I believe it is a myth to say that separation of powers is a requirement for good democratic government at the local level. When Montesquieu wrote about separation of powers he was lecturing to the British form of government which combines legislative and executive powers under Parliament. I think this confusion of powers makes sense in county government.

My own recommendation for a growing urban county is to have an elected executive, but to make him first among equals. He must then be supplied a professional administrative officer whose job would be to compile the budget; to supervise personnel, accounting, and data processing; to settle interdepartmental disputes; to develop a good management system, and to provide his elected official with intelligent information. This would leave the elected executive ample time to think, to reflect, and to provide policy leadership for the community.

Discussion

Question: Dr. Kelly, do you propose that the chief administrative officer be responsible solely to the elected executive or to the group of which the elected executive is the first among equals?

Dr. Kelly: He should be appointed and fired by the group, but supervised and responsible to the elected executive. The county governing body, in other words, has both legislative and executive powers. At present, Prince George's County has a five man board elected for four years. The board elects the chief executive who is paid considerably more than other members, is full time, and by law, is responsible for the administration of the county. One of the problems has been that the chairman who is elected by the board can be removed at any time by the board. In practice this has meant that the chairmanship is rotated every two years. A reorganization commission is now suggesting this is not good procedure. One person should have the responsibility for four years. Often it takes at least a year to get to know the operation, especially if you have a whole new board. The chairman should be elected at large by the people and not be removable by the board.

Question: How does the chief administrative officer form differ from the county manager form of government?

Dr. Kelly: The most important difference is that the chief administrative officer does not have the power to hire and fire department heads since that power resides in the board. A chief administrative officer can recommend to the board the dismissal of department heads. The county manager by definition *is* the administrative chief for the county. Under this system there is a sharing of power because political responsibility is focused on the chairman who has some executive responsibilities, but administrative responsibilities are focused on the county administrative officer.

Question: You did not mention in your discussion on forms of government one where a strong mayor would have the right to appoint the administrative officer.

Dr. Kelly: This would be the case where there is an independently elected chief executive with power to hire his administrator. The quality of the administrator hired would depend upon the chief executive and he would be responsible only to him. The professional administrator generally prefers to work under the county manager system where he can negotiate with several bosses and where the charter gives him some specific powers.

Question: Mr. Roos, would you briefly mention your programs of intergovernmental relations and then your own thoughts about the responsibilities for an intergovernmental relations position, particularly within the county organization.

Mr. Roos: In the St. Louis metropolitan area there is a fragmentation of local government. We have 164 separate local governments within our county, including 95 municipalities. There has not been much success in achieving a formal merger of these various large local governments. The relationship between the city of St. Louis and St. Louis County has not always been the best because many people have left the city. There are racial problems involved. We have set up a regional council of government, the East—West Gateway Coordinating

Council, which is functioning quite effectively. It consists of the local governments of the entire metropolitan area on both the Illinois and the Missouri sides of the river. This group coordinates those areas of service where area-wide cooperation and coordination makes good sense. We maintain our own sovereignty, and it is a voluntary association, but nonetheless quite effective. It is working on an overall land-use plan which is a basis for rapid transit planning, and is developing a sewer plan and a recreation plan. We must work together if our area is going to get federal funds. I am personally opposed to federal involvement, but the federal government has made one major contribution. It forced us to set up this mechanism and it is creating cooperation in St. Louis County.

There is a municipal league of cities in St. Louis County. It has a committee of the fifteen largest cities with which the county government has developed a good working relationship. The opposition to our efforts to improve our area has come mostly from the small municipalities where officials frequently fear the big county is going to overtake them, destroying their identity. In response to the need or importance of a chief executive, I think you have got to have one personality to take the lead and be able to speak for the county point of view. If you have a board it has to speak as a group; you do not have the salesmanship that is necessary to represent the country's interests. I think you have to have a person with some power to sit with the mayors of the cities and work out these problems.

Question: I wonder if you might discuss relationships with the state and the federal governments.

Mr. Roos: Our entire air pollution control efforts are tied to the state, which makes the rules. The planning function for the entire area involves federal funding and our health functions all involve funds from the federal government, as does the war on poverty program in St. Louis County, which is administered by a nongovernmental board of directors. I think one of the weaknesses of the poverty program in the St. Louis area is that we are not as locally responsible as we should be. Our office of Economic Opportunity program spends about sixteen million dollars a year with no political responsibility, only a lay board of fine citizens. If somebody goes south with the money tomorrow, nobody is going to be voted out of office, nobody is going to be held accountable. The same is true with our metropolitan sewer district. These people are appointed and not elected.

Dr. Kelly: We have an interesting development in Maryland. A constitutional drafting committee suggested the idea that county government should be the primary form of government. In Prince George's County there are twenty-eight incorporated municipalities and the largest one has a population of 25,000. These small municipalities perform a few services, such as garbage collection and snow removal. The drafting committee has recommended that municipalities be the creatures of the county. You can imagine the problems this has created in our relationship with these municipalities. We have a municipal league within the county and prior to the constitutional convention meeting we had good relationships. We meet together to work out various problems on an administrative level. There are supplementary efforts on the political level since many of the mayors are active in partisan politics and seek out their political friends on the county commission.

We also have a council of governments which includes counties in Maryland and Virginia and the District of Columbia. Elective officials represent their jurisdictions. One of the problems is that most of these people are so tied up with other responsibilities that there is a danger that the council staff will run things. The council has been very successful on noncontroversial matters. For example, by the end of the year all the jurisdictions except the District of Columbia will have adopted a new air pollution ordinance. The District has a real problem because many federal installations are polluting the air and cannot be controlled by the District. The Council of Governments has also worked effectively in major areas including water pollution control.

Probably the most successful cooperation has been in police protection as exemplified by the establishment of a new metropolitan police communication system. We are talking about a three billion dollar transportation system for the Washington metropolitan area. We have a long-standing Washington Suburban Sanitary Authority established in 1919. It has received some criticism because it makes decisions affecting the growth patterns in Prince George's County over which elected officials have no power. Last year the elected officials did something about it. Now a five year plan for this agency must be approved by both Montgomery County (a county bordering Washington, D. C. to the north and west) and Prince George's County. We also have a metropolitan park and planning commission agency but it may be split up because of dissatisfaction with the joint planning approach.

Question: Dr. Kelly, I think you are in the wrong town to sell a strong elective executive type of government because we have both a city government and a county government where the chief elected official can be outvoted. On the other hand, you point to Mr. Roos and say the "only objection you have to the elected executive is that it's a man-killing job." Yet, compare Mr. Roos's job with the President's job, requiring political and executive responsibilities for the entire country.

Dr. Kelly: Mr. Roos has pointed out that someone should speak for the county; the chairman speaks for our county because she has the support of the board. At the same time she can use this board to help her politically and administratively. I think the executive should be stronger but still share its powers with the rest of the council. The demands on the elective officials to meet with civic and professional groups are extreme. We have to split this up and it has worked out very well. The drawback that I see between the elective executive and the council is not that it is a man-killing job, but all too often a stalemate develops or you have the "buck-passing" that exists in some counties where they have an elected executive system. I think if you can avoid this problem you can still get the benefits of a vocal political leader which I believe is needed for good administration.

Question: It seems to me you have been living under an ideal set of circumstances... I mean if your council is supporting your executive, your opinion has been colored.

Dr. Kelly: Yes, this could be a problem. Generally one of the major points brought up is the problem that exists between the Congress and the President. We have had strong presidents with support of their parties, but I think this type of separation of powers on a local level is not necessary.

Question: Mr. Roos, you mentioned your need to go to the state capital for a full home rule authority. Is this in the Constitution or the Statutes of Missouri and specifically what needs to be done in this area?

Mr. Roos: I would think the best way to get home rule is with a constitutional provision. Some have toyed with the idea of having county authority given through statutory authority. If this is done and you then want it changed to a broader type of home rule, you have to return to the legislature to give you that authority. What we sought in the last legislature, and what has been sought by preceding county administrators of both political persuasions for the last ten years, is the right of broad constitutional authority for the people of a county to establish the type of government they see fit and give the county any authority that does not contravene constitutional and statutory limitations. For example, we had to go to the legislature to get special permission for the county to administer a county-wide air pollution control program because all municipalities could not do it. We have only limited authority and I think constitutional home rule authority is the ideal way of solving our problems.

Dr. Kelly: This question has caused us some trying experiences. We tried to distinguish between home rule and charter government for political reasons. The Maryland legislature has given Prince George's County some home rule and flexibility in what we can do. There is a provision in the constitution that a county can become a charter county by going through a procedure of electing five men to write the charter. Since 1923 only four counties have taken advantage of this procedure. The reason is that it becomes such a political battle. The impression is created that the charter writers are trying to replace the incumbent elected officials which has not worked well. Therefore, the constitution drafting committee put in a section in the new Maryland Constitution that would require *all* counties to become charter counties by 1972.

Mr. Roos: By lack of home rule, if one wrote his own charter he would still be limited by the state and by the powers given to the county government. For example, we have eighty-five separate police departments and a county police department in St. Louis County. We have just completed a thorough study recommending a reorganization of responsibility with the county providing supportive services to municipalities having certain local police functions. If we had home rule the majority of the people in St. Louis County could vote for this police reorganization. Under the present limitations though, we can do nothing unless every police department and every police chief agrees to reorganize voluntarily and you know the chances of that happening. These are the limitations we have and I think they are unfortunate.

Question: I would like to ask Mr. Roos to comment on the method of electing the county council. I understand you have seven that are elected from districts. Have you given any thought to having some or all of them elected at large?

Mr. Roos: Yes. The *St. Louis Post Dispatch* has been a great advocate of having a number of the seven elected at large. We have opposed it because it would be a duplication of the executive who is elected at large. Why duplicate his functions at the legislative level?

Question: Dr. Kelly, I understand your elected executive is not as strong as that of St. Louis County. Are the other members of your board of supervisors elected at large?

Dr. Kelly: Yes, they are. I think this is one place Mr. Roos and I disagree. I think the real mistake is to have only districts represented on the council. Each commissioner elected from a district feels that is where his allegiance is and it doesn't take long for him to forget that he is also a member of a county board. Continuing crises occur about such problems as roads, police protection, or where you put the health clinic. All too often the solution is to build two clinics, creating an inefficient duplication only to solve the political dilemma.

Question: Is it true that even if you have a charter home rule it would not solve the problem of your eighty-five police departments and your hundred odd cities?

Mr. Roos: If we had complete home rule we could appeal to the wisdom and intelligence of citizens who could vote on any change they wanted. I am convinced that you can reason with the citizens and take cases to them, whereas frequently the officials of the smaller municipalities are extremely inflexible. Home rule gives the people the authority to act. However, the political partisans from our county where these little domains exist have had considerable help in Jefferson City and have been able to block our efforts.

Question: Then the only solution to county government is to eliminate the municipalities.

Mr. Roos: It has been made very clear that you can't. It is not politically feasible in St. Louis County. Many of our larger municipalities are able to perform local functions more effectively than one county-wide government would. The philosophy of our administration has been that of a partnership of county government, which has responsibilities for area-wide services, with a few larger municipalities. For example, in police protection the county should have the responsibility for the communications, training, central records, and other back-up services beyond the capabilities of any one municipality. I still think the police officer who knows the neighborhood and knows the front and back door of the business establishments is more capable to provide local patrol services.

Dr. Kelly: California counties have had some real success with the so-called Lakewood Plan where the county provides services to municipalities on a contract basis. When a political jurisdiction is established, it takes a long time before it can really perform. By the contract mechanism in the case of police service, engineering service, or purchasing service, you can cut down the overlapping responsibilities, the overlapping staffs, and reduce costs. We have a central purchasing system; we are trying to work out the arrangements for a service charge so the municipalities can use central purchasing. I hope we can make the police force the size we think it should be so we can contract with some of our municipalities for police services.

Question: Do you have a chief administrative officer in St. Louis?

Mr. Roos: Yes, I have an administrative staff. I have a chief administrative officer who is appointed by me as county supervisor. We also have four or five assistants on the supervisor's staff who specialize in contacts with various departments. In other words, I can see no reason why a chief executive cannot surround himself with competent professionals.

Question: Don't you think there should be a professional man, trained in the art of government, who controls the executive functions? When the chief executive is an elected position, this qualification is not controllable. I am worried about a "political animal" controlling executive functions.

Mr. Roos: If the people elect incompetents, they will have a poor government. We have had administrations, Republican and Democrat, in St. Louis County that have been solely political and have not lasted. The people voted them out.

Dr. Kelly: I do not think Mr. Roos and I really disagree. We both see the need for two things: focusing the political responsibility and having someone who is trained and qualified to be responsible for administration. We are now spending four hundred thousand dollars on data processing; if you do not have someone who knows something about computers you may very well be wasting your money.

Question: Would you care to comment about partisan versus nonpartisan elections?

Mr. Ross: I believe that the chief executive ought to run under the label of Republican or Democrat in a large county. I think nonpartisan elections are always partisan elections becuase the parties function behind the scenes anyway. But, people ought to be able to see the label instead of this terribly confusing nonpartisan system of electing people in larger cities and counties.

Question: We have been talking about executive leadership. How were you able gradually to reduce the variety of independently elected officials?

Mr. Roos: It took a breakdown in government. One year tax bills did not go out so we did away with the elective collector. That led to the establishment of a Department of Revenue. In 1966, we succeeded without fiasco in eliminating the elected highway engineer. Our next charter change will presumably eliminate all elected positions except the prosecuting attorney, members of the council, and the supervisor. Some of the people are already up in arms. It's disturbing to me that people who label themselves "conservatives" and who are opposed to the intervention of the federal government in local areas still oppose efforts to improve local government to make it effective and workable.

Question: What is the trend in Prince George's County?

Dr. Kelly: Not only in Prince George's County but throughout Maryland the new constitution proposes doing away with all the elected officials except the commissioners, the prosecutors, the state attorney and the sheriff, who is a constitutional officer.

Question: How about assessment in the two counties represented by our guests? Is the assessor an elected official in St. Louis County?

Mr. Ross: No. The assessor and collector were elected until this tax collection failure. Now there is an appointed director of revenue. The assessor is in charge of both the assessing and the collecting functions; collection and assessment employees under him are now merit system people.

Dr. Kelly: In Maryland we have a state merit system but we supplement it to get good men, making it in effect a county system. The clerical staff is on the merit system and the state assessors are on the state merit system. They reassess, or try to, every three years. We have an assessor that is appointed. We submit three names to the state committee and the governor appoints him. Whoever is appointed must be trained by the state.

Question: What tax sources would you propose for metropolitan counties?

Dr. Kelly: Our property tax is statewide. I think Maryland has the best ratio among counties of any state. All of them assess at about 60% of market value. Our tax rate is $2.90 per hundred. We have a shared income tax which is collected by the state and rebated to the counties. We also have a transfer tax which is one half of 1% on real estate valued over a certain amount.

Mr. Roos: I would like to see us given the same taxing authority that municipalities have, because as an urban county we are providing many municipal services. Specifically we asked the last session of the legislature for general fund increases. We are taxing at the top of our present authority. We asked the legislature to grant us the right to levy a county-wide cigarette tax and a tax on gross utilities receipts both of which are agreed to by all local interests. These increases didn't get out of the committee. St. Louis County is no different than the City of St. Louis in its requirement to provide police services, health services, hospital services, and I don't know why we should be limited. Perhaps there is some reason to limit rural counties because their functions are limited, but I do not know why urban counties do not have broad taxing authority.

Implications for
Metropolitan Planning

The Planning Role in Urban Decision Making

Robert L. Williams

If planning does nothing else in a community, it forces up issues. It also attempts to create organized, constructive debate upon those issues. Coming out the other end of this process, in one form or another, are, hopefully, a series of alternatives which seem to reflect the broad public interest and the major long-range objectives and goals of the community.

Let me describe what I think is the nature of community planning today. The American planning movement has a fairly short but very dramatic history. Planning is almost pure democratic process, and therefore one of the most frustrating and nerve-wracking functions in local government. There are checks and balances built into local planning that are almost unbelievable in comparison with other functions. Planners don't have two thousand years of history and evolving acceptances like public works directors or tax collectors. Planning's roots extend back to the Industrial Revolution, but it started essentially with the City-Beautiful Movement at the turn of the century. It developed further in the New York studies of slums, light and air controls, the beginnings of zoning as a land control or regulatory device, and the experimentation of the 1930's with "green belt" cities. Planning has progressed through various phases but in the mid-1940's there was a major breakthrough. There had been a lot of deferred public works development, projects that had been laid aside in order to throw our maximum resources into the war effort. A second thing was that people who had come to the larger cities, particularly those along the sea coast to get into the shipbuilding and airplane factories, didn't go home after the war. We had, in effect, tremendous metropolitan growth that caught people in positions of responsibility off guard.

Those were abnormal times, and our whole approach centered on how to survive in a highly dynamic, fluid and critical situation that confronted our central cities. The "move out," the decentralization of the central cities, was one of the direct effects. Why the flight to the suburbs? I would say because of cheaper land, the opportunity to start fresh, the search for privacy, and perhaps to flee from some of the physical and racial problems of the central city that had accumulated over the war years.

The mid-1940's represented a major personnel breakthrough in the American planning movement. If I had a chart I could show you the membership growth of the American Institute of Planners since 1947. It shot nearly straight up after the mid-1940's. As you know, one of the central prerequisites of a profession is that it respond to public need. Planners are products of urbanization. By 1947 there was a public awareness that complex problems of great magnitude were smothering the American city. There was a need to gain leverage on these problems. The device chosen was comprehensive planning. Now, government didn't create comprehensive planning. It is, in effect, a management tool. It was lifted without shame from corporate business.

City government is also a major corporate undertaking. To think in lesser terms would be both fallacious and dangerous. In the late 1940's we had agitation for improvements coupled with a lack of financial resources and a fantastic backlog of public works projects to be either improved, extended or replaced. Much of this work was needed below ground where it just didn't have visible or political impact. The post-war construction boom created a major outcry for a comprehensive approach to all these problems. Compounding the urgency was the question of transportation needs.

One of the traditional myths about planning is the "cloud nine" myth. It is naïve to assume that planners can engage in the planning process and not be somewhat pragmatic. As a management tool, comprehensive, long-range planning is a most pragmatic process. It protects both public and private investment because it provides a logical framework for expenditures. As a management tool, it has none of the connotations of "cloud nine." Aimless daydreaming is not vision, but directed vision attempts to beyond the immediacy of governmental crisis, to provide some of the long range parameters of development that must be considered within any particular urban area.

This factor catapulted community planning into the decision-making process. But planners are not making the decisions. Planning has a supportive role in decision-making It ought to be at the table where the basic decisions of community development, growth, and change are made because it is part of the kit of tools available to decision makers, especially the elected officials. It has been said that the role of a planner is to so support a politician that he conducts himself like a statesman. In that sort of situation, everyone wins.

Planning is also in the decision-making process because it helps to reduce variables and to introduce stability into government business. It certainly is in a position to assist decision-making in the selection of significant factors and to reduce the number of alternatives available. Practical alternatives contain the basic potentialities within a community. So much for the *art* of planning.

The *science* of planning is on a different plateau. It involves application of the lessons of technology and the newer tools that are part of the decision-making process. The science of planning takes planning alternatives and helps to indicate which will most likely be the best solution. It attempts to provide a cost effectiveness ratio. Planning is in the decision-making process also because it represents a reconnaissance function of great value to a community. It operates the same way in corporate enterprise. Planning relays information back, providing pertinent feedback information and suggesting the implications of various possible decisions.

In a large part planning is tied back to the goal-setting process that must go on in every community. The establishment of sound goals for a community makes the preparation of a comprehensive plan almost an anti-climax. It is also fundamental that we have broad-based community and citizen involvement in the preparation of community goals and that these goals be made very clear in terms of their potential impact on the community.

Berkeley, California, for example, developed one of the early prototype community goal programs as a prerequisite to actually carrying out its comprehensive planning program. One of its goals read: "Our community should be the intellectual center of the San Francisco Bay Area. We do not intend our community to be an industrial empire. We think it has tremendous opportunities for recreation because it is on the shoreline. It is in a good location relative to San Francisco and the Golden Gate." These goals set the economic, cultural, social and institutional framework for the Berkeley community. That's how important and fundamental goal-setting can be. The process is akin to giving an architect a list of specifications and telling him: "Develop alternative sets of house plans that will meet my particular needs within my resource limitations."

Here is another example; the city of Alameda is an island with seventeen miles of shore line in San Francisco Bay. This shore line is an economic asset, but it was not being developed properly. Only about one-half per cent of the waterfront was open and available to the public, and that part was usually the ends of streets that stopped at the shore line. There was no public beach development. A goals program was undertaken to help develop the waterfront alternatives. Now there are several miles of good public beach, but only because the fundamentals of community purpose had been considered. The city's strong and weak points were critically appraised. Development followed. Alameda wasn't trying to be all things to all people. If Berkeley wanted to be the intellectual community, Alameda wanted to be the waterfront and recreational community. Alameda had a natural asset, in other words, that the other communities around the Bay didn't have without artificially creating it at fantastic public expense.

I have advocated that the planning commission in certain communities should be reorganized into a community or county *goals* commission. This role requires a good rapport with the elected officials. It would move commissions away from their traditional zoning and quasi-judicial roles. The job of the staff planner and the planning commission is to work in conjunction with the elected officials to develop alternative, comprehensive plans that faithfully carry out the most accurate interpretations of community goals. Goals should make a community stretch. They must go beyond what most people think would be the projection of the status quo into the future. They ought to reflect what is important to the community. There are new techniques that help us determine that.

An aspect as important as planning and politics is planning and intergovernmental relations as it relates to politics in the process of promulgating policy. Because comprehensive planning or community planning usually establish some sort of developmental framework, they take a wide variety of forms. But, more and more, we are beginning to see planning processes as instruments of policy. Developmental policy and comprehensive planning policy are now being considered as a necessary prerequisite for functional or specific subject planning.

One of the reasons for this is the impact of intergovernmental relations. No community situated within a metropolitan area is independent of its neighboring cities and counties. Open space and recreation, air and water pollution, transportation networks, and a variety of other things are common to all units of government. Planning represents one of the bridges through which intergovernmental liaison and developmental dialogues can be developed.

I had the privilege of serving on a couple of the advisory committees for the Association of the Bay Area Governments in the San Francisco area, one of the first prototypes of a metropolitan council of governments. This trend represents a thread of hope for our urban centers. Otherwise, things would be grim. Most metropolitan area governments do not have a constituency; they don't have an adequate treasury; they don't have the internal governmental structures; and they don't have the mechanisms and the institutions to recognize metropolitan problems and opportunities and do anything effective about them.

California is a very strong home-rule state. Often to obtain a unified approach to a problem within the metropolitan San Francisco Bay Area (nine counties and about eighty-five cities) it was necessary first to find a common enemy. The common enemy in California was the State. Local leaders said, "Look, if we don't solve this metropolitan problem for ourselves, the State will come in and do it." This is one reason the Association of Bay Area Governments has been so successful. Many jurisdictions joined ABAG for entirely different reasons, some because they felt that the metropolitan approach to metropolitan problem-solving was ideal, necessary and a fundamental truth. Others joined because they didn't want the State to preempt; a third group joined because they feared the State might establish a port authority equivalent to the New York Port Authority in the belief that this could cream off all the profit-making and dividend-producing activities.

The federal government's programs at least require comprehensive planning as a prerequisite to receiving money from many of the functional programs intended for the metropolitan area. But isn't it ironic that despite federal emphasis, planning still represents probably our weakest function in local government? It is being strengthened. You have a new metropolitan planning commission in the Kansas City area. This is very healthy; it is essential in terms of undertaking a metropolitan approach to metropolitan problems. But planning often has no relationship to ultimate accountability. Councils of governments, composed of accountable elected officials, provide a linkage that I think is very important. The council of governments approach is at least one that offers some hope and some new direction.

I opt for regional action on regional problems. We need new governmental structures, new instrumentalities or institutional bases upon which we can undertake metropolitan programs and insure proper follow-through. As a case in point, I am fearful that this is not going to happen in the interstate highway program. The Highway Act of 1962 requires that there be a "continuing planning process" established after a metropolitan highway network is established. I don't know of one metropolitan area in the United States that actually has wrestled through this problem and come up with a solution as to how it will shift into planning overdrive after the interstate program ends. How will the metropolitan areas carry on the continuing planning process? It's a process which few have really considered seriously. Also, no one has said how it will be financed. The states or some other group will have to operate the system and continue the planning process. We may be in considerable trouble because metropolitan areas have no constituency and they have no treasury. I would lay that at your feet as a problem of considerable proportions.

Much of what I have been saying re-enforces the comprehensive planning requirement and the fact that we expect both public and private investment to be able to relate well to it. Many federal programs, especially at the metropolitan scale, are established along functional lines — the highway program, the open space program, even Model Cities are only partly comprehensive in their approach. All of these are somewhat functional and each has a comprehensive planning prerequisite, but federal definitions of comprehensive planning differ from program to program. They don't match up. The requirement is different and thus is interpreted and applied differently.

To the Bureau of Outdoor Recreation "comprehensive planning" is very simple. To the BOR the term means you've got a federal, state, regional, metropolitan and a local open space and park and recreation program, and they relate well to each other. They *are* integrated and they *do* work well. But open space and park land uses are only a portion of comprehensive land use relationships. Herein lies part of the appalling danger of some of the federal programs. They are very highly functional in character. They each have responsibility for establishing planning requirements. Planning and strong intergovernmental relations, particularly at the metropolitan scale, can bridge some of these programs. This calls for cooperation and coordination, exchange of research data, establishment of metropolitan data banks, and a better system of exchange of intelligence.

The intergovernmental relations aspect of planning is not sufficiently emphasized. As a director of county planning I found myself doing more metropolitan planning in the San Francisco Bay Area than I was county planning. Not only were we interdependent as a major county of one million people in the region, but we had a leadership role. At that time I believed, and still believe, that metropolitan counties are a legitimate subregional level of government. In terms of providing research data and other information needed for comprehensive planning, as well as for other reasons, this still makes sense. But it was from my vantage point as a county planning director that I really got into some of the major issues of metropolitan development and growth, and began to see that councils of governments or other new mechanisms and structures had provided a new direction to go.

What is the alternative? In the Bay Area it happened to be special purpose districts. The play was that you set up a special purpose district with a board of directors composed of elected officials. The result was one on air and water pollution, one on transportation, one on open space and shore line development, another on water control and a variety of other functions. Eventually these might be amalgamated, not into a metropolitan government structure, but at least into a canopy of limited activities that could be closely related, one to the other. Having the same people sitting around the same table and discussing these matters makes sense. These people, of course, were not only accountable to the region and to the metropolitan area, but were obviously also accountable to their own jurisdictions and to their constituency.

Most of the people in the metropolitan areas are sophisticated about this. They want metropolitan solutions to acknowledged metropolitan problems, and local government is in a position to give them the leadership, if it can establish the machinery.

How then can we make local planning relevant? Some of the new tools are PPBS, which stands for planning, programming, budgeting system. This is a technique that anyone who is involved in the planning process or in management or in government decision-making levels has been using for many, many years. But PPBS is a fresh approach. The PPBS approach takes planning out of limbo and moves it toward programmatic considerations. Conversely it forces the budgeteers and the money people to think in terms of programmatic and longer range terms. And so planning, programming, and budgeting systems, at least to me and to the American Institute of Planners, suggest a revitalized management approach to complex urban and local problems. I applaud it because it makes local planning relevant and puts it into the decision-making process.

I know planners who hide behind the computer. They will computerize something to death. They will dissect it so fine that it chews out all the flavor of the issue. So much time may be consumed by this procedure that the solution becomes irrelevant to the problem. But, hardware, computers, and other techniques of this sort help us to move up to the second plateau, from the art to the science of planning. Computers help define alternatives and the subtle shading between alternatives. This is useful to policy makers and that's where planners are trying to get, where the decisions are being made. Hardware is a support tool which has useful applications. In a highly dynamic and constantly changing situation in which there are many inputs regarding complex urban problems, there isn't any one man or even any group of men who can come up with all the alternatives without the aid of technology. It isn't going to make the decision, but it is a tool which, like planning itself, can assist decision making.

Likewise simulation models, gaming, and other new techniques require a high degree of recognizance. What is pertinent? What is significant? Any subject can be overresearched. Selectivity can make data meaningful, pertinent, and applicable to a given set of problems or conditions. Planning can be made relevant because there has to be consistency between the policies, the programs, and the daily decisions on those policies and programs.

What are some of the bridging roles of planning? I think one is in the time scale. The terms of elected officials rarely exceed four years. In comprehensive planning we talk in terms of decades. So, there has to be some meeting of the minds on these longer range goals and objectives in community planning. One of the roles of planning in bridging the time gap between long term objectives and the shorter political scale is to contribute to political accomplishment in terms of development programs. This can affect the establishment of priorities.

Planning can also bridge the public and private sectors and does so very frequently. The "customers" of the planning department are as much from the private sector as they are from the public sector. Much to the chagrin of the public official, they have their own public forums and their own press contacts. They make news for good or evil in planning. Therefore, I think planning has a bridging role to play in self-defense.

Planning can also bridge the aspirations and the resources of a community, and between experimentation and evaluation. This happens in subdivision design, transportation systems and downtown and urban renewal programs. There has been something new, something fresh added. Model cities are built on this concept of innovation and breakthrough with new ideas — not just refinement and polishing of the traditional approaches. A hundred million new people will have to be accommodated in this country in the next forty years. We can't utilize the same old systems and the same old techniques. More experimentation is needed. A research and development approach to urban problems must be encouraged, and planning is part of that process.

One of the most democratic processes of local government, ironically enough, is one of its newer functions — community planning. It provides an opportunity for involvement of the public and not just as an escape valve for the emotional issues which most developmental matters seem to engender. In a very constructive way it can involve all people and groups of people in many different ways. How to read that involvement or how to interpret what people are really trying to say is a difficult matter. I think these are the bridging roles of planning.

Perhaps a word about the use and misuse of implementing devices such as zoning is in order. Although zoning in many communities is off the track, and there has been a lot of misuse of the technique, it still has a great deal of value. I see zoning as a protection device like an insurance policy, rather than as a regulatory or restrictive device. More and more as we use performance standards and other sophisticated ways of looking at land as a resource, we're going to see zoning come back.

The true role of the planning commission may be as a goal setting and policy advisory group to the elected officials, a close support group of top level citizens who think comprehensively about the total community. There is a new crisis in the planning commission that is being ignored with all the talk about getting top management in government, defining its role, and relating the decision-makers and the elected officials to a technical support team. A new development director is needed who is a canopy over the community development function, the zoning codes, the planning function, and the urban renewal agency. Several communities have this now and yet there is little realization that this changes relationships between the elected official and the professional planning staff. No one seems to be looking at what the implications are for the appointive bodies, namely the planning commission. What I'm hoping for is the reconstitution of the planning commission into the goal setting processes of the community on a continuous basis. This isn't a one-shot sort of thing; this is a type of activity that ought to be going on critically and constructively in every community all the time.

Let's take a look ahead a few decades. The planning issues over the next fifty years are going to include several of the ones we have mentioned. Without going into too much elaboration they should be summarized. Major changes in metropolitan form will occur. I'm not talking about governmental structure, I'm talking about the way metropolitan areas grow and change. Will our present suburban pattern of development continue or will there be something new as an alternative such as new town development? This would take types of controls and types of metropolitan planning at a sophisticated level that we haven't seen yet. We must study carefully and soon, with a real research and development approach, the environmental tolerance level in the American city — tolerance levels about housing, about transportation, and about density.

Many of us apparently are willing commuters, ready to drive our cars while breathing exhaust fumes, moving ahead at five to seven miles per hour for forty-five minutes twice a day. I think there are tolerance levels about these things. Much of this apathy is because we haven't shown the American public any better way. There *are* ways to cut commuting time. There *are* ways to solve some of the transportation network problems in our American cities. But, these tolerance levels really haven't been established. The housing density in Hong Kong is 3000 persons per acre. That is ten times the density of Manhattan. The Chinese have a tolerance level that is influenced by their culture. We haven't made these sorts of studies yet. When people say in zoning questions that "this density is too high" — I respond by asking too high compared to what? The discussion degenerates immediately to a debate of human judgment, one man's word and experiences against those of another.

We are living now in a society where what we're really doing is avoiding disasters and achieving minimums. This is what planning and apparently local government are doing today. The people will soon be demanding that we move above these minimums. This applies in air and water pollution most particularly because in both situations people feel very strongly. Maybe the tolerance level is lower there for physiological and psychological reasons. We are more sensitive to those types of pollution than we are to visual pollution in terms of wires and billboards, clutter and dirt and other things so indigenous to our American cities. Environmental tolerance levels must at least be established before acceptable standards can be set. Perhaps a new basis for regulation of human activity and development within an urban setting will emerge.

We must learn to apply the scientific breakthroughs. Little effort is being made to convert new knowledge for urban development applications. New fuel cells could conceivably free housing units from the umbilical cords of water, light, and sewage lines. You could reside anywhere that you could reach by your transportation vehicle. Desalinization will have a very heavy impact on urban living. Planners are hip-shooting on all of these things; we can't tell you the implications of technology as yet.

We have a long way to go in translating these technological changes in terms of land use, socio-economic relationships, and the whole urban pattern. There are environmental question marks. I think we will have to learn much more about man and his basic needs, values and interactivity. We spoke earlier of community values. We've got to be able to do the same for man as an individual. His privacy requirements, his need for variety, his need for choice, his need for cultural attainment and growth, not just for survival or for mere accommodations, must be better defined. Planning is therefore going to have to be more than advisory. It can be part of the decision-making process, but its inputs will have to become more interdisciplinary. We have serious questions on "optimum" environment, what it is, what it contains, and who is to determine it. I'm not in favor of "technocracy" — I don't think that technologists are going to be in a position to run the country and make the decisions having human dimensions. I still believe the democratic process, through elected officials, is the best approach, particularly in the urban setting. But the elected officials must learn how to use the specialist.

Long-range planning is sound business. As sound business it has its pragmatic aspects. However, we must also be visionary — in the sense of not being afraid to think ahead, or to examine our assumptions and aspirations. Human environment is all important. It is human environment within a physical structure that we talk about in comprehensive community planning. This physical environment must be used to enhance human activity. Research can help us define and perhaps work toward optimum environmental levels in terms of community growth and development. Our affluent society demands fulfillment. It demands environmental stimulation and harmony. It is within the American city that this is either going to occur or not.

Discussion

Question: What degree of permanence do you attribute to the community plan? You give the impression you are very attached to the existing plan, whatever it is.

Williams: I think there is a vital point in terms of making a plan effective and useful as a management tool and as a support function to decision-making. Therefore, its use, or its misuse, is of vital concern to me. I object to politicians using the plan as a straw man. One of the key roles of planning is the assistance in the preparation of community policy and of basic goals. Many people talk of the master plan or the general plan as something sandwiched between two covers and deemed effective or ineffective in various communities. But to me a plan or a group of developmental policies has validity only to the degree that it has been promulgated, and officially established under due process. When community leaders talk about their health policies, police policies or fire protection pledges, they are firm and conduct themselves in keeping with those policies. But, in planning the ground rules are quite often different and you find that planning policy is used to perhaps go in a new direction. Any time I hear someone say in a public meeting, "Well, it's merely a plan," I gird myself. I say, "That man is just about ready to circumvent the plan." Why doesn't he say it's merely a policy? I can't think of anything that's more dangerous to a city or a county than having a comprehensive plan (or a developmental policy) that is obsolete or that doesn't have broad support. It can work against the public interest. It can boomerang. It ought to be up-to-date and it ought to be critically reviewed, challenged, assailed, tested, fired at, and constantly made a highly dynamic useful working instrumentality of the city or the county. If it is, it should not be merely a political straw man. That's what the plan is, it is a developmental policy.

Question: What is your evaluation of the Program-Planning-Budgeting-System approach?

Williams: I've mentioned that PPBS is not really a new direction. It's a new nomenclature, but it's a standard approach that has been used for many years. Everyone had his own terms for what is now called PPBS. It's part of the planning process and it's part of the linkage between planning, programming, and budgeting. I think it makes a lot of sense. Former Secretary of Defense McNamara had given it dignity and some momentum at his level. I would anticipate that it's going to find its way into most other levels of government. I've said PPBS is a good direction in which we ought to be going.

Question: How critical do you think the suburban-central city conflict is?

Williams: One of the things wrong with metropolitan county government is that it rarely acknowledges or recognizes its leadership role in the metropolitan setting. Conversely, it does not recognize its interdependence with the other governments. I think there is a myth in the central cities *versus* the suburbs approach because the real decision-making and crucial decision-making is on the fringes of our urban development. Increasingly, it will be in areas where these important decisions will be made. There is a question whether we will continue the suburban sprawl or whether we will try new patterns of metropolitan development such as "new towns" programs. The answer lies in strong intergovernmental coordination.

Question: One of our greatest problems on a metropolitan level is financing programs that involve big expenditures and many jurisdictions. Do you have a bag of tricks that is going to help us out of that situation?

Williams: Planning is an element that links long-range planning and long-range fiscal programming. I think they have to be laid side by side. Planning links long-range planning to long-range fiscal programming by removing some of the cyclical effects. It helps to remove political dynamite such as raising or lowering taxes from year to year. These things shake the faith of the constituents. It is valuable to time these long-range goals to a long-range fiscal plan. This is over and about general budgeting considerations. It is also something that planning can do for the metropolitan financial problem that can be politically helpful.

Question: Pursuing the idea of a plan as a framework for implementation in specific terms, could you give us an example of what you mean?

Williams: Let's take a plan for transportation. Within a comprehensive plan, there may be a transportation element in which there may be several counties affected. Each county then develops its own transportation plan in accordance with that part of that plan that applies in its jurisdiction.

Question: Are you saying, then, once you've agreed on a plan you ought to stick to it, is that the point you make?

Williams: In terms of day-to-day decisions and in terms of public investment, yes. That's the framework not only for public investment but also for private investment as well. Now, you can change a plan. I'm not saying you write it out for all time, but you ought to change it under due process and there ought to be a rationale applied to why you're changing it. In other words, if situations change to the point that policy changes, that's legitimate, provided it is legitimately changed.

Question: Where you need some sort of private initiative to achieve the planned objective, would you accept as one reason to change the plan the fact that for some reason private initiative has not materialized? In other words, what would be your reasons for changing the plan? How would you determine if you should depart from your original plan?

Williams: The ultimate test on any plans, either for changing them or preparing the plan itself is that it serves the public interest. A plan is a series of interdependent policies. A lot of public investment is going to be made on the basis of that plan, in the community facilities, water extension, special purpose districts and other jurisdictions. It begins to lay down a pattern of developments to which private enterprise can quite frequently accommodate and should accommodate. Now, when you get into zoning, or the speculating type of investment, this is another question entirely. I see zoning in a very positive sense — it is as a protective device rather than as a regulatory device telling you what you can or cannot do. I think we're beginning to see stretch and flexibility and more creative zoning techniques, particularly performance standards. Planned unit development zoning is especially helpful on large scale developments where there are multiple land uses.

Question: In your experience do metropolitan issues get identified on a metropolitan level? Is there any hope for implementation of planning solutions on a metropolitan level?

Williams: I have never experienced any metropolitan area where officials couldn't quickly identify metropolitan problems. They also knew that they had to affix metropolitan solutions to these problems and develop metropolitan action programs in order to overcome them. Unfortunately, the metropolitan areas usually lack adequate mechanisms. Planning at the metropolitan scale often is in limbo. That's why I get so excited about councils of governments like the Association of Bay Area Governments because it is at least a thin silver thread of hope that we might be able to do something beyond just having a debating forum on metropolitan issues.

Question: Would you comment on town hall meetings and their success or failure as a means of developing community goals?

Williams: I think it was partially successful in Berkeley but it went too long. Berkeley was really one of the first in the country to go into goal setting from this direction and in this depth. The town hall meetings broadened involvement so that everybody in the community was included. Remember, however, that probably the average educational level in that town is at least two years of college or better. It's an intellectual community.

Question: Is there a better way or another alternative today?

Williams: Yes, but I wouldn't say that it's an either/or situation. It's using the town hall for its limited values that I have attempted to describe. I have a bias in favor of limited but judicious use of town hall meetings. But, I've also seen them boomerang. I've seen this happen in ethnic situations and in Negro slum areas, where either a Negro or a white man came in and said, "These people have asked me to speak for them," but the people didn't know him from Adam. And, all of a sudden here was the planning commission providing a new public forum (with a great deal of press and publicity and video tape backing them up) for people who alleged and presumed to be the leaders in the area. What do you do? Do you challenge them right there? You have to screen hearing material for what it is really worth.

Some of the new attitudinal surveying techniques are useful. I don't know if our censuses are ever going to get to a point where they can go into some of these things. I'm interested, for example, in the membership of the American Institute of Planners and trying to determine pivot points of career decision-making. What makes a man go one direction in the profession versus another? Why does he specialize rather than staying in general practice? These are things that would require new and very sophisticated attitudinal surveying techniques. There is research going on, but the urban decision-making use of these survey techniques is just in the beginning stage. If we could put a good research and development program together on some urban planning problems, then maybe we could solve something even as mundane as our garbage and refuse disposal. (We're still handling our garbage and refuse the way they did in the Roman army camps 2000 years ago.) There are going to have to be technological breakthroughs. One of them is the survey technique.

I think there will be a variety of other ways of determining public attitudes, individual attitudes and functional group attitudes. The planners don't know much about this. We're relying on others. The future pattern will probably be the interdisciplinary team approach using a variety of technical skills. These teams will start with public administration management because that's where the translation has got to occur. While management in cities and counties has a very key role in leadership, it has to build the sort of team-skill that can attack these issues from a variety of points of view. I've seen it happen with public health officers, public works directors, planning directors and finance officers quite often. Getting into the trend of these new programs, we might look at PPBS (Planning, Programming, Budgeting Systems). Everyone is systems-oriented now. We see PPBS as making planning relevant by bridging between planning and implementation. Management takes a very pivotal role in this. This is where the action is. It's the marriage point for long-range goals, aspirations of a city, resources and the financial capacity or other capacities (skills, etc.). That's why I think the Planning, Programming, Budgeting Systems approach can be very useful in making planning effective, which it has not been. I will be the first to admit a flagrant failure in most communities of the planning function becoming relevant.

Question: From the trend of your remarks thus far it would seem that you see planning primarily as a physical planning device and yet isn't this really called the secondary role?

Williams: The end product of planning, I think, and I come from a designing background, still is physical environment. This, to me, is the end product of all this activity. There has to be a tangible result in the planning process. We seek an improved environment. We seek an environmental product in which people can interact and where human activity within an urban setting occurs and flowers.

Future Manpower for Urban Management[1]

Nathan D. Grundstein

I am not an expert in any particular set of functional problems. The problems that concern me are an interlocking of three things. One is the general design of the organization for urban management. Given a design of a structure, certain kinds of things follow. My position here is that the American firm in the period of 1901 to 1925 worked out a fundamental pattern of organizational design for the nationwide multi-purpose, multi-product corporation. And in the period since then, it has fitted both the technology of management and a human capability — the general manager — into that design. This interlocking of three things, the general design of the organization itself, the technology for managing this structure, and the human capability — the management competence — to work and realize the potentials of the technology and the organizational design has never been resolved for the public sector. This paper is on the applicability of these three things to the city and metropolitan area: (1) the management design, (2) the applicable technology, and (3) the human capability. Their interconnections are the substance of the paper.

Cities are again at one of those stages in time when the conjoining of (1) The reperception of the manpower for urban management and (2) The redesign of urban management has a great deal of significance for future developments in urban management. It is a twice recurrent stage in the history of urban management since the turn of the Twentieth Century.

In each of these stages the social form that this conjoining has taken has been an expression of the relationship of a professional component of urban manpower to political control of urban management. The present stage must also work out this conjoining of urban management manpower and urban management redesign as an expression of the same relationship. What is likely to be different, however, is the social form that will be imposed on future urban management, because the working out of the relationship is already taking a different path than it has in the past.

The value of briefly reconstructing the constituent elements and the social choice outcomes of these earlier, recurring stages in the history of urban management is its utility for demonstrating how the future of urban management will differ from its past. Twice before — once in the case of the municipal engineer and once in the case of the city manager — the relationship of a professional component of urban manpower to political control of urban management has been confronted and worked through as a stage of social choice in the development of urban management. To describe and characterize that confrontation and choice is, in effect, to establish a reference base by which to comprehend their recurrence now for the third time in the history of urban management, when the strategic professional component of urban manpower is the urban planner.

This interlocking of these three components is presented for the metropolitan area for the third time in the Twentieth Century. The original presentation of this choice of system design, technology for management and human competence for management, was precipitated in 1894 by the municipal engineers who were the first professionals of urban management.[2]

Engineers comprised over ninety per cent of the membership of the American Society of Municipal Improvements, which was organized in 1894. The Society's constitution stated that the Society would seek "to promote the best methods to be employed in the management of Municipal departments, and in the construction of municipal works . . . ." It could fairly be said of the municipal engineer that at that time he "was the only recognized formally educated individual of any consequence employed by cities." Nevertheless, the municipal engineer turned away from the problems of municipal management. At this period formal city planning was only beginning to emerge and was not picked up by the municipal emgineer as part of his professional competence. Instead, the municipal engineer focused on developing the engineering technology relevant for a variety of public works and municipal improvements − notably roads and pavements, and sewage and sanitation.

At the same time, he began to develop a professional career path that increasingly led him away from association with municipal management. We know this not only form the utterances of municipal engineers in their official proceedings, but also from the sharp rise in the membership roster listings of titles as consultant engineers. As a consultant, the municipal engineer could retain the city as a client, but occupationally he was not subordinated to the dominantly spoils system of political control of urban management.

The choice of system design, technology for management and human competence for management was precipitated a second time by the city managers who represent another group of managerial competence, who also brought to the city a particular type of organization design and who had in mind a particular technology for management.

The introduction and acceptance of the ideal of a city manager came as an innovation in structural form for urban management. The professionalization of urban management is really the core of the city manager concept. What is to be noted, however, is that it perceived the professionalization of urban management as a manpower problem only if a compatible structural form by which to redesign urban management existed as a given. That structural form was also a way of constraining political control of urban management, which was taken to be a necessary condition for the professionalization of urban management. The organizational primciple of specialization of function was applied to the management of the city, so that the professionalization of urban management was, in effect, the professionalization of an urban function. Unlike the municipal engineer, the competence of the city manager as a professional was not independent of his position in the structure of urban management. Necessarily, therefore, the city manager would have a more constrained professional career path than the municipal engineer. He could develop territorial mobility as between cities, but he could not develop occupational mobility outside of urban management.

At this point some comparisons are both possible and relevant.

1. What we have are two instances of the response of organized professions to the management of the city.

2. Both represent instances where the response of the organized profession to urban management was the outcome of a perceived relationship to party, partisan politics and political control in the management of the city.

3. The response of the municipal engineers was a strategy of maintenance of an autonomous professional competence that existed anterior to and independently of urban management, and the rejection of functional subordination to political control of urban management.

4. The response of city managers was a strategy of structural redesign of city government that would establish the necessary conditions for building an autonomous professional competence focused on urban management, and the acceptance of a structurally constrained functional subordination in the performance of this professional competence to political control of urban management.

5. For both professions — the municipal engineers as well as the city managers — the strategy of withdrawal and avoidance of party based political control of urban management resulted in a functional profession- alism, which took the form of organizational enclaves of science oriented technological competence. Both professions could be built into a functional structure of urban management, and urban management itself was but the management of an aggregate of bounded functions.

6. In the context of the occupational career paths that were open to each profession, urban management as an option for career choice had a different significance within each profession.

7. While one professional group (the municipal engineers) emerged before the advent of city planning, and the other professional group (the city managers) emerged after the advent of city planning, in neither instance were they influenced in their respective approaches to urban management by the implications of city planning for urban management.

Urban planners are now the critical professional component of urban manpower. It is due to contemporary urban planning that the present stage in the history of urban managmment is different, and that the conjoining of urban management manpower and urban management redesign must be reworked anew. What now exists is the possibility for breaking out of the earlier, established relationship of professional manpower to political control of urban management. That outcome will be determined by how the urban planners work out the social form that will express their appropriate relationship to poltical control of urban management.

Up to the present, the profession of urban planning has had no definite conception of urban management. To be sure, it has wanted the inclusion of the planning function in the managment of the city, which has meant establishing a functional enclave for city planning. The point of the matter, however, is that a functional enclave within the structure of urban managment only expresses the earlier social form that the relationhip of professional manpower to political control of urban management took on. It represents the older strategy of withdrawal and avoidance of party based political control of urban management that was accepted by a functionally committed professional manpower. It takes for granted the going structural pattern of urban management for the utilization of planning.

An organizationally adaptive strategy intended to find room for one more function within the structure of urban management is quite different than a strategy of confrontation of politically controlled urban management. The latter will require urban planners, as the critical professional component of urban manpower, to articulate a point of view about what urban management should be like in order to utilize effectively the science oriented technology of urban planning as it is now developing. It is precisely at this nexus of choice of strategies that contemporary urban planning has arrived. It is a choice that can fix the lines of development of the future manpower for urban management, for it is a choice that links the manpower for urban management with the design for urban management. The two have always been linked, and the character of the linkage is such that the professional manpower components of urban management will develop within a social form that is a response to the design of urban management. The effects of this linkage extend into the education of professional manpower for urban management, and thus the future education of the future manpower for urban management will feel the effects of the choice of strategies.

It is no longer acceptable to think of urban planning as existing within a functional enclave located within a structure for urban management. Urban renewal opened the organizational paths through which contemporary urban planning could escape the constraints of the functional enclave within which traditional physical planning for the city was confined. It is this emergence since 1947 from the confining boundaries of a functional enclave that is the distinctive organizational development of contemporary urban planning. In retrospect, this emergence was a necessary condition for urban planning to provide the measure for urban management. The question, which was once whether urban management any longer had the option of existing without urban planning, now became: What kind of urban management was appropriate, given a requirement of urban planning in its contemporary form? It is through an understanding of what is indicated by this different and later question that we can comprehend what the future manpower for urban management will be like.

The consequence of the sustained Federal investment in urban planning is that urban management has passed through the screening provided by the analytics, the documentation, the processes and the implementation of urban plans and planning. At the same time, the range of non-functional experience with urban management by contemporary urban planning has brought the latter into working contacts with the entrepreneurial, the strategic, the fiscal, the allocative, the investment, the operational, the coordinative, the areal, the representational and the decisional aspects of urban management. What emerges from all this as the appropriate kind of urban management is something that can be characterized as tightly coupled (or tightly linked) management. It is a kind of urban management that is the product of a design for management, of a focused management technology, and a level of capability of the manpower for urban management. The objective of urban manpower policy should then be to raise the level of capability of urban management manpower sufficiently to make tightly coupled urban management practicable. The capability level of the future manpower for urban management then becomes the criterion by which to approve all subsequent measures to develop that manpower.

Unlike the earlier historical stages involving the municipal engineers and the city managers, the professional competence that is now involved does not exist anterior to and independently of urban management, nor is it an autonomous competence existing apart from poltical control of urban management. By sketching the contours of that competence and the generalized structural pattern in which it will be utilized, and then relating the foregoing to professional career options we should be able to glean the milieu in which the individual and social development of the future manpower for urban management will happen. The number of determinants is small but powerful. We know from the urban economists (such as Professor Wilbur Thompson) that urban management technology will exhibit some relation to urban scale because the problems of urban management are related to the scale of city size. The management problems of a tightly coupled system of urban management are more likely to be critical for the larger than for the smaller end of the urban scale. Moreover, scale is associated with complexity so that we can expect a different order of complexity in both the problems and the technology associated with urban management at different magnitudes on the urban size scale. We can take these differences as presenting learning requirements for different stages of professional development, although I concede that it is not now possible to speak with the desired preciseness about the content of the learning requirements. From the vantage point of occupational paths as career options for professional manpower, what is possible is a career distribution of occupational movement that can be time plotted along the range of urban scale. This distribution may be thought of as sequences in a progression of learning stages, but it is not to be identified as the only occupational path open for manpower development.

A related occupational path is organizational rather than territorial. In addition to scale associated problems, urban management technology exhibits the problems associated with organization specialization of decision. It is not only the analytics for decision, but the social structure and the processes for decision that enter into the development of the future manpower for urban management. The social environment of urban management in the future will be changed by the effects of structural changes that have their source in the tighter coupling of urban management with urban planning. Given the expanded ambit of concerns, given the revised instrumentation and methodologies, and given the broader range of professional specialities that have been included within contemporary urban planning, we can expect a concomitant change in the scale of the organizational overhead for urban management. Changes in structure will follow changes in organizational scale. Indeed, something like the emergence of the structural differentiation between the general management (corporate staff and group management) and divisional management (operations) that has taken place in the organizational design of the modern corporation will make an appearance in urban management.

It will mean not only an increase in the magnitude of the investment in the organizational overhead (here again urban scale will be a limiting factor), but also an expansion of career options for urban manpower. As for the latter, it may be assumed that there will be significant management performance differences as between structural levels that will present learning requirements, and that these learning requirements can be matched with some measure of stages of professional development. Nevertheless, one cannot now speak with the desired explicitness about the transformation of decision problems, social structure, and processes for decision into differentiated learning requirements for urban management manpower.

We do know that there are manifest differences between the entrepreneurial politico-managerial level of management and the program client-area level of management. The former is subtly being transformed into a man-machine system, and the importance of the analytic relative to the bargaining processes of social decision appears to be gaining. At the same time, we do not really know much about the particularized flaws through which at this level, options are generated for urban choice, or scanned against a variety of criteria, or the coupling between urban planning and urban management takes place. In short, as of right now, if we set about deliberately to develop a top level management capability in the future manpower for urban management, what there is of value to transmit would be pretty much shrouded in doubt — to say nothing at all of the effectiveness of the mode of transmitting and learning it.

At the level where programs are consumed by the client as need related services, the spatially associated phenomena of urban management are taking on a wholly new meaning. In the past, urban services were viewed as the product

outputs of functional activity, which could be managed by being organizationally rationalized into sequences of acts and then iterated within the constraints
of organization. The Green Books supplied the models for functional management. What has taken place, however, is the collapse of all of the urban services
parameters that once were taken for granted, and this has had pervasive effects
on the content, the organization and the personnel for the management of
programs of urban services. There has been a trade-off of technical competence
for other values, namely the representation and employment of service
beneficiaries. In particular, there has been both a dilution and a revision of once
accepted standards of professional competence in service fields through the
increase of paraprofessioanl personnel. Moreover, organizational representation
of service beneficiaries has meant that the spatial decentralization of urban
services has supported their becoming territorially politicized. The analytic tools
(models, etc.) for the planning and management of services are really
instruments of aggregate analysis for use of the politico-managerial level rather
than program implementation aids at the point of service consumption. In
terms of the future manpower for urban management: What is the expected
occupational path and organization mobility of the paraprofessional? What are
the career options of management manpower in the service programs (spatial —
that is, clientile-mobility? Program mobility — but spatial immobility?
Organization-structural level-mobility?). What are the learning requirements
connected with effective performance in the management of urban services?

The urban professionals will separate out into (1) The Nationals and (2) The
Locals. These terms describe categories of career patterns for the urban
professionals. The Nationals are those who will have access to occupational paths
which will enable them as urban professionals to move between urban
jurisdictions on a national (or sub-national) geographic scale. Their careers will
lay in the urban industry — which is both an aggregate of jurisdiction and an
aggregate of firms constituting an employment market for the urban professionals. From a motivational standpoint, these nationals will be searching for paths
of rapid, upward mobility, both social and organizational. Their competences
will be generalized (inter-jurisdictional and inter-areal), adaptive (responsive to
the variances of different jurisdictions and areas) and social (effectively
accommodated to differences in leadership types, leadership styles and decision
structures).

The Locals of the urban professionals are those whose occupational paths will
be constrained within an urban jurisdiction or within a local aggregate
(metropolitan area) of urban jurisdiction. Their careers will lay within an urban
jurisdiction within a locality, but modified by the possibilities of intra-local
mobility provided for the urban professional. From a motivational standpoint,
these Locals will accomodate to queuing up in a "waiting line" of organizational
opportunities for upward mobility. It is doubtful whether the structural base for
intra-local mobility will provide a significant alternative to the "waiting line" as
a career path for the Locals. Their career problems will be those associated with
"waiting line" opportunities, including the equitable (seniority) and status

(salary differentials) constraints on organization mobility through a waiting line. Their competences will be locally specific-fitted to the social environmental particularities of a particular jurisdiction or of a local area. The locals will also tend to become bureaucratized around position and task specialization.

In addition to accomodating to a "waiting line" of organizational opportunities, the Locals of the urban professionals will have to accomodate themselves to an influx of the paraprofessionals. The introduction of the paraprofessional into urban management will represent the application of a manpower policy for dealing with structural unemployment in the cities. The accommodation of the Locals to the paraprofessionals will take two forms: (1) competition for "waiting line" opportunities and (2) a revision of the competences that are accepted as the hallmark of the urban professional. It is particularly in the urban services that the paraprofessional will be fed into the channels of urban management. A revised structural pattern for urban management will take into account the changed composition of the professional manpower for urban management.

The pattern of structure for urban management into which the urban management professionals will fit should not be visualized in any specific organizational form. Rather, it should be thought of in terms of some primary components that are capable of taking on a variety of organizational forms. Each of these components will have its own differentiated part to play in urban management. Each of these components will have its own social composition. Each of these components will have its own information channels. Each of these components will have its own class of problems and decision processes. It is not a task specialization but a social specialization of function that will give patterns to the strucutre for tightly coupled urban management. What the coupling of urban management to urban planner will require its structure that is adapted to different orders of function, as represented by each of the competent complexes.

The primary components (derived from a social specialization of function) are three in number: (1) The Entrepreneurial (Politico-managerials), (2) The Urban General Managers, and (3) The Program operationalistis. The urban management professionals-both the Nationals and the Locals-will relate differently to each of these components, simply because the social utility and the technical contribution of the professionals will be different for each. The group of Politico-Managerials who will comprise the entrepreneurial component of urban management will represent a contingent and personalized social structure for urban management. They will be individuals of diversified motivations who will be playing a variety of career games and who will be the contingent by-products of political control of urban government. The sources and the modes of inclusion and utilization of technical competence within the group of Politico-Managerials is critical for tightly coupled management. The inclusion of the professional within the social composition of the entrepreneurial component presents complex questions of team formation. In terms just of a desired level of technical sophistication, professional Nationals will be preferred to professional

Locals. Still, more than just this is involved, for it is not only the level of technical competence, but also the social utilization of that competence that is relevant. The expertise of the future manpower for urban management will be more systematic about social utilization capabilities within the structure of the entrepreneurial component of urban management. It is these capabilities that will determine how effectively the technical competences of the urban professionals who are the Nationals can be adapted and accommodated to different jurisdictions. It is at this structural level above all that the conjoining of the political and the professional in relation to a class of decision problems involving entrepreneurial options for the city illustrates the choice of manpower and management design strategies.

The component of urban General Management is structurally underdeveloped and lacks organizational form in the existing pattern of city government. However, the link to urban planning will compel changes in the modes of urban management, for it introduces changes in the technology of urban management. The urban General Management Component is an alternative to the cabinet of departmental officers and to the staff of the office of the urban chief executive as the structural component for urban management. The component of Urban General Management will represent a relatively greater investment by cities in plan relevant management technologies and the structure for their utilization than presently is the case. The plan relevant management technologies are those which have to do with program design, resources allocation, spatial or areal decentralization, environmental monitoring, fiscal and investment strategies, multiple program coordination and management control. These are management technologies that will be integrated into information systems for urban management decision. Moreover, these are management technologies that are objects of science oriented inquiry by the management science profession. The analytic base — or the logic — of these technologies cannot be learned on the job, but their organizational utilization and their application to the content of the urban management problems of a particular urban jurisdiction can be job learned. In all likelihood, the urban General Management component will serve as the testing ground and supply the occupational paths for the urban professional seeking to move into the politico-managerial (entrepreneurial) field of urban decision. It is the structural link between the entrepreneurial and the program operations components, and within it are located the plan relevant management technologies by which the transformation of the decisional output of the former into the expected activities of the latter can be done.

The Program Operations Component will present a number of intractable problems for urban management. Program operations interlock area and clientele (or recipient) with the services content of programs. For purposes of program operations, the urban jurisdiction will be disaggregated into territorial units and program differentiated clusters of spatially distributed recipients of services. Unstabilizing tendencies can be introduced by spatial factors and clientele motivations encountered in the management of service programs. Area has a representational as well as a managerial utility. At the same time, programs are differentiated responses to a range of need and aspirational levels of the service beneficiaries. Territorial control enables the service beneficiaries to impose their own aspirations on program management at the level of program organization and operations.

In the Program Operations Component there is the likelihood that occupational paths for urban professional manpower will become either clientele specific, area specific, or program specific. On the whole, these favor occupational experiences that will bias the urban professional towards becoming a Local rather than a National. The clientele and area specific occupational paths are also those most open to the paraprofessional. It is less inter-program mobility than a type of experience that will provide opportunities for multi-program relatedness learning which will open occupational paths to upward mobility, whether as a professional Local or as a professional National.

The extensive diversity of program fields (Health, Community Development, manpower, Family Services, etc.), coupled with their interrelatedness, precipitates problems of coordination. Operational coordination is a managerial part of the planning implementation. In urban management, neither analytic coordination nor operational coordination are, as yet, highly developed competences. Knowledge of the appropriate combination of organizational forms and social processes with technical and socio-political skills for coordination will be included in the competence of the future manpower for urban management. Urban planning will require from urban management that it have the competence to put into effect area focused, multi-program, urban development strategies within some framework of comprehensive planning.

In Sum: Urban planning is the reference base for the design of future urban management. The future manpower for urban management has been viewed in relation to a type of urban management that is characterized by its being coupled to urban planning. The coupling of urban management to urban planning is a matter about which cities will no longer have any choice. What is of concern is the level of capability at which urban management should be able to function in order to be effective when so coupled. The level of the capability of urban management is the general objective. The future manpower for urban management can be related to the desired capability level of urban management.

Urban management design is in actuality a choice of manpower development strategies. The design of urban management has always influenced the lines of development of professional manpower for urban management. Urban planning is the reference base for the design of future urban management. The coupling of urban management with urban planning means the redesign of the former, and this redesign can be articulated as the form that urban management should tend toward in order to be able effectively to utilize urban planning. The focus of professional education for urban management can now become the capability level of a distinctive type of urban management.

Discussion

Question: When you talk about Locals, are you confining the government to one specific unit or including the possibilities of the developing field of intergovernmental relations? If the latter, what do you see as the training potentials for management types who would be capable of working in this new realm?

Grundstein: I defined Locals as those persons dealing with single jurisdictions or a small aggregate jurisdiction within a territorial boundary such as metropolitan areas. The fundamental reform of local government would not come and did not come through Councils of Government or Metro governments or any other structural device. It's being forced upon local government by the federal government through an allocation mechanism. The fundamental simplification of local government would come through the federal government forcing the local government to organize to receive allocations of monies. This will reduce local government from an In-party system, that is to say, an infinity of participants, to a relatively small, limited number of participants. The structure itself will police the internal claims of the participants so that when it comes to the federal level there is a very small number of requests for funds. In this way, we can develop a certain rationalization of the allocation of resources. Two things will then emerge: (1) You are going to need a technological base for assessing relative claims. Why is city X's claim more important than city Y's claim? Right now, you don't have an analytic base for fundamental social decisions which delineates one allocation as against another. (2) The federal government itself, in terms of its regional organization for purposes of program coordination, lacks a good analytic base. Therefore, it never really knows whether it's optimizing or suboptimizing. Optimizing is of course difficult and I think the most we can hope is for a higher level of suboptimization.

What about opportunity for Locals within this aggregate of jurisdictions? I believe that as you develop an analytic base for allocating resources through the federal government in the local areas, you are going to get into the general management structure and that these Locals would become Nationals. Insofar as you move into the functional activities of local governments, these people are Locals and they would become either program specific or clientele specific. All systems are going to divide into either entrepreneurial, general management, or program operations, or nothing will happen, which is the present system.

The developing intergovernmental relationships now are a set of general management structures, such as the intergovernmental council. What they lack is an adequate technological base, or a technical and informational base for making the decisions that they say they are going to make. You're all bargaining without analytics. If the federal government came to you and asked the Mid-America Council of Governments to provide an allocation pattern for twenty-three million dollars spent among twelve services which will optimize the development of this area, I'll bet you couldn't do it. Instead, you find the twenty-six guys whose income is below the poverty level who don't have a park and you request three humdred thousand dollars to give them a park. What about the opportunity costs? Is that more important than an allocation for purposes of developing a hospital in an area?

The big mistakes are made at the top. When you made the big mistakes at the bottom, you can live clean and work hard but all you can get is an incremental gain. The demands of the public sector are so incredibly great that you've got to get the intelligence level functioning or we will just use up every single dollar that you've got. Nobody is going to give away his discretionary money. I'm for the public sector getting something and meeting certain public needs but not for giving up my discretionary money. There's an infinity of demands out there. What you must develop is the general management structure for the intergovernmental area capable of dealing with special choices which will move toward optimization of the development of the area. The analytic people are people who are ultimately going to be Nationals. The functional people are going to be Locals and their movement between one area and another will still keep them Locals. Does that answer your question?

Question: Not quite. These trained management types who would be advising the politicals I think are boxed in to the job that they have been committed to perform. I think these management people who are working for one government are trying to do as good a job as they can within the one government. Even if they see the totality and become Nationals in proficiency, their job is still prescribed by their employer. I am wondering how people who are confined can be made to see the total picture and whether they can move toward something larger such as a restructuring of government or a more efficient intergovernmental cooperation. Do they have the avenue open to them to even recommend to politicians the more efficient way of providing functions?

Grundstein: Two things are happening. I don't think there will be a fundamental change in local government strucrure. The structural changes are going to come through the allocation mechanism primarily through the federal structure. You can't think of this as a fixed bundle of management types. New people are feeding in all the time, in fact, moving into new kinds of positions so that your older people who are not capable of fitting into the new structure are falling behind. The system has a certain amount of civilized quality about it. These people are no longer in the fundamental decision processes. Furthermore, some political types search out analytic types to get assistance but it is done now on a informal basis. We need a better, more formalized recognition of this. There will be a fundamental transition problem, for the older managers who are trained in functional task specialization. I don't know what to do about that, and I don't know about the process by which we might retool them.

Question: I have two related questions. On the entrepreneurial level, will developing an analytical base be an in-house function or will it come through the allocation system of the National technicals? If it does come through the National technicals, what, in fact, is the use of having any Locals at all?

Grundstein: The thinking ground for your general management people provides you the base and gives the in-house technical competence that enables these people to participate to some extent. There's a lot of supplementary data that you have to get out in any one kind of study in your general management area. On really big problems it's rare that the city has the bundle of technical competence that is needed in-house, it usually must go out of its own resource pool. Sometimes it doesn't trust the local level of competence, or alternately the local level is wired in to certain kinds of people, or the structure won't let them go. You get a combination of outside technical Nationals supplemented by assignments of technical Locals from the general management level. That's where your learning takes place for the people who are going to keep custody of the high level technological competence in the area. You can't afford the Nationals anyway over a long period of time. They're too costly. They keep moving on until they eventually have to make some kind of commitment. They ultimately either head for a consulting firm because of the pay or they go to a university in order to have a civilized environment to work and live in.

Question: It seems to me that a lot of this discussion is predicated on the idea that structures are important. My own experience indicates that they are losing their importance and are becoming nonstructures. Kansas City offers an excellent example of this. The entire juvenile offender structure has been changed just to get rid of a juvenile judge; a whole city government structure has been changed just to get rid of a particular person. It seems to me that the structure is based upon certain ideologies which have disappeared so that the structure itself is rapidly disappearing too.

Grundstein: Organizational structure is now malleable. It follows strategies but the social division of function is not that malleable. A neighborhood group cannot make social decisions for Kansas City, no matter how it is structured. A neighborhood group can make claims on the social decision structure in the sense of values which support the allocation of resources, but it cannot make that decision for Kansas City. I didn't give the entrepreneurial area specific organization at all. I said it was a social division of function and it will develop its own structure. The other point is that you may pay too high a social cost in order to get rid of that offender. In other words, you tore up the place in order to do something that should have been dealt with some other way. It could have been handled more sensibly.

Question: Yes, but it seems to me that way of operating is more and more a reality and that structures are correspondingly less and less a reality.

Grundstein: It's only a reality because you don't have another way.

Question: I would agree then. Another point that I wanted to ask about concerns urban management as a subsystem of the decision process. Let me give you an example: I live in Kansas City, Missouri. But I am closer to the State of Kansas then I am to downtown Kansas City, Missouri. So, if I would try to influence the air pollution policies, I could get a change in Kansas City, perhaps, but it wouldn't benefit me because Kansas City, Kansas, would have no air code. It seems that the larger structures are really out of touch with reality and are forcing people to abandon them.

Grundstein: This indeed is a most serious question for management science. On the analytic side we would call this a question of epistemology, involving the theory of knowledge and the question of the real world. There is no one reality. Reality has an infinite set of dimensions and there is therefore a spectrum of aspects of reality with which different persons are in more or less close subjective relationships. The problem is moving from an individually experienced reality, such as hot or cold, into a general or socially experienced reality. There is a problem of pollution in Kansas City that's an aggregated type of problem, and it is real from the standpoint of a social aggregate. You can show that there's a dispersion of a certain amount of foreign matter of an injurious character in a certain measure of density in a certain unit of air, distributed spacially. That's an aggregate reality. It is reality. If, however, you tell me that you, located spatially in this area don't subjectively experience that reality, it is not real. It's not real for you, but it's still real. The problem of why you need the political managerials is precisely to deal with the multiple demands of reality. The system cannot respond to every aspect of human reality simultaneously.

That's what relative preferences are. If any of you have children, you will know that each child represents a single subjective reality source and that the problem of dealing with multiple realities represented by your children is a problem really in the management of the family and the development of your child. There's some analogy of this to the city. There's an infinity of realities out there because there's an infinity of human experience. But every human experience is not so unique that it cannot be related to another human experience. The definition of poverty as an income less than $3000 for a single person is an aggregate definition of poverty. But the cultural experience of poverty is not necessarily identical with every person having an income less than $3000. Therefore, the subjective experience of low income is not the aggregate reality, it's an individual reality.

A city is a social aggregate and the claims for a personalized, subjectively experienced real values, in relation to the aggregate of experienced reality in the city, is what gives the administrators headaches. As soon as the administrator has one person to deal with other than himself, he has the moral problem of choosing what reality he will accept. What you are saying is that the system is not very well geared to dealing with multiple realities which exist in something as complex an aggregate as the city. I agree with that.

I think what we will have to do is raise the level of capability or, in terms of absolute demands, I want mine! I don't know about yours, but I want mine! The question is, what are the social costs you are willing to pay for yours? I assume you are going to come up with some kind of boundary. If you tear up enough things, people will say, "Well, that ought to be a better way." Pollution is real. It's real for other people as well as for yourself. It, however, may not be as real for you, therefore, you'll be willing to make a trade-off. Suppose, therefore, we get into a bargaining position with you. Pollution's not a real problem for you but your housing is terrible. On the other hand, my housing is good but pollution is terrible for me. Want to trade off realities? What do you want me to give you to improve your reality of low housing so you will improve my reality of bad air pollution? Along come the technical people and say "What's the cost of a trade-off?" What do I have to pay in order to make this kind of trade-off? Trade-offs are a way of dealing with multiple reality. One of the failures of urban social decision processes is its inability to deal with the level of capability for the kind of questions that you're raising. And in the alternative, individuals will tear up the place. Have I responded to you?

Question: I'm not sure!

Grundstein: Have I confused you others on this? You have lots of things out there. Your so-called problems are really aspects of human realities. Pollution and transportation are social utilities — things that people want out of human existence. Housing, recreation, community facilties and education are really ways of organizing human existence, to get certain kinds of existence, to get certain kinds of social utilities. The ideal system is one in which no person has to sacrifice his wants for other wants. That's known as the Praeto optimum. The real world is unable to function in respect to a Praeto optimum.

Question: Let's take it on a pragmatic basis. You are a city finance director and find the major sources of industrial taxation are scattered throughout several other governmental units. One community is almost completely industrial and has a very low tax base. More industries are leaving your central city and going to the periphery into this small city because of its preferential taxes. In terms of other urban services which require funding, you are not able to tax this wealth of resources which goes to make up the economy of the total area. People live in one place and work in the other. People work in one place and they have to spend inordinate amounts of time traversing across the metropolitan areas to get to the job. As the finance manager you have no way of tapping into the resources or even to suggest to the politicals alternatives to be able to provide the services that are needed by the people living in this area. How can a manager perform his function in such a complex multigovernmental situation?

Grundstein: You've been working on this for a long period of time so it's not an impossible situation. It's surprising things that have been done, considering the situation. It's not an unexamined problem at all. We looked at this in some detail in Pittsburgh when we were doing a renewal simulation model in the problem of costing out investments in renewal and of financing renewal projects. There are a lot of options out there. What we discovered, however, is that the political likes to work on certain options which he likes to conceal. Finance is a problem in strategy and there are choices. Up to now, on the whole, politicals have attempted to keep the analytic base and the options for financing undercover. At the same time, the analytics do have kinds of options that they can afford.

If you are saying, however, that you will always match revenue with service needs, forget it, you never will. Human claims are infinite. Your problem is some allocation of resources. Remember the people that got trapped in General Electric in the conspiracy to fix prices? This poor devil is making somewhere around seventy thousand dollars a year, but he felt trapped! His kids were going to Switzerland, you see, and they had their finishing school, and his wife had to go to Europe, there were trips around the world, and so on. His needs weren't met and he had a characterological breakdowown in order to guarantee his income.

You aren't going to solve that problem with that kind of attitude. That's a stance toward the universe. That has nothing to do with the management of resources. You never solve anything ultimately, either. The question is whether or not you tend to get better. That's really what your problem is. Over time, are you in fact capable of dealing with a different set of problems at a different and higher level of effectiveness? If you're getting better, that's pretty good. You're dealing with things now that you couldn't have dealt with at all fifty years ago.

Furthermore, when I was young, the problem seemed to be that of nobody working — poverty. I was trained for periods to prepare for a lifetime of poverty. Today it's a period of affluence that you are trained for. You never know what may come up. Nobody seems to be any happier, as far as I can make out. Your problems change, that's all. So if you are thinking in terms of a static universe, and if I do certain things, certain end products are going to come out and everybody will then reach an equilibrium state of satisfaction, you are doomed to disappointment. The one thing that we know about human beings is they are essentially a disequilibrium mechanism which can't stand to be in an equilibrium state. We generate dissatisfaction.

Question: You say the test is whether we are getting better?

Grunstein: Over time, I think we can deal with a different and more complex order of problems.

Question: The riots tell me that we are not getting better in the big cities. How do you explain the first really violent response that was seen since World War II in terms of developing competence on this political managerial level to respond more intelligently to social pressures and social demands? We are not getting better, if you use riots as your witness test, and I think you've got to use the riots as a major test of the competence of this department.

Grundstein: Maybe you've got to, but I don't have to. I don't know if I have an authoritative explanation so let me simply give my view of it.

The level of investment has been too small, in terms of contemporary problems. Also, you've never been future-oriented. You're always working on past problems. Take the problems of Cleveland, for example. Cleveland missed the boat starting in 1950 with respect to industry. Cleveland never changed its land use patterns to permit the development of industrial parks within the city. So, for fifteen years, industry located outside the city. This began to generate a self-perpetuating cycle in which people formerly living in Cleveland moved out to the plants in the suburbs. Then residences were constructued in the suburbs, and more industry came in because there were more workers there. The service industries followed the workers in the residences, then more industrires followed people, more services, and so on.

Transportation came in and began to link-up transportation networks between the suburban nodes. Cleveland was not dealing with a future problem at all. The political system rewards loyalty, not competence. Everybody who was neglecting the technical problems for the development of the city and making the wrong social decision were, because of party loyalty, being moved up into judgeships, cabinetships, and whatever other things they get. The fundamental social decisions were not future-oriented. The level of investment in the techincal competence was pretty bad.

There's an historical stage in cities when you are working on the current problems. You go back to 1900 and you will find that the initial problem of the cities was to get out of a poltical corruption so inept that you couldn't even deal with the fundamental services. You couldn't get your garbage collected, streets cleaned, the houses kept burning down, and disease was rampant. The initial investment in cities was to get an organizational structure which would enable the performance of minimal functions of rubbish, street cleaning, health, housing construction, sanitation, and so on. That job was done, but the melody lingers on. That is, the technical functional competences are still being fed into our schools of public administration.

Not only are the political people guilty of not dealing with future-oriented problems, but so are the educators. Universities are not very adaptive mechanisms. The profession of public administration made a terrible failure in terms of not directing its people to future-oriented problems. The profession of public administration as an educational system is today merely an acolyte of federal grants. They run where ever federal grant is given becuase it's a way they finance themselves. Therefore, they haven't built up any technology for future-oriented problems of the cities.

I want to congratulate the residents of the central cities on their intelligence. The city got so bad that they finally moved out. This is the way of telling political and managerial people that you're failing and I'm leaving! I don't know how to do your job but I know what I have to do — I'm going, Mack! And they went by droves! And they are still going! It's the greatest decision ever made! If you don't know how to run your city, I don't either! But I'm going some place that's a little bit better! They went and they are still going. The problem with some of the central cities, like Cleveland, is not density but vacancy! There's lots of land. I don't know what it's like in Kansas City.

Question: How do you explain certain breakdowns in the capability of the community today to respond to pressing social problems? What is there in the current leadership structure in the way of the community organization that has brought about this lack of effective response to this breakdown that has occurred in the relationship between the leadership in the community and the other groups in the community that are making demands? There is a certain kind of alienation from the so-called leadership structure.

Grundstein: I want to stick within the limits of my ignorance in some of these things. In the interest of personal honesty, I'm going to have to say I can't answer this because I don't know that much about it.

Question: Let's change the question a little bit. How will this political managerial competence come into being in a given community? It doesn't exist at any great extent today. How is this particular level going to come into being in a community in a better sense?

Grundstein: Let me talk about some things that I think are taking place. It's pretty impressionistic. There's a change of generations taking place. I don't have the number handy, but by 1970, three-quarters of the people that were in government starting in about 1933 are either going to be retired, voluntarily left government, or dead. There's also a change in age groups in the population which is going to be reflected in the change in the composition of the structure. In the end, long live biology. Change in age groups really means change in relationships between elements of the population. So that's one method by which the change is taking place.

There also is a change in the rate of movement of people through systems. The average age of heads of large firms is going down, for example, so that the rate at which people move between systems is more rapid. People in the top level systems are in closer relationships to ideas in their community, and the relationship to the external world is closer. Older persons have a problem of jumping between generations.

The second source of change, aside from the movement of different age levels into positions of dominance, is the influence of the federal government. It works mainly through the allocation process, and that is forcing the cities to put their money in what we call future-oriented and developmental-oriented activities. That's what the model cities and urban renewal are. One problem is that it forces a dependence of local finance on federal financing, and federal financing is usually unstable. If you cut off the federal money, where would the cities be in this activity? They all need credit, as far as I can tell. Over a long period of time, the federal government is not stable in terms of funding local activity. But right now, one of the influences for change is the amount of funds that the federal government is pouring in and the way in which it has allocated that money to planning activities. By planning activities, I really mean social decisions concerned with the development of the economy and social decisions which require technically based and analytically based information. That's another source of change.

The federal government as yet, does not have a policy with respect to cities as such. It does not yet have a policy with respect to relative advantage between metropolitan areas. Should it prefer San Francisco to Kansas City? That problem has not yet been faced in terms of what we call metropolitan area competition.

The third factor that results in the change is subjective attitudes toward human existence. This is particularly true of low income groups which have abandoned passivity in relation to social needs and are much more vociferous and much more organized about the allocation of resources. This has introduced a whole new set of aspiration levels and a whole new set of social claims which have forced traditional allocation processes to shift. All this has been accompanied by changes in social behavior.

Where do I find no change? I don't find conscious strategies of change within the institutional structure of urban government itself. I find the real institutions have changed. What we are undergoing is a period of institutional invention. That's why the entrepreneurial area is important. It's really undergoing a tremendous period of institutional invention. You now have intergovernmental councils, metropolitan area planning councils, and regional hospital planning councils. The changes that are coming about are in the quasi-governmental area, in the more limited functional programs that cut across and have freed themselves from bureaucratic structures. The formal governmental apparatus is pretty well change-insulated.

Question: Are you saying that this political managerial competence is growing up outside the city governmental structures?

Grundstein: Influenced mainly from the outside. Your political group includes representatives from industry, influentials from local power groups in the community, either ethnic or nonethnic, or industrial or nonindustrial, as well as your elected city council. The city council now takes its place as only one among the political group of the city. My position is that they need something similar to the Council of Economic Advisors of the President. And they have to be taught how to use these people. You not only need a city council, but you also need fundamental socioanalytic groups similar to the Council of Economic Advisors for the city council. They have to know how to use this information and feed it into the set of social choices. That's a real institutional change that's lacking here. Now, the city managerial structure itself needs to learn how to function in terms of projects and teams and not in terms of functional tasks. And it needs to be reorganized as it can deal with the area problems, on what we call a multiple-program, multiple-coordinated basis. The whole basis of internal management in the city has to change. Where do I see that the technicals come from? Well, the best teacher is not necessarily the university at this point. I would hire a consulting firm to serve as my management change agents within the city around a specific program. As a matter of fact, I know where it's being done. This is really what your problem is. You have to change the style of management and for this you need a consulting group to show you how it should be done.

Question: What about the in-service function?

Grundstein: They don't have enough in-house competence yet. I would ask universities themselves to make a link-up with a small number of key consulting firms and go through a series of case histories, involving model cities, management changeover, project development, urban renewal, resource allocation, housing development, and change in health services. Those are a very selected group of case histories. How the problem came up, whom you worked with, what were the social problems of getting the thing defined, what were the analytic techniques used, why were they good, why were they not good, what were the implementation problems, and what kinds of learning were required? They would have to be done on a very intensive basis.

Question: Are you saying that the area concept of urban management will work on problems as defined by the citizens rather than as defined by the managers?

If this is true, is it necessary then to develop a management team to serve the needs of this area? Are we building up a multiple program team which has functional structures?

Grundstein: The problem of areas is reconciling them with comprehensive decisions. It's not all one or all the other. The difficulty with physical monopolistic planning up to now is that it has never taken enough options into account. The demand for something like aggregate planning where your planning technicians are linked into areas and clientele is a recognition of social demands and values that the central system never recognized before. The problem is to link up areal demands with comprehensive plans and to let the comprehensive plans take into account some balancing off of areal plans. Area can't do everything by itself just because it is linked up. The south side needs the income base provided by the north side or the east side. On the other hand, the manageability of the city is essentially becoming a series of area-based, multiple-program strategies. It's no longer a series of uniformly administered functions. You have to collect garbage at a different rate in one area than you do in another area.

Question: Then you're saying that the desires of the people in the area should shape the response of the urban manager.

Grundstein: They certainly should be taken into account to a greater extent than formerly. If you cannot meet them, you've got to say so and show how they clash with the general comprehensive plan for the city. They certainly should be taken into account where possible preference should be toward recoginzing them. You are going to have to assess the feasibility and the relative importance of these claims.

Question: I can think of a specific case of the model cities area here in Kansas City which is now slated for strictly industrial development. The people who live in the area don't want to shift to an industrial area but rather maintain and build up residential characteristics. But the planning function here said that the area should be eventually an industrial area.

Grundstein: I would put a team of analytic and political types on to it. What you give me is polarized — it's either/or. I want to see whether we can get some set of solutions which is not either/or. And I want the political types and the analytic types to be linked-up with people in the area. Look at a whole new series of options and you have a tremendous educational problem. If you can be saved, you have to show them how; if you can't be, you have to tell them why; and maybe you can even save pieces of it. The problem now is really to educate vast segments of the urban population with respect to these social decisions. These decisions can no longer be made by a limited number of politicals operating from a central decision apparatus because the choices to be made are much too fine in relation to the grossness of the choices.

Question: You are assuming an urban management capability of a magnitude that is beyond the cities at this point. The problems are so numerous that we don't have the manpower to do this type of analysis. I don't know how many years before I see this type of personnel available to us.

Grundstein: I don't know whether it's as bleak as that. If you work out a strategy for this and work out some relative priorities you can then try it on a test basis in some areas. I think you have to use this as a point of entry in a learning situation. You can get some funding for it, if not from the federal government then from foundation sources. The Ford Foundation, for example, gave $175,000 or so for the study of development problems of small cities. There are things out there. The problem is to try and get a learning situation and see whether or not you can generalize on it. Rather than numbers of people, I think it's the way in which you apply existing technologies of the social structure in that area that is important. Let's take an example. The question is whether or not to include this area in the model cities program. You go to the model cities people out there and say, "Look, this is the problem. This is what I want to do to resolve this question. I want to approach it this way. I estimate the types of people I am going to bring, and the structure by which I am going to deal with the problem and it's going to take this long." You can also ask that for purposes of submitting the application. We will submit it one way but we will reexamine the issue once the project is funded. There are all kinds of options out there if you can get to the right guy.

Question: You are looking at it from the other side, and it seems to me that it's a problem of educating the professionals rather than the inner-city people.

Grundstein: It's both sides. You have to educate the inner city too.

Question: It seems to me that the professionals are really out of touch with the needs of the people in the inner city. One of the best examples I have seen is the circus called the O E O Mental Health Center. The professionals on the board are saying that they want to talk about health services, and the people from the inner city on the board are saying they want to talk about jobs at the mental health clinic. When you walk into a place, a neighborhood organization, you don't find a list of health services, but rather a listing of the jobs available. The professionals are simply out of touch with reality.

Grundstein: Suppose I put it another way — any approach to these questions which polarizes the positions of the parties automatically makes the problem insoluble.

Question: But the question is who sets priorities? The priorities in the ghetto are not health services but jobs. If the professionals set priorities as health services, they are not meeting the needs of the people in the inner city.

Grundstein: There are a lot of options out there. Here again you give me a polarized solution. As a manager, I will avoid polarized solutions like crazy because it gives me lots of problems. It makes for great dissatisfaction for those who are on the other end. For example, one of the areas of Boston went to designing a housing project by itself using the poverty population itself. They got a delegation of authority, hired their own planners, hired their own contractors, designed the project, and got it through the central planning committee, and supported it through them through the federal government. Now there's a case in which you allowed them to work out the problems but not polarize it. *We're* going to build it, not *you're* going to build it. You've got to avoid polarization. Out of this, you can show them that jobs are one of the problems.

Question: You don't need to show them that, they know it already.

Grundstein: Yes, but that's not the only problem.

Question: Well, it is to them. You can't sell health services to somebody who's starving — it just doesn't matter. It's important to me because I have a nice job but it's not important to somebody who doesn't have a job.

Grundstein: Then, you've got your solution. If you tell me you can't, then you've got to do what you can. I always have a problem with going in and saying that you can't. Because we know then that a great deal of human choice is contingent and that it depends on how the thing is brought up.

Question: I am saying that the important question is: 'Who sets priorities?' Whether professionals are going to set priorities for people or whether people are going to set priorities for professionals.

Grundstein: Suppose we ask how it's set and not who sets it. In East Cleveland, Arthur D. Little and Company had a series of meetings in which technical people came into neighborhood centers and raised a whole series of questions about the problems of the neighborhood and what activities should be undertaken to deal with them. Lots of stuff is out there and it's never been brought together. We have to deal with value differences in polarization such as you are talking about. But I am going to resist you. Social choice is full of an infinity of options and a good man finds them. And if you let them polarize, you've got lots of problems.

Question: Isn't one of the problems that you're discussing here the inadequacy of data to help make the decision of this either/or? Take this model cities decision concerning location. Wouldn't one possible method of agreement be that the model cities area should be those blocks which have the worst conditions? If so, you have to spell out what *worst* means. High infant mortality, lowest income, greatest dilapidation, whichever of the half a dozen items you need. And then on a block-by-block basis, collect data using the computer as the analytic tool that would help make the decision. Blocks that end up in the model cities area would be the ones that people quantitatively would agree to. What do you see as the place of the computer as a management tool, and I'll confine it to the area of data collection? There are a myriad of agencies, as you say, who are all doing their jobs and collecting their own data. The possiblities of an integrated data system from which all management operators can use this common pool as a basis for decision making seems to hold vast potential.

Grundstein: There's been a certain disillusionment with data banks. The second consideration is cost. We know behaviorally that different sets of decision makers use different sets of information with respect to different value choices. One of the problems in the design of the data bank is that you cannot possibly get all combinations of information for all combinations of decision makers for all combinations of problems. It's impossible — one of the problems therefore that we have is bounding the field. With respect to what kind of outputs generally is what kind of information relevant? We've never really solved this problem. You can't design your information system until you have some idea of what end products you want. Data by itself is not enough.

Another point is the relationship of social decision to data. Data never concludes anything. Social decisions are a compound of strategies, value preferences, and relative importance of difference values. Everybody's values and the weighting of the value choices are not necessarily on the same plan of equality. The strategies are the way in which you define the problem or what problems you allow to come up for decision. The set of social decision processes are the way in which the human actors relate among themselves to come up with some kind of decisions.

If you take any one component such as data, and put it into a set-up which has at least a half a dozen elements, nothing may change. The decision makers may move around to the little black books and personal sources of data. This is where our failure occurred at Pittsburgh.

We had an urban renewal simulation which was computerized, but we could never link-up with the way in which the political authority of the city of Pittsburgh actually made decisions. With models of financing urban renewal projects, we showed them that fiscal decisions are really strategy decisions and how they could be done in relation to financing urban renewal. But that wasn't the way that they wanted it decided. The way in which they decided fiscal problems was related to the way in which they maintained sets of options which could be utilized in order to maintain certain sets of support and to allocate resources within the city.

The human being, if I'm permitted the obvious, is awfully complex. I really respect this and there is not one piece of hardware out there that is going to hold him. The problem that you are asking is what is the level of investment that I want to put into hardware for purposes of getting an information system that I can demonstrate is going to give me certain kinds of benefits in relation to the social decisions I want to make.

There's a loss of glamour of central data banks at this point. There are a lot of technical problems in constructing these data banks. They're still killing us. The literature that's coming in on data banks now is awfully critical. They are too costly and haven't been linked up to managerial processes. These are the things that are troubling us. Educational problems of users have not been licked at all.

Question: You said that we should be looking toward new techniques, and yet what you've said about the decisions for the selection of urban renewal areas in Pittsburgh follows old techniques. These are mainly political decisions based on power and on benefits for self-aggrandizement. If new management is going to educate the power structure to make better decisions, I think that these new technologies have to be used.

Grundstein: That was our failure as technicians in relation to politics but it wasn't their failure. We did a beautiful job of laying out the logic of social decisions, but not the empiric of social decision. Interestingly enough, however, we lost the war, but won the battle. A new group in the political structure is coming in now and is beginning to utilize what we said ought to be done, but they are learning in their own way and they have taken over control of the hardware. So we lost the war and won the battle and in fact, we showed them how it ought to be done.

What they did is put in their own political type who's learning the system. One of the fundamentals of human beings is trust as well as competence. You've got to have both. We lost them, but we learned about them. It was our failure as technical people in not making up with them. It could be done and it's going to be done but you need a new breed of cat.

You need your politicals, but you need another set of politicals. You need a political type who's not afraid of the analytic types, who can look at analytic information and understand it. You need management development programs for high level political types not for third-level bureaucrats. It's a terrific education problem with the politicals. That's what really takes place when you bring in high level Nationals out of consulting firms. The really good ones are saying you have to change the type of management.

One of the failures of Cleveland is it brought in people who did projects for urban renewal but who never really influenced the managerial structure. They took projects and threw them in a file cabinet. And no one paid the least bit of attention. You can't do this without changing your style of management and the people that come in use your technology and social decisions to educate the managers. You just can't come in and capsulate yourself in technical analysis, file a report, and leave.

Question: In the case of Pittsburgh, who were your entrepreneurials?

Grundstein: We had a relatively simple set-up. The late David Lawrence linked up with the Mellons so you had the political and economic together. Everything else flowed and fell in line. The Mellons owned a great deal of downtown and they would walk into tenants of firms that they owned and say you are going to move downtown into these buildings, and they did. You didn't have a problem.

And so far as the political structure following through, Lawrence took care of the city. We found, however, that we couldn't get implementation on certain kinds of renewal projects particularly in the utilities field. The engineering side and the utility side in the capital investment of community facilities is relatively inflexible in terms of changeover. We could never get the political party to send the word down to restructure that particular organization so that we could coordinate with a rate of investment in construction of housing and utilities. We cracked up on the implementation side.

Question: I feel that in the case of local government, if the elected legislators really want to plan and manage social change badly enough that somehow it will get done and they will find technical assistance. Apparently, in Pittsburgh, you had no lack of desire, but it's just another problem for your local government.

Grundstein: There's been a study of local governments done quietly for HUD by Arthur D. Little and Company on how planning is utilized in local government. They found that they don't go to the planning commissions. One of the problems is the rate of response to your local planning structures. The critical problems of planning come up when the rate of development of the cities is at such a speed that you need technical assistance and they can't get that kind of technical assistance from your local planning structure.

Question: The fact that most planning staffs have no one competent in the area of social planning indicates to me their inability and lack of desire to do anything except react to social change. When they want you badly enough they will come out again to find the technical resources.

Grundstein: You're going at it in the American way so far which is peaceful in the end. In the regional hospital planning, the university planning, the intergovernmental planning, I think you are correct on that, but suppose they want to start, then who's there?

What we need are politically adaptable and poltically skillful technical people who know how the political decision process operates and how to feed their information into it. I will say that some of the problem is the problem of will. Are you willing to make the investment in the activity? It may be that we have to reach a level of incompetence in this area and make sufficient mistakes so that the thing cracks up first to mobilize people's commitment. There's nothing like riots to start you thinking all over again but it means you are working on past problems.

My occupation and personal commitments tend to make me think that there ought to be a better way but my realism always says that there's an alternative to a better way and that's a bad way, like riots. But schools cannot accept that as a basis of action. We have to say that there are better ways of doing things that enable you to deal with problems as they are developing, and that are consistent with certain democratic conceptions that are reflected in the organization of your local government. However, it may be like penicillin and venereal disease. The venereal disease rate keeps going up though the cure for it is readily available because the social structures are so disorganized. It's a dismal view, but it's possible.

Question: The use of PPBS by local government produces alternatives for choice as one of its products. To me this seems to create a decision process whereby the council is forced to choose between alternative courses of action. Do you think that the political structure likes to make these choices when there is a conflict that could result from this? Wouldn't they rather have no alternatives rather than generating conflict within the political structure by choosing between a variety of alternatives?

Grundstein: One of your problems is to feed up options in such a way that you do not polarize opinion. That's a social skill. There's a good illustration of this problem now going on in New York City where they have developed a display system for dealing with certain alternatives. These required groups of teams working over two weeks to thirty days. Don't feed up information in such a way that you polarize your response. This is the way in which you utilize information.

You can feed up the series of options but in such a way that you don't precipitate public conflict over it. Also, it's a question of timing when the options become too formalized. If you do it at the last minute you may not give them enough freedom of choice. How much lead time do you give them before it's necessary to decide?

Using certain social manipulations that are legitimate, you can take the administrator off the hot seat. If you put him in a position where he has no chance at all you've got a problem. You have to use this thing with some sense of the dilemmas of social decision makers at the highest level. If you come in and release your report to the press as to what the options are, and these are polarized options, and you throw it in the lap of the city council at a public hearing without prior consultations, you are dead. Nobody operates that way. It is a question of soical conditions under which you both formulate and feed in the options for decision.

Question: Well, this is true, if you have the opportunity to take the time to understand how you want to present these options, or if you have the time to grasp what the real options are in terms of how they are going to be viewed by the council. You might not have the same perspective as the city council.

Grundstein: Therefore, what we need is a set of learning processes for people coming into the general management level to demonstrate how political managerial decisions are made and how to use the apparatus without wrecking it. This part of their competence can be called social utilization capability.

Question: I think that there is a certain set of assumptions that the older generation of professionals and planners in office adhere to, which don't jibe with reality. The assumption that you shouldn't serve up a set of options which does not polarize opinion is not the method of operation anymore. Most of the younger people operate on a series of forced confrontations. That's the way action has gone from what I've seen. Not from serving up a series of what I would call pablum, but from really defining an issue and forcing these people to choose.

Grundstein: But you can get conned when you don't think you can do anything any other way.

Question: I'll dispute that. Confrontation is a whole new method of operating that is a style of life. It is really coming to the fore and the older people have an awfully hard time dealing with this. I think younger people enjoy it as a style of life rather than just a way of getting things done. You said before that human desires are limitless but that is not true of all young people. For example, my father has a hard time living on just $50,000. I would have a hard time doing it too because I wouldn't know how to spend my money. I don't want $50,000 and I'm not going to try to get it, you see? There are a lot of young people who feel that way.

Grundstein: I must say that the single sample is too small for such a generalization. It's a mighty big world of young people out there and there are still those that are upwardly mobile and want to move into certain social structures.

Question: I agree, but not in the same terms as their parents.

Grundstein: No, thank Heaven for that. Handling conflict is part of the competence of the newer generation. The older ones never recognize conflict; they always stress teamwork. But still it has the problem of maintaining the boundaries of the structure. If you want to have a series of revolutionary councils running Kansas City, that's one way of operating it and it is possible. I don't want to rule it out. You may have a big housing construction program after it's all over. But it's possible to run it that way.

Question: I would like to generalize on some of your earlier comments. My concern is whether we might get ourselves in trouble later on if we do develop a differential between nationally oriented and locally oriented technicians. I am assuming that the nationally oriented technicians are going to get bored after they develop on the local level and will bubble up at the top on the federal level or in the consulting field. They will then develop uniform federal policies which could conceivably mold the nation into a bland sameness. Today we at least have competition among metropolitan areas. I'm not saying this is an imminent danger, but I can see this is a potential danger. My concern is the survival of competition within urban areas rather than always trying to come up with a regional approach to everything. You gave the example of the poor deciding their own housing project. An example would be letting the hospitals compete with each other. It costs more money maybe, but you might end up with a better health system when you are finished. We do have to compete to try to do a better job.

Grundstein: That's an approach. It's an entrepreneurial choice. They found in California, for example, when they located highways that the hospitals followed the highways and the users of hospitals followed the highways. In other words, people followed the easiest transportation route to a hospital. All the hospitals in the cities, therefore, tend to die. The committee was then asked to finance hospitals. The question became which hospital to give it to? That's why we had the regional planning board in Pittsburgh, which was extended to Cleveland, New Orleans, and perhaps other places, because the problem of investment in these services is really such that unless you control it the level of investment becomes uneconomic. You pay opportunity costs. You're paying the cost of the project you might have gotten if you had made better choices in the original allocation of money. Since there is only limited money at any one time – in 1950 or 1970 there will be more money, but as of 1955 or 1965, there's a certain boundary limit – what you want to do is to minimize your opportunity costs.

Question: But aren't there certain public areas that you can quantitatively define as levels of care and levels of services and distribution, and others that you can't standardize or quantify? What, for instance, is a quantifiable, acceptable level of health care? Even the doctors can't tell you whether this is good or bad care. What concerns me is someone on a higher level defining health care for a local level. This is a sort of health care that everyone has to achieve; we will penalize the one institution that wants to approach it in a different way.

My concern is getting back to the top in our political structure. I see instances where there are top policy makers in Washington who've got their own viewpoint and my concern would be that we have enough competition to insure different choices at that level, to make sure something doesn't get screened out which has a lot of merit. My concern is that trained and nationally oriented technicians aren't all poured out of the same mold.

Grundstein: If you pour every important technician out of the same mold to handle positions in the bureaucracy, the profession can become pretty standardized. However, the problems are dealt with at the top. Low control government doesn't solve the problem and local government can't solve the problem. You've got to define what the problem is first. The technically trained man, the general management man, or the manager in the local area has to know how to operate under different conditions. That's the skill you give him. Not that he has a uniform way of operating, but he knows you can do some things in Pittsburgh that you can't do in Kansas City, and that they have decided to do things differently in Kansas City than they do in New Orleans. That's the only way I could respond to that.

Question: How do we get this entrepreneurial man at the very top to seek the additional training that you're talking about so that he is then capable of making maximum use of analysis and other kindred items? The mayor, or the manager, or the chief ward leader are the people who now are in the entrepreneurial spot. How are you going to get them involved in wanting to seek this additional competency?

Grundstein: First of all you are going to have to talk to some of them and identify their group. That's not so hard since Hunter's techniques with identification. Your top social decision structure is close to, if not the same as, the community power structure. You have to cut that down somewhat into the social power structure or social decision structure. You have to talk to these people, go look at these classes of problems that have come through them, and begin to be perceptive about what kind of information to utilize. Who do they rely on to decide? We call these mapping information processes.

Question: How do we convince them that this is really going to work? I don't really dispute any of this, but how do we convince the key entrepreneurials in practice?

Grundstein: We have to show them that it's helpful. We have to show a kind of utility, a payoff that is relevant. You can try this out in the location of your high speed automobile transport network, for example.

Question: If you take one thing like highways, or health care, suddenly you see all the concomitant relationships. These are so far beyond our methodologies and our procedures and our informational abilities, that we really can't do a competent job to demonstrate to this individual that he should make use of this sort of thing. It's like the chicken and egg in terms of the development analogy.

Grundstein: In Cleveland, the business people insisted upon it because the business people are the primary sources of hospitals. In Pittsburgh, they've heard about it and they insisted that a structure like this should be set up to defend them against claims for corporate funds for hospitals. Then they set up their own staff structure. We have an interesting phenomena when the business people say, "Look, by gum, we need a better way!"

Question: There is undoubtedly some value to the computer and yet the methods used and means and research tools are still being developed.

Grundstein: I'd hate to have to wait that long. What I think you need is a group going out to a key number of cities for a certain kind of technology you can trust. And you can get some idea of the relative effectiveness and the conditions of utilization of these technologies and go to a limited number of consulting firms that have looked at some case histories, San Francisco, New Haven, Boston, New York City, and Chicago at least have some well documented cases. I need to take an in-depth look at what was done in the utilization of new management technologies and the problems of social decision, given the class of problems that they tried to deal with.

Question: All they really did though was narrow down certain choices. They were still the major governmental sort of thing requiring the skilled artist to come in and choose among the alternatives.

Grundstein: You must have depth, I don't care what else you have, depth is part of everything.

Question: So, we are back to this breed of cat you bring into the public service and this is the art of the second level. So we are at full cycle?

Grundstein: No, you're not at a full cycle. If you get a different breed of cat it remodifies it, but the modifications are critical. A breed of cat which can't use analytic types and does nothing more than develop information is one breed of cat, but the breed of cat that can use analytic types is quite another. Richard J. Daley, Mayor of Chicago, fascinates me. He represents a cross between an old line political type that can use analytics but he never loses political control of the system.

I am awfully fully curious about how they do it and how was it utilized in San Francisco where the specific analytic technique was used to project housing needs. What happened to that? I don't know! All I read in the articles is about what the technique was and how it was put forth in San Francisco and how it could have solved this problem. But I don't know what happened! You should study the case history and failure of urban renewal to determine what is the matter with it. I think a lot more is out there than can be brought together. I think you can do some hothousing on this. You can bring in special development crews for your top levels. It's a real problem of transformation of utilization of information. What information do I get if I use this model?

Question: I don't quite buy the idea that power structures for the entrepreneurial group are that easy to identify. The experience that I've had is that it varies tremendously among communities. Pittsburgh is vastly different from any structure in Cleveland and certainly from Kansas City. And it seems to me that before we reach this level something has to be done with the social organization of an entrepreneurial level. This is one of Kansas City's problems. I don't think that there is any high enough degree of organization so that people in the managerial level or people who are attempting to influence the entrepreneurial level can really reach it effectively and work with it.

Grundstein: All right, I'll buy that. You want to start with an identifiable, bounded group, already identifiable as being involved in certain kinds of social decisions which involve the development of that city.

Question: Did you say that the Nationals would probably define the problem but the solution would probably still be at the local level?

Grundstein: The problems are solved at the cities level because the problems are defined by the cities in terms of a specific set of decision makers in a specific area. The federal government is basically an allocation apparatus and it defines only the general boundaries in which it will give money. The Nationals will come to supplement your high level politicals.

Question: Yes, but if this thing ever develops, the Nationals would make the decisions defining the problem.

Grundstein: No, they would work with your politicals in providing an analytic base and options and getting the thing back to the federal level. They wouldn't necessarily define it. They would help you define it or put numbers on it, or give you options. Your Locals finally determine the problem because they live with it and are linked up. But they need an analytic base for this social decision process.

Question: Do you think that the analytic base on the national level might be so overwhelmingly dominant that it might actually define the problem as though the Locals wouldn't be competent to do so themselves?

Grundstein: I don't think so because you have to use your Locals and the consequences are local and there's a lot of information that's never available to anyone except the Locals.

Question: Then you wouldn't say that this is a danger?

Grundstein: No, you need to know that they have to supplement you. As a matter of fact, in some areas neighborhood groups are learning how to use technical high level people. What may happen is a flip in which your clientele in certain areas may become stronger technically than others. With respect to managerial structure, they'll bomb you, that's what they'll do. Because they'll talk from a technical base about their aspirations that you don't even know anything about, and you are going to have to rush out and get some technical people and check it out. That's what advocacy planning is.

Question: As you outlined it, there is an analogy between the private sector and the public sector. The private sector being the corporation with its board and its top manager, and the public sector with its policy making structure and its top manager. I assume that in the private sector the top manager has an official relationship as the manager and he also has a social relationship. He has an unofficial way of communicating with the top policy makers. I know this is not true in the public sector because, besides your decision makers and your top manager, you will not only have to deal with your officially elected people but also your quiet leadership. You have no mechanism to communicate with them except public meetings, through official legislation and so we have to find a mechanism in the public sector. The manager is not in the right social structure. They artificially put him in there by buying him memberships in the right clubs so that he has the opportunity off duty to start influencing these decision makers.

Grundstein: You have to do that at the entrepreneurial level. In universities, departmental chairmen and deans are given club memberships, but they never give it to professors. I think it's relevant. I have to agree that in this community you can't go to two or three people on an informal basis and engineer decisions, decisions are not made in this community on that basis.

Question: Are we to use club membership as a tool for getting to the effective decision-making process? This is a rather sad comment on the state of our community or any other community. We know right away that there are certain exclusions of groups from the right club compounding the problem of the polarization of the black in our own community as well as any other community that is fighting discrimination. If the situation is as described — what does this tell us about Kansas City? Is there really no power structure in the sense that there may be an old line one in Philadelphia?

Grundstein: You have your own kind of social structure and it is neither good or bad. I am here, you are here. That's it. You have to take it as it is. It doesn't make any difference it it is good or bad. If you don't have a power structure that is a unique case from my standpoint.

The New Technical Competence for Urban Management

T. R. Lakshmanan

In preparing this presentation on the relationship of analytic technology to urban management, I realized the difficulty of doing justice to the topic and decided to protect myself behind a series of definitional hedges. Let me begin by saying that I owe certain distinctions to Dr. Grundstein. Referring to analytic technology as the bundle of technologies that augment the relevant informational basis of decisions in urban management, he hierarchically classified the three levels of that management as (a) political entrepreneurship, (b) general management, and (c) program operations. While flexible — and certainly not mutually exclusive — these three levels are primarily concerned with, respectively, "what to do," "why do it," and "how to do it." Much of what follows will reflect this distinction.

Dr. Grundstein gave the impression, however, that he was largely concerned with intrajurisdictional areas. My own experience, on the other hand, has been related to regions, to metropolitan areas where there are multi-echelon governments and where the policies of those governments are considerably affected by federal and state governments. My remarks here will, in the main, be colored by this interjurisdictional slant.

In that such interjurisdictional areas are extremely open, those managing them are concerned with the coordination (in a physical planning sense) of public investments and space. Similarly, in any metropolitan area, there are multijurisdictional problems, since what happens in one jurisdiction has effects in another, producing a whole range of interconnected, interjurisdictional consequences through such strategies as coordination and "cooperation," in the context of personal interplay and meetings.

Reference to some concepts from welfare economics reveals, however, the inadequacy of this approach in dealing with interjurisdictional effects. One such concept is externality, wherein events taking place in one jurisdiction produce costs and benefits in other jurisdictions which are "external" to the actual physical happening. Air and water pollution exemplify the many cases where externalities become important in metropolitan planning and management. A second element is that of incidence — of who is to benefit from and/or pay for the application of policy instruments or public actions. We are not only concerned about actual magnitudes of impacts, but also their incidence dimensions. What will be the incidence of costs and benefits of a public program by population group, by economic sector, by geographic area, and by time period?

A third important consideration is the occurrence of economies of scale. In discussions of public investment, one hears increasing talk about joint purchase and use of facilities to achieve economies of scale. These effects are important to any decision to invest in metropolitan areas.

A fourth aspect is the complementarity of public investments. One such investment may, in addition to producing benefits and costs of its own, increase or decrease those available from another type of public investment. Two types of public investment thus may have a synergistic effect, where each works to increase the effectiveness of the other and benefits increase as complementarity increases. To take a somewhat primitive example, the simultaneous carrying out of a library program for housewives and a library program for children will likely attract more attendance to each program than would the carrying out of either program alone. Building a highway to a park is another example. This principle can be applied within a single jurisdiction if, as Dr. Grundstein suggested, the urban area is divided into smaller parts, like Model Cities neighborhoods or other geographic subdivisions, in order to increase local participation. If metropolitan management is to be effective, then it must think about these interjurisdictional and intergeographical effects in terms of the above four aspects.

Returning now to Dr. Grundstein's management hierarchy, let us attempt to use it to describe this complex set of effects. First, each management level has its more-or-less characteristic orientation.

The managerial entrepreneur is structurally oriented, is concerned with the basic question of functions. What, he asks, is it that this agency should do, what should the government be concerned about, and under what institutional framework should these questions be addressed? Here is sought and developed the total rationale of the system. Here the system is "structured." The concern is with simplicity and broad rules of learning behavior.

The second orientation, at the level of general management, is analytical. General management is concerned with questions of why one instrumentality may be preferable to another, given the concerns expressed by the entrepreneur. This choice of programs, of investments, requires analytical information on the impacts of the available alternatives.

On the third, the operations side, the information orientation is most important. Such information is to reflect how, and how well, the chosen programs or investments are, in fact, achieving their objectives. Of course, any sort of division between structural and informational analysis is highly arbitrary; but, for this classification, it is the emphasis that is important.

Let me now elaborate on the informational requirements of these three strata. The political entrepreneur must make broad decisions about the priorities about which he should be concerned, and any analytical technology that is to be relevant to his decision-making must be at that same, broad level. The concern of general management, on the other hand, tends to be area- and program-specific. At this level, analytic technology must relate to available methods of achieving aims, and answering questions, proposed at the higher, entrepreneurial level. The third level, then, requires information on the actual efficacy of the programs being carried out. Here, the analytic technology must seek to endow that information with additional meaning by relating it to the choice of subject (political entrepreneurial) and the choice of how to look at that subject (general management).

Having developed these general points, let me now describe a case study concerning the linkage between the political entrepreneur and general management.

I will first cite a study just finished in Puerto Rico because, in view of the special institutional framework and the context of planning, it offers a case in which my points can easily be made. You will see the analogy between our experience in Puerto Rico and the variety of metropolitan experiences.

We were asked, in Puerto Rico, to recommend a set of analytical models and the requisite information systems to help the Planning Board and the various government departments address themselves to varieties of planning issues. In defining the scope of this complex problem, we found that a very important element was, simply, to develop a strategy for looking at it. We attempted to articulate the problem as it would be seen by the decision-makers, by Planning-Board members, the Governor's office, and the various department heads — all at the political-entrepreneurial level — and to relate their view of the problem to what general management personnel could do in analyzing the problem. In defining the context of the policy issues coming up for discussion, we realized that the way in which such issues were being raised in Puerto Rico flowed from the nature of the development process and that the dynamics of the economy flowed from the resulting settlement-pattern changes, population migration, population growth, and resulting changes in welfare levels. So, to define the public issues, it became necessary to understand the development processes themselves.

In general, Puerto Rico offers one of the success stories of the development field. Its growth, in twenty-five years, from poverty to income levels comparable with those of some European countries has nevertheless been accompanied by tremendous population increase. Since economic development is a highly competitive affair and tends to occur in those clusters of skilled population and available capital which are found in urban conglomerations, the city of San Juan has become an increasingly potent attractor of that economic growth, as well as of migrant population.

There seems now to be a major gap between the modern, growing sector in San Juan (and, to a lesser extent, in Ponce) and a lagging sector outside the urban areas. This gap poses two kinds of development problems, which can be called "adaptive" and "developmental." First, the explosive growth of the cities results in great demand for investments in public facilities. Moreover, as planning and investment succeed in coping with crises in housing, education, transportation, and social services in the cities, still more people are drawn to those cities. This attraction is brought about both by the existence of the products of that investment and by the increased economic viability conferred on the city by its infrastructure investments. This traditional problem of physical planning in response to economic growth, John Friedman calls "adaptive planning."[1] The other problem is, then, the need to develop the periphery, to counteract the tendency of urban centers to sap the economic potential — capital and skilled labor — of the countryside. In this field, planners are concerned with stemming rural out-migration and producing income-generating activities in the hinterland. This concern may be called "developmental planning." Neither the adaptive nor the developmental activity is, of course, altogether specific to either urban or nonurban areas. Developmental planning must continue in the cities if their rapid growth is not to turn into equally rapid decline, and adaptive planning must take place in the outlying areas in response to social pressures there. Nevertheless, the dichotomy is real, as is the fact that successful planning of one kind will create added demand for the other.

In Puerto Rico, because of the stage it had reached in the development process, the scale of the island, and its unique institutional framework, we felt it necessary to merge the development and adaptive planning streams. In doing so, there was created a planning framework which related island-wide macroeconomic planning to microanalytic spatial planning or, in other words, related macroeconomic targets to those of microanalytic spatial planning.

To illustrate, let me take the case of decentralization, a general issue generating much debate at the present time. No one is quite sure to what extent centralization or decentralization affects the economy or living standards in the San Juan area, but there is agreement on the physical costs of traffic congestion, facility shortages, pollution, etc. In a growing economy, areas of high density may be immediately advantageous, but the long-run spiral of their social costs cannot be ignored. If, then, decentralization is made desirable by such social costs, the question becomes one of how much decentralization and in what form. The choice may be to attempt to spread economic activity uniformly over the island, or instead, to concentrate on certain of the apparently more viable growth centers at the expense of others. As phrased, the parameters of the issue are migration and the growth of new urban areas. This is not, however, the way the problem should be framed.

To the contrary, the problem is to identify the chief goals underlying planning for the island as a whole. Migration and the growth of new urban centers are not goals, and for that matter, neither is decentralization. They are, instead, instrumentalities available for use in approaching those goals. To look upon them as instrumental objectives is to approach the problem in a different manner, one reflected in the chart on page 176.

As the chart shows, we felt that there were three major goals underlying all island planning efforts: (a) to maximize gross island income, (b) to improve the distribution of that income, and (c) to improve the level of community services available to the residents of the island. In achieving these goals, then, such

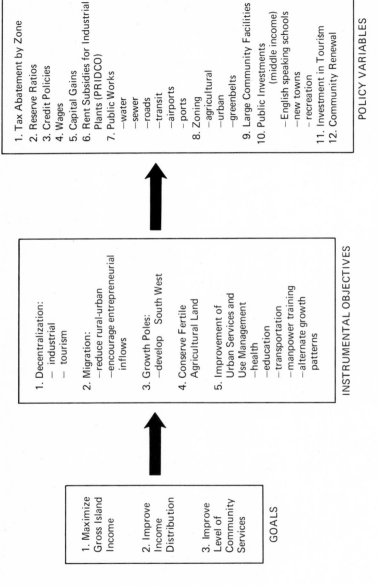

Figure 9-1 Goals, instrumental objectives and policy options in Puerto Rico.

GOALS

1. Maximize Gross Island Income

2. Improve Income Distribution

3. Improve Level of Community Services

INSTRUMENTAL OBJECTIVES

1. Decentralization:
   – industrial
   – tourism

2. Migration:
   –reduce rural-urban
   –encourage entrepreneurial inflows

3. Growth Poles:
   –develop South West

4. Conserve Fertile Agricultural Land

5. Improvement of Urban Services and Use Management
   –health
   –education
   –transportation
   –manpower training
   –alternate growth patterns

POLICY VARIABLES

1. Tax Abatement by Zone
2. Reserve Ratios
3. Credit Policies
4. Wages
5. Capital Gains
6. Rent Subsidies for Industrial Plants (PRIDCO)
7. Public Works
   –water
   –sewer
   –roads
   –transit
   –airports
   - ports
8. Zoning
   –agricultural
   –urban
   –greenbelts
9. Large Community Facilities
10. Public Investments
    (middle income)
    –English speaking schools
    –new towns
    – recreation
11. Investment in Tourism
12. Community Renewal

instrumental objectives as decentralization of the economy to a point corresponding to the population distribution are to be sought. This objective relates to the goal of improving the distribution of income. By decentralization of industry and tourism and through tax policies, subsidies, and public investments, the incidence of future growth can be made to reach the lagging rural and small-town population.

Another such objective is control of migration between regions of the island in order to (a) slow migration from rural to urban areas, and (b) encourage the flow of skilled labor and entrepreneurs from San Juan to other growth poles. Still another is the encouragement of development at other viable growth centers, a strategy explicitly involving intraregional concentration of economic and social-overhead investments to create environments attractive to both industry and skilled professional, managerial, and technical personnel. A fourth objective, the conservation of agricultural land, relates to the goal of maximizing gross island income and stems from concern with the uncontrolled expansion of urban areas into fertile agricultural areas. A fifth, the improvement of community services and use management in large concentrations of population, reflects the concern, primarily, of adaptive planning. It includes, as a concern related to infrastructure investment, that of designing appropriate land-use patterns.

The policy options listed on the chart should be self-explanatory and are in many ways analogous to those available to urban and regional planners here. The following chart places them in the context of overall economic planning, in a manner general enough to be applied to any planning activity.

The scope of this framework, which was adapted from Tinbergen's work,[2] is to pose goals of economic policy and to investigate means of achieving those goals. First, there are the "targets" of economic policy — level of employment, per capita income, distribution of income, balance of payments, etc. — the achievement of which will depend, in turn, upon two other sets of variables. These other variables are divided among those which are not controllable (United States gross national product, interest rate, mean wage in New York, etc.) and those which are (the policy instruments at the disposal of the government, such as, in the case of Puerto Rico, tax, wage and credit policies). The model shown in the chart on page 178 helps estimate the net effect of a unit change in each policy instrument upon each target variable.

A point worth making here is that, while Tinbergen alleges that the side effects of a given action (those not related to the goal at hand) are "irrelevant" to a given planning problem and can be ignored, these same side effects are of great importance to adaptive planning. In other words, the pursuit of one set of goals gives rise to side effects, which effects may, in turn, become the targets of later planning efforts. What may be viewed as a side effect for island-level developmental planning (e.g., urban congestion) becomes, from a systems viewpoint, the valid object of a further inquiry for decision-makers at the urban level. This was one of the several reasons it was felt necessary to approach the planning issues in Puerto Rico from a systems point of view.

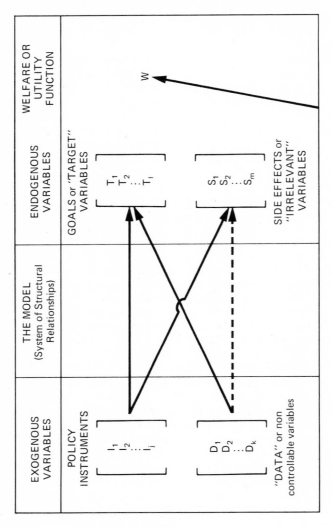

Figure 9-2 A framework for economic development planning. (Adapted from Tinbergen)

This illustration should spotlight the essentials of an analytical technology appropriate for linking the political entrepreneurship level (Planning Board Member, Bureau Chief, etc.) with general management level (Director).

To develop the same illustration one step further is to identify the new technical competence at the general management level, as follows:

Figure 9—3 is an attempt to relate an illustrative set of policy issues in Puerto Rico to some effects or impacts of these policies and to identify the sequence in the analysis of these relationships. Illustrative policy options and plan alternatives are indicated on the left hand side of Figure 3; the effect types, which are the consequences of alternative policy options and plans are next shown; and the three other boxes (enclosed by double dotted lines) show the "generic" models that would be appropriate for estimating the effects of these policy options. The first of these boxes sets forth the classes of economic and spatial concepts ranging from growth considerations to local "comparative advantage" (as modified by access, facilities and agglomeration effects). The box just below lists various types of models and the box on the right, the alternative data requirements for the concepts and the models. It will be noted that the policies listed both in Figures 1 and 3 span (illustratively) the options available to the Planning Board and other agencies responsible for different functional areas and geographical levels. Thus are encompassed the policy instruments open to the functional departments, such as education, health, highways, etc. Similarly, some of the policy options open at such different geographical levels as the Island (e.g., credit policies, reserve ratios), region (tax abatement, new towns, etc.), metropolitan (water, sewer, community facilities), and municipal (zoning, renewal) are listed. In terms of the planning orientations, they pertain to the gradiational macroeconomic development; Island-wide concern at one end and microanalytic physical-spatial (adaptive) orientation at the other, with an emerging regional-planning focus that merges the developmental and adaptive viewpoints at the intra-Island level.

Again, the list of effects that have to be measured to elucidate the policy options in Figure 9—3 comprises a variety of economic, demographic, social, and physical variables that bewilder by their magnitude and different incidence dimensions. In other words, the variety of effects must be measured as incident at different geographical levels and upon different population or economic groups. Such measurements of effects would draw on a broad list of economic and spatial concepts, as expressed in various analytical models (Figure 9—3) and calling for a range of rich data.

Figure 9—3, then, is a simplified way of posing the impact measurement problem and identifying the analytical requirements in skeletal form. But the requirements, even in skeletal form, span a wide range of complicated concepts not all easily understood. How does one organize and manage the process of further specification of the requirements and the design of appropriate analytical models?

This question surrounds the management and evaluation of large complicated systems in general. Theorists, in recent years, have attempted explicit formulations of ways of partitioning such complex systems into elements and

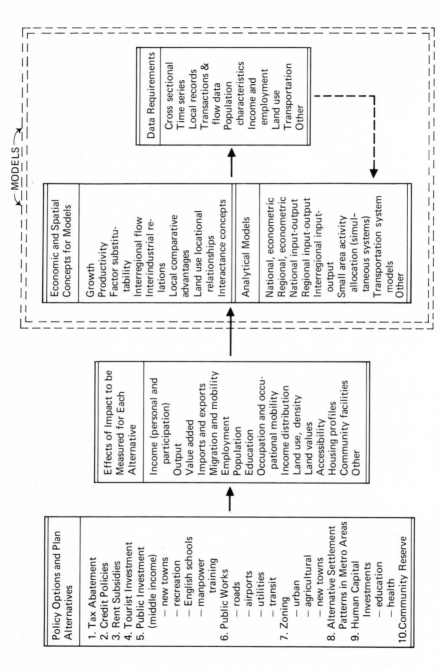

Figure 9-3 Public policy issues and role of analytical models in Puerto Rico.

subsystems for effective decentralization, but within the span of central management. But how does one partition such a system to render it analytically more manageable?

The problem of partitioning has not only a management aspect, but also a "causality" aspect. In other words, how does partitioning a system into components affect the relationship among the components? This aspect has been discussed by some theorists in the context of hierarchical systems in social sciences.

This suggests development of an efficient manner of decomposing or partitioning the effects and developing analytical schemes (Figure 3) that are tractable. First, it seems clear that the planning system as outlined in Figures 1 and 3 is a double hierarchical planning system — one organized by function and by geographical area. Further, in view of the mission of the Planning Board and the need for comprehensiveness in approaching developmental problems, it would seem that partitioning the system along functional lines will be less desirable than doing so geographically.

What would seem, then, an efficient strategy would be to pose the planning issues, the policy variables, and their effects and associated analytical requirements at each of the following geographical levels:

- Island
- Regional
- Metropolitan Area
- Municipal or intraurban

As these issues are addressed at each of these levels, however, the analytical work must provide mechanisms for relating issues between geographic levels. Two other criteria may also be required of analysis — that the work be interdisciplinary and that it be operational. (By operational is meant quantitative analysis that is implementable at reasonable cost.)

Given the broad strategy and these criteria, the following observations may be made. First, the planning issues will be addressed at different levels in the hierarchy. In such hierarchical modeling systems, the structure is one in which the results produced at a larger geographical level (aggregative model) are expanded in detail (sector and geographical) by models at the lower levels. The design and implementation of such an analytical framework will not be an easy task. If the analysis should be highly reliable and readily useful in policy formulation, it would need to be elaborate, expensive and extravagent of scarce manpower and might take several years to implement.

In view of the operationality criterion, however, this complex modeling system could be broken into "submodels" of which the interconnections are so planned that individual submodels can be amended or replaced without redesigning the whole system. This would result in a modular model system in which existing and easily modifiable parts of the overall requirement package could readily be delivered, while certain component models would be held for long-run developments.

Discussion

Question: As I view the possible models, there seem to be three classes: (1) the ones that you call national or regional econometric models would trace flows of money and savings to investment capital from region to region. (2) The input models trace flows of materials, trade goods and materials to be employed in the manufacture of goods, consumables to physical things, from region to region. And then, finally (3) the small area of activity allocation in parks. This is a broad generalization, but it does trace the development from area to area, and all three must maintain some degree of balance. How would you modify that as a guide to the world of economic modeling at this time and this place? We've got flow of money (capital), we've got flow of goods and the traditional *Leontiff* input-output model, and then we have the migration and transportation models, and residential models where the people want to live. There's only so many tricks that you have and what I'm asking is what would be taxonomy of the technical tricks?

Lakshmanan: The way in which you combine them very much affects your own style. You are right in saying that the stock of models available is very limited by the regional and by the industrial model. The model I'm recommending deals with multiplied effects. For instance, public investments to help Tennessee or Arkansas may conclude with the money ending up in Michigan, since most of the money is not public. It's not a contract investment, there's no way to hold it inside. So, the interregional and interindustry effects are very important, and they are captured by the interregional and the interindustry models. We are attempting to do something that most of the larger scale macromodels have really not attempted. They have no special component exclusively built into them. They are macroplanned, developed specifically for one task. What we are attempting to do is to take models built for other purposes and try to feed them in. These are series of approximations.

Question: Getting more local and specific, take the example of the Model Cities program in Kansas City. Now, you laid out some physical planning variables and some economic variables. With the Model Cities program you run into some additional factors such as social and even political variables. What prospects are there for applying the new technologies to this problem?

Lakshmanan: You have in the Model Cities program a problem that deals with political trade-offs and socioeconomic and physical planning effects, but have found out these models are based much more heavily on certain economic theory concepts which have been developed on a larger scale level. By stringing them together we make some sense out of them because of the way we are able to exploit developments in economic theory. At the small area level, dealing with those various issues, I don't know how many explosive particles of model systems can be developed. More useful, perhaps, in the case of payoffs, is the way in which you structure your decision system. In other words, as money being spent on the system like Resource Allocation and Priorities Analysis (RAPA), the resource analysis program that the Office of Economic Opportunity developed. Your payoffs are much greater than actually running through developed models of various kinds.

Question: I wanted to hear a little bit more about this incremental findings as opposed to positional findings, particularly if it has something to do with postponement of value questions.

Lakshmanan: If I could put a label on what I have said thus far, it would be excitingly relevant. I would like to make three or four points which perhaps should have been made earlier. My basic assumption, in looking at the question of the role of analytical technologies in urban management, was that the big mistakes are really made at the top. So, what you should do, in terms of introducing analytical technologies and using whatever help they might provide in improving urban management, is to attack at the top. There is so much needed everywhere that you are concerned with, and so little ability almost at all levels, that probably your best payoff might be at the top level. That is the underlying assumption behind my comments.

One other related point is that when I say that big mistakes are made at the top, the concern naturally shifts to what sort of questions should be looked at, in the sense that a PPBS system would look at the problem. You are not only concerned with questions of relating to one functional area, but also of relating urban management in the top level, you are concerned about two things among alternative major function areas in which you wish to put your resources. In this context the primary questions are not: public safety, or crime. Police departments, I am told, are very efficient, having helicopter teams and such other investments, but is this the best way of spending money or are there other ways? Nobody can really say that any analytical strategy exists to answer these questions. I don't want to give a pessimistic impression that analytical technology is of no use to management. Analytical technology, properly structured, with enough resources and time has great potential use to these areas. Right now, the level of development is such that some of these questions are of more help in facing the problem rather than in answering it.

Of course, you cannot really structure the problem unless you begin to answer some other questions. I suppose one of the major questions in public management is, how do you allocate your resources among different kinds of public investments, and what sorts of trade-offs do you establish when investing in one area and another area? Some of these things I transitionally looked at when I talked about complementalities or joint effects of various kinds of public investments. As you can see, most of these concepts are taken from economic models and economic concepts. We now realize that most of the things we are looking at in urban management have many more social and economic implications than once believed.

In discussing social indicators, there is now talk of preparing a social report just as preliminary preparation for an economic report. What are some of the things you will put in those things? Here again, the question is defining your concepts. I recently came across a book by an Englishman named Atkins, on the question of social deviance and juvenile delinquency in developing areas. There are great tensions brought about by rapid growth and by rapid economic growth and by social organization change resulting in much deviant behavior. Deviance is a multiple-cause problem. You can look at some of these statistics and information systems as a part of this new analytical technology, since information is available in quantities never before possible. People who previously did not report some deviant behavior before, now report it because it is no longer considered socially reprehensible to do so. There is a better reporting system today than it was before. Demographic changes also affect this data flow. You have interbred social statistics as backgrounds. Some reflect actual changes in crime and others simply reflect the new way in which data is collected.

To get to your question, you asked me about incrementalism. Planners have generally subscribed to the rational deductive model. In simple terms this means you somehow come to an agreement as to your goals and objectives, and to achieve these goals you have alternative policy options. By collecting information on the impacts of these alternative policies and then comparing these impacts, you develop the social welfare function. I don't know how you develop it, but you develop somewhere a welfare function and you choose the set of instruments that gives you the sort of impact that you like — here I am defining it by welfare function. There is a tremendous cost just in collecting information for all of the alternatives which is implied in this model. There is another school of thought put forward a few years ago by Charles Lindblom, which rather than describing what the planner thinks the world is, looks instead at how the decision makers actually make decisions.[3] They are attacking problems in series, one after the other. The power of politicians is not vested in one decision-maker. Most of these models of decision making are from the point of view of the firm. **Question:** I would translate this idea of incrementalism into specific information systems steps. Rather than one integrated information system for the metropolitan area, we would expect a multiplicity of these, one for each power base, one for each self-interest center which needs its own information to make its own plans. Gradually, these staffs would among them build up a respectable data base for the metropolitan area as a whole and at some later point some merging combinations might occur. And the data would be collected for solving rather specific decisions.

You may contradict me here, but coming back to "the soul of fools" work on stimulating the '60 and '64 elections, where they used old Elmo Roper entirely, his old survey data and political polls. They didn't ask for any of this data, the data had already paid for itself because Roper published it and made his money. He just plowed the way. But there was enough identified with the data that they were able to go in with strong theory.

Lakshmanan: I agree with you and would point out the fact that I don't think that there is a danger of one large information system in the metropolitan area replacing any other system. I don't think it is going to happen or, if it should happen, that it would be desirable. Any piece of data is interpreted by each user in terms that are relevant to him. Take the case of the National Income Accounts, a lot of data is being collected by the federal government. This is data that has been felt to be very useful since our experience in the depression. In the

1930's when we had the depression, we would like to have had a lot of unavailable information. As a result of Keynes' theory income accounts data was collected. Subsequently an economic model was developed in the 50's. By the late 50's and early 60's, we had enough data and enough analytical technology to handle the sort of questions we really needed to answer in the 1930's. We can somewhat manage our economy in the 1960's at the level of the problem we faced in the 30's.

Question: You take a fifteen-year lag between perception of the need and accumulation of the data base, then by 1983, we ought to be ready to handle crime in the cities.

Lakshmanan: We ought to be ready to handle people in any area too, in 1983.

Question: I gather that you feel that planners' advice is not being heeded by top decision makers. Do you have any indication that that may change?

Lakshmanan: This is becoming less and less so. Planners are beginning to realize that they should state their problem, not in terms which are acceptable just in professional lingo, but in terms that are also relevant to the decision maker. For instance, if you pose the problem of decentralization as one of *concentration,* I don't think you are really asking it in an operational form. Decentralization is not a goal but is an instrumental objective to achieve some other goal. Decentralization becomes meaningful only in terms of a larger goal. Planners are beginning to state things in terms that are relevant to the decision makers.

Question: Do you have experience in this regard with the models that you have developed in a consulting capacity?

Lakshmanan: I can give you one or two examples. In one case, this sort of system was appreciated most by the chairman of the planning board rather than some of the top level planners. We felt gratified by that, although it may be that his enthusiasm stemmed more from a sense of duty than actual comprehension. All our models were developed within a specific position context. For instance, the sort of model that was developed for Baltimore was concerned with defining the sizes, the locations and the timing of a set of regional shopping centers in the whole metropolitan area for the next twenty years. Given a certain distribution of population, income, and consumption patterns, what would be alternative sets of shopping centers that can be added? This model is now being used by real estate developers. If they add to a shopping center here, in a given time period, what are the effects? What kind of sales will be generated, how does the location affect existing shopping centers and so on? There is a further interesting question here regarding privileged information. Who should get the information, who should not get it? The basic problem is the accessability of the private sector to data developed within the public sector, and each case must be handled individually.

As new problems arise, we are still collecting more data but it is a continual fight to keep up with tomorrow. We don't have any analytical apparatus to deal with the problems of the regional area, we are specifying, we are collecting data, maybe in the late 60's we might be able to solve this problem. Data is not going to be big enough and we are always going to be behind because data is useful only in the context of a purpose.

Question: The intriguing thing about the systems approach is that it is comprehensive. Don't you need, therefore, a most comprehensive model encompassing your economic variables, your political variables, your social variables, and what may be called cultural variables? If one relied on the incremental approach, would not other parts of your system become disjointed? For instance, the President's riot commission report on the cities clearly established sets of interrelated conditions as causal factors. Don't you need a most comprehensive, completely macroaction type of model, which secondarily can be broken down into subvariables and used for community computer facilities? The results hopefully should be a comprehensive plan which leads to massive cooperative effort at all levels — geo-economic, political, social, cultural, and governmental. The trick is to establish linkages among your variables and also among these three levels of political entrepreneurials and decision makers and so on.

Lakshmanan: Philosophically, one cannot disagree with you that incrementalism takes away from the comprehensiveness, and therefore it is less than perfect. But, if you are waiting to develop a full-blown comprehensive system you are not only allocating a whole lot of resources in the process, but there are also tremendous opportunity costs to those resources. How much comprehensiveness can we afford given the present state of public investments? By improving health planning, for instance, you automatically generate a high degree of demand — induced demand. But what do you do when the demand overreaches your ability to deliver the payoff — that is, the supply of health care? It very much depends upon what resources you have, and analytical technologies cannot solve the resources problem. They can make obvious the impacts of making various kinds of choices — if you allocate so much, if you assume this level of ill-standards, what is the impact? But the technologies in themselves cannot provide substitutes for resources — technology is an analytical rather than a service device.

Question: I'm looking here at the model developed in Puerto Rico. Could you conceive of the technical consultant, saying to the policy maker that he would not work on say, economic development, because racial and social integration had not yet occurred and that without integrating them, the economic variables would be unmanageable?

Lakshmanan: In a study for the Detroit metropolitan region, we were specifically requested to produce a distribution of population by racial composition since this is an important factor in guiding development in the area. The variables that are chosen in a particular context may be dependent upon controversial political issues. In terms of analytical technology being a useful adjunct to the three levels, planning is helpful in the political process to the extent that it deploys a technical base for issues that are raised. The role of a technical, analytical competence in management must be kept in perspective since so many of the decisions in urban management are ultimately political. While the technician can clarify technical issues analytically, he cannot dictate political decisions. Some believe that the major problems are political rather than technical, and that the issues are not being raised at all and we are addressing ourselves to the wrong problems.

Question: You are so familiar with the technology, I suppose you would take this for granted. Some of us may not realize either the capabilities or the limitations of simulation techniques. There are tremendous capabilities, but the goals of comprehensiveness and integration are a tremendous burden for this technical capability. I'm thinking of a study done for a west coast city, which attempted to look at this housing market in a comprehensive manner, for a fairly large metropolitan city. The study took at least over a year to complete, and after they completed it the costs were so high that they weren't really able to check it out very thoroughly to see if it was reasonable. They made a few runs but without sufficient data to run it. After they turned it over to the city planning department, there was a period of eight months in which it just lay dormant because the city couldn't afford to run the model either. One of the inputs was harder to estimate than the output of the model itself. This input was migration of people into the area. The output had to be inaccurate since the input data was flawed.

Lakshmanan: You are raising a question of facing the problem in a technical way and I can give you an example from CONSAD where a good analytical development was frustrated because of the administrative necessity of developing parts of it at different levels of capability. We were prevented from presenting that model in terms that were relevant to the top decision makers by intervening general management levels who wanted to view it for strategic purposes as a very powerful black box which could produce all kinds of answers. Any black box that didn't meet these requirements was completely rejected. For two years, that model was just filed away after an expense of two hundred thousand dollars. The problem was a question of the way in which it was presented to the top level menagement.

Question: It seems to me you've urged two things upon us, neither rejection nor acceptance of high goals immediately, but rather a gradual movement from our present position, undertaking specific projects for fairly short-range purposes at the various decision centers, wherever they lie. And using whoever will fund them. Simultaneously we should develop a comprehensive continuing long range plan for the development of our information resources in the metropolitan area. It seems to me that the ideas we have applied to long-range physical planning are applicable to our information systems also. We know about capial investment, where do roads go, and where sewer systems go. We have a lot more influence in some things like zoning or other specific rules and regulations. Therefore, there must be investments in information resources that we have available even accidentally by letting a major contract. Have I gone too far?

Lakshmanan: No.

Question: I'd like to ask a question about the formulation of goals in the Puerto Rico study. You have three first order goals that were the governing parameters for the models, for the whole family of models. There must have been some goals implicit in the Pittsburgh model — some of them perhaps nonissues, things that we know only from an analytical standpoint for instance, our understanding of social systems and social, economic and special systems are important variables that influence the system in a significant way. We can't really simulate or model anything if we don't include these. I can see dimensions of the goal coming in from both the analytical side and coming from the political--administrative decision-maker's side. When you go into a place like Puerto Rico, how do you operationally establish your initial goal structure on which you're going to base the rest of the work? Where do these goals come from and how are they formulated?

Lakshmanan: Let me illustrate it with two examples from the Puerto Rico and the Detroit study. In Puerto Rico, of the three goals that we have come up with, the first two are to increase income and bring about a better distribution of income. These are basic goals generally considered in any development of economic analysis. The third goal of social welfare is implied in physical planning. We also tried to put in more goals and to state them in an interrelated way. One of the things we initially talked about was the settlement pattern. The way in which the settlement pattern in various cities relate to each other as they do in an advanced economy, is a very important factor but it is really an instrument for achieving these goals. We arrived at this intuitively by discussion rather than in a formal fashion.

In the case of Detroit, involving a land use and transportation study, locals helped us structure the process of goal formulation. The way we tried to help them was to articulate the problem of goal formulation in a formal fashion, believing that goals come out of issues. We started with such things as when you talk about issues, an issue concerns the present state of affairs, the desired end state, and the means for achieving it. From this definition, if you say that decentralization is an issue and you are concerned about the present state of your affairs, is decentralization really a problem? What are the significant questions? Future desires limit how much decentralization or conservation you want. And the final question, what are the means you want to achieve them? From these derived definition points, the locals look at an issue.

It is also important how the issue comes into the public focus. Certain issues come out of bureaucratic processes and have been highly engineered. I've been dealing with traffic planning for a long time, long before the land use and conservation study. All we had then was the problem of how to put a road through or put a signal through. There were city accidents, in six months, we put a stoplight. Today, you have got certain rules of thumb in the same way they used to work. The source of issues, the context of issues, the way in which this issue is incident is extremely important. Raymond Vernon has pointed out that issues tend to get raised in society dependent upon whom they affect.[4] Pollution is a very good issue on which much money is going to be allocated. It has been said that the transportation problem has been defined, not in terms of a mobility problem in a metropolitan area concerning everybody, but rather as a way of solving the particular problem of getting the suburbanite to his work place in the center city. Coincidentally, planners and problem solvers are professionals who live in suburban homes and commute to the city. So the way in which problems are posed is dependent upon who poses them and upon who has the social responsibility and the opportunity to pose them. Issues affecting low-income groups, such as poverty, are structured too often from the viewpoint of the planner rather than the afflicted group.

We must begin to distinguish between certain contextual goals and primary purpose goals. For instance, one way of improving transportation is to have so many highways that traffic moves flawlessly. At the same time, this may destroy the central city area. You can put highways through provided the urban renewal areas will let you put them through — it's a contextual goal. We structured the problem so that they can locate goals in relation to their problem. We provided the conceptual framework for looking at them.

Question: I disagree to some extent. This discussion is perilously close to the trap that sociology fell into which made it irrelevant for so many years. If we're talking about goals arising from issues, we ought to think of issues in terms of things that ought to be discussed, not just those that are being discussed. How close are we to having some completed examples, some good case studies that we could take say, to a school superintendent or a school board member and he could see immediately the value of the technical operations?

Lakshmanan: Let me first answer the two questions that you raised in your comments. I was not saying that when you look at a problem you should fall into the sociological trap of being value free. Planning is really a political activity in that you are allocating resources and you are protecting values. So I'm not saying that we should be free from values.

Question: No, I didn't interpret that. I just thought the emphasis was transient.

Lakshmanan: On the other point, in terms of the usefulness of existing models for, say, education. There are several kinds of problems that an educational planner might face. One might be such a simple problem as how many pupils will there be in the next twenty years and their geographical distinction. There are models that are now available for him to predict small area population increases.

Question: I've seen some great hypothetical examples, but what we really need right now is something being done that we can show this school district.

Lakshmanan: One of the problems of the school board is the question of designing facilities so that you can have multiple use of a facility. This is a micro problem. But at the macro level, in terms of assessing the educational goals by comparing one kind of a training program to some other kind of training program, you can ask them such basic questions within the wall of allocation of resources. I am not acquainted with such models if they exist.

Question: If we go into the industrial area, like locations of plants, warehouses, and factories, I think you can find there instances where the analytic study pays for itself over and over again. Imperfect as it may be, the computer model lets you look at the whole thing and relate a lot of tedious details. For school systems, such models remain to be developed, and this means a long-term commitment of money, personnel, and time.

Question: I just want to, Dr. Lakshmanan, if I may, strengthen the value point here because I see it again as a problem of linkage, especially as the public administrator is concerned. It's a question of the *is* as much as it is the question of the *ought,* so the behavioral approach and a computer approach are compatible. There may, however, be the danger of stopping at one level. I don't think we can afford to stop at the informational level but must find a way of linking information to action into policy, not only in terms of what policy *is* but also what policy *ought* to be.

Lakshmanan: I agree with your point that urban management policy should not only be oriented to what *is* but what *ought* to be. What should the innovative concern in decisions be based upon? Does this imply an authoritative allocation of values? Is the public administrator really responsible in our social system for that kind of value allocation, or is it done in the political process? What the administrator can say is that if X is allocated in this fashion, these are the consequences.

Question: Into traditional American public administration we kidded ourselves that there was a dichotomy between policy and implementation.

Lakshmanan: I'm not saying there is a dichotomy, that every time you say something, you are building your own value system. But institutionally, are we set up so that the public general management level person administratively makes decisions that involve actual allocation of values? Or is it part of the political process?

Question: As I see it, because of the way we are structured politically, the people in the system are not particularly concerned with comprehensive planning. Do you have any suggestions as to how the structure could be changed so that it would be more amenable to comprehensive planning?

Lakshmanan: I'm saying, first of all, and descriptively saying, that they are not addressing themselves comprehensively. I'm not sure what the answer is to that. The basic problem is to find an appropriate definition of comprehensive that we can live with, that is implementable. For instance, the PPBS approach is in some measure comprehensive. If we would engage in developing a design for regional PPB systems much could be accomplished. A PPB system is concerned with relation of planning and programming, within the parameters of a governmental unit that has jurisdiction, that has a budget, that has an executive. Regional planning does not have an executive, you don't have a regional government, you don't have a regional budget. Apart from all the conceptual problems, we have to think about such intangible qualities as regional shadow budgets and things like that. But, as I pointed out earlier, when you look at the regional planning problems, to make a regional PPBS work, you must define what your regional PPBS is to be concerned with. Should it be concerned with externalities, be able to talk about incidents, be able to talk about scale economies? We found that there were a lot of problems that are central to regional planning that are also central to PPBS. It is easy to talk about externalities, it is a lot more difficult to actually measure what an externality is. The problem with comprehensiveness is in framing the content of comprehensiveness in ways that are feasible. There are both the conceptual and the analytical difficulties, and that is why I am advocating incrementalism as an operational necessity.

Question: Do you have any suggestions for changing the political structure in such a way that it would be more amenable to comprehensive planning? Are there structural changes that you would advocate?

Lakshmanan: Are you suggesting things like regional government or something of that sort?

Question: I think that would be a fairly obvious one at the upper level. What are some lower down that you think might be changed?

Lakshmanan: For many years planning grew larger in scope, from local to metropolitan to regional planning. Now this trend has been reversed with such things as the model cities programs, or the community councils programs. By moving back to a neighborhood concept we are acknowledging the ineffectiveness of previous planning efforts. But this is not structural reform.

Question: If you take the two comprehensive views of planning and programming is there a danger here of developing a closed society rather than this open society that we have?

Lakshmanan: I don't think that there is a tremendous danger involved although there may be tendencies toward that. If the decision-maker at the top level does not understand it, he can always freeze out resources. Nobody is going to allocate resources unless he understands how relevant it is. So it is up to the model builder and whoever are the investers, to explain what he is doing in terms that are relevant.

Question: Recent studies of power and decision making, particularly one of Robert Presthus on two upstate New York towns, concluded that a relatively small number of persons play coveted roles in most public decisions.[5] In one case the economic power structure was more important, in another the political power structure. The question is how analytic technology ought to effect these relationships?

Lakshmanan: Are you really saying that models would at least have joined these power structures?

Question: I said something like that, yes, although I personally don't think it has to be.

Question: We may be kidding ourselves here. I think we have a little bit of evidence with respect to the way in which computer technologies have been used in industrial corporations. There's no question that they have strengthened the top levels of management at the expense of middle management. If there is some analogue in the social system, it is conceivable that there will be a group of decision makers who educate themselves in the technology, who use this education as a way to enhance their own position in the system. As a result of successful uses of the technology, they can gain greater access, greater control, and limit access to other people in the system.

Lakshmanan: I share your point of view that information has power. Obviously, all these analytical technologies give you a certain reservoir of information. The people who allocate resources to give the information have eroded the position of middle management, to secure enough power for itself. Top management has a way of reaching out and getting it from these computer boys. The way it is being utilized is still a political problem. It's a danger to beware of.

Question: Because there is presently power being utilized in this area, the model system may change the power in some way and it may even tend to open up things. Models that are being used now may be primitive, but their sense of values is influencing decisions. What you may do by introducing analytical bases is not create power, but rather you change it, and you may even open things up.

Question: In any case, what you've done here is to put more of the authority back at the level where society expects it to be accountable and maybe we should make that analogy with political and social power structures.

Question: In the most advanced forms of the species available in the past, the military command and control system, when the top level people wanted to get an iron grip on subordinates with the computerized system, the system was almost made worthless because the lower echelon instinctively conspired to distort the data to protect themselves. The Strategic Air Command command and control system is said to be such an example.

But you can get a counterbalancing of this information power. Recently AT&T went before the FCC on a rate case and they bought an enormous computerized data base from Standard and Poors, a twenty-year financial history on 2000 firms. They analyzed it with the computer, made every possible chart to support their contention that they needed a rate increase. The poor FCC could have been snowed under, but they had access to the same data problem. They had also purchased the copies for their consultant and he generated other charts. They had paper all over the place. But that's the same power relationship working in the opposite direction.

Question: I raised the possibility that a place like Puerto Rico may have one group who do have this expertise and they don't have the other group of experts to counterbalance them.

Lakshmanan: Puerto Rico had planning boards set up in 1942 which planned the development process in Puerto Rico. At that time, they were set up to look at economic planning, social planning, physical planning, all in one agency. No other planning agency was given such authority and they never integrated. Some agencies did. One division did all the data work and planning and another did the zoning cases.

Question: The second part of my question is whether you have run into this type of thing as you've gone around working?

Lakshmanan: Not recently. In the early 60's a few eastern cities and only a very few midwestern and west coast cities talked about models. With other people, you had to first of all sell yourself as a person, then sell your idea.

Question: Are all these models based on a computer capability? Is there computer capability tied in with the use of the model technique?

Lakshmanan: Yes, most of them are. But many of these models use most computers available and standard available programs. They do not involve ultracomplex computer equipment. All you need is a standard computer.

Centralization vs. Decentralization

10 Councils of Governments: The Potential and the Problems

Kent Mathewson

It is not very long ago that when I spoke on councils of governments I had to begin with a rather detailed explanation of what they are. I recall quite clearly that up until about a year and a half ago I was able to name each of them from memory. There were, after all, fewer than ten such organizations until that time, and the oldest was less than ten years old.

Then suddenly, the times and the concept became right for one another, and hundreds of new councils have been created almost overnight. I noted just the other day, for example, that seventeen new councils have been established in the State of Texas alone, a state which has only twenty-three metropolitan areas in all.

Indeed, it is now just about impossible to keep track of the growth and the development of the council of governments movement. It is very nearly correct simply to assume that in any urban region in which there is a number of cities or counties which share common problems — and that includes virtually every metropolitan region in the nation — there is likely to be a council of governments either already established or else in the discussion and planning stage.

This tremendous growth of a government institution which was unknown only a little more than a decade ago has three major bases. The first relates to federal grants-in-aid programs and their growth as a source of local support. There are, you know, more than 450 different federal grants-in-aid programs which provide cash assistance for local and state government programs of a great many types. With very few exceptions, these grants for many years were made on individual application and with very little in the way of coordination either at the federal or at the state or local level. Then, in the early 1960's, Congress began to realize that its programs of assistance to local units were not having the desired impact. Its members became aware that the lack of coordination may have been one of the principal reasons for this lack of success.

Accordingly, in 1962, Congress attached a requirement of regional cooperation between local units of government as a requisite for obtaining highway funds. The Federal Aid to Highways Act of 1962 required a "continuing comprehensive transportation planning process carried on cooperatively by state and local governments" in all urban areas having a population in excess of 50,000.

From that point on, federal money became increasingly dependent upon interjurisdictional cooperation in hospital construction, in housing, in water facility and sewer construction, in open space and land use programs, in airport development, and in most other areas for which federal suppport is so essential to our local units of government. This, in turn, produced a growing need for some kind of regional organization which could assure the federal authorities that regional planning considerations were being taken into account. The regional approach became a reality and the need to view many local programs as regional programs became a very serious and often unprecedented task.

In many localities there were regional planning commissions which might have been able to fill this need. However, most regional planning commissions have long suffered the defect of not being truly representative of the people. As a consequence, they were not automatically accepted as being capable of achieving the purpose intended by the federal legislation. In the Detroit metropolitan region, for example, our own Regional Planning Commission — and I would hasten to say it was one of the first and one of the best staffed and financed in the nation — did not include in its membership persons who could officially speak for the residents of our region. They were excellent people, well qualified and dedicated to the regional planning functions, but they could not arrive at conclusions or make commitments which represented anything but their own opinions and desires. No one of our more than 350 local units of government felt in any way bound by any of the Planning Commission's deliberations. We have had innumerable instances where these deliberations and the regional plans which they represented were literally ignored by independent units of government.

This, unfortunately, has been characteristic of regional planning agencies throughout the nation. And these agencies have also had other built-in defects. Some of these defects relate to the legislative enactments which created the agencies, others to fiscal problems, still others to the lack of rapport between many professional planners and many practical politicians.

So the regional planning commissions have not, by and large, been an easy and automatic answer to the problem created by federal insistence upon regional coordination as a prerequisite to its grant-in-aid funds.

The second major reason for the recent growth of the council movement has been specific federal legislation which has offered to finance the operations of the councils themselves. The Housing and Development Act of 1965, for example, authorized grants to "organizations of public officials . . . representative of the political jurisdictions within a metropolitan area . . . for the purpose of assisting such organizations . . . to develop regional plans and programs . . . "

This provision not only provided funds for regional planning which did not have to come from local sources, but it also made quite clear the fact that subsequent federal programs would be increasingly insistent on area-wide reviews by all local units before additional federal monies would be forthcoming. Indeed, the Demonstration Cities and Metropolitan Development Act of 1966 has borne this out.

The third major reason for the sudden growth of the councils of governments, however, is the most important of the three in my own opinion. That reason is simply that urban development in this nation finally reached the point where the need for interjurisdictional treatment of many urban problems became so evident that all of the old obstacles to interjurisdictional cooperation had to fall away. The depression of the 1930's and the war of the 1940's retarded urban growth, but during the 1950's there was so much construction and expansion that the very nature of our cities and suburban areas changed. By the 1960's the old picture of a city surrounded by a thin circle of suburbs and then by miles and miles of farmland and forests had literally disappeared from many parts of our nation. The word *metropolitan* became very common and even words as *megalopolis* began to be heard. Entire areas — the several hundred miles from Boston to Washington, D.C., for example — became one great urban sprawl. And this was not limited to the industrial northeast. Texas has twenty-three metropolitan areas: just imagine that — the wide open spaces so famous in song and memory of the Saturday afternoon matinees — with twenty-three metropolitan areas!

With all this it became readily apparent that our existing governmental structures were hard pressed to accommodate themselves to the changing conditions. What worked well in the urban - suburban - rural days does not work in the era of the metropolis.

It is no longer true, for example, that an individual city can handle its own air pollution problems. On the contrary, no city which is immediately and closely surrounded by numerous other communities can protect its own citizens from the effects of pollution regardless of how hard it tries, what laws it enacts, or how much it spends on the enforcement effort.

Nor is it still true that an individual city within a metropolitan area can provide public transportation facilities for its own residents. On the contrary, comparatively few workers today reside in the same community in which they work. A city transit system is useless to them. If it exists, it can only continue to increase fares in the effort to stave off financial collapse while the number of riders falls and while increasing numbers of individuals clog the streets and highways in their private automobiles.

And it is no longer true that a city in a metropolis can cope with its own financing problems. On the contrary, when surrounding communities drain off its higher income taxpayers and its best tax producing industries, when competition for revenue sources is more important than quality of services, when one community has the tax base and its neighbor has the poverty, then cities experience very serious financial problems and their residents pay the penalty.

It is no longer true that a city can handle its own traffic problems. Being surrounded by many other communities whose land use and traffic patterns fail to take into consideration those of their neighbors, most cities can only continue to add more signs and signals, to post more one-way streets, to continue to prohibit parking, and to strangle slowly in the congestion.

And it is no longer true that a city can cope with its crime problem as it could in years gone by. Criminals can commit a crime today, cross the street, and be in another jurisdiction. If they have planned well, they can drive five minutes longer and put two or three more jurisdictions between themselves and the scene of their crime. The police are at a real disadvantage in these cases. Their radio systems, their modus operandi files, their personnel deployment, are all restricted to a single community. But there are no similar restrictions on the criminal. When the police in one jurisdiction get to know his methods, when it begins to look as though one more holdup or burglary or auto theft will be his last, then he simply moves on to the jurisdiction next door. He can do this dozens and dozens of times without ever leaving his home base — each time selecting a community where he is unknown and unexpected.

I could go on and on to speak of what the uncharted growth of our cities has done to cripple us in efforts to deal with water pollution, to dispose of waste, to provide decent housing, to give all of our children a decent standard of education, to provide adequate health and welfare facilities and programs, to zone land properly, and to do a great many other things. There is little need to do so. You recognize the problems or you would not have established your own Mid-America Council of Governments and you would not be here today.

We have more than two hundred metropolitan areas in our nation today. There are some 3500 cities within those areas, some 2500 townships and some 300 counties. They are all having these problems. And many of them, as I have noted, are turning to the council of governments approach in the effort to do something about them.

This, I believe, is the right approach. Even if federal grant-in-aid programs were not involved, even if councils could not get federal operational support for their day-to-day activities, this would still be the right approach.

There are those who would disagree. Some, for example, still feel that the regional planning commissions will suffice, that a council of governments is an unnecessary additional agency. Of those critics of the council concept, I would simply ask whether their planning agency is doing a good job of resolving those regional problems which require interjurisdictional action. If so, then I would quickly agree that a council of governments would be superfluous. But if the answer is in the negative, if congestion and blight and pollution and the other area-wide problems continue to exist and to grow despite the efforts of the planning commission, then I would say that these critics should face reality. They should try a new approach before — not after — some crisis occurs.

At the same time, I do not mean to imply that this is strictly an "either/or" situation. In the case of our own Southeastern Michigan Council of Governments, we did not really abolish the regional planning commission in favor of a council of governments. Technically speaking, we revised the membership of the planning agency and altered its structure and its functions somewhat, in order to convert it into a council of governments. The Council, in other words, has been created by altering the Planning Commission and changing its name accordingly.

So far as the former members of the Planning Commission are concerned, they have been superseded as directors of the agency by individuals who represent the local units of government which form the membership of the Council. But they have not lost their expertise and their experience. They now serve as members of the Planning Advisory Committee of the Council of

Governments, and they provide an invaluable service. My own conclusion is that their value to our region has grown, as has their sense of accomplishment, now that their efforts are truly meaningful in terms of governmental participation and implementation.

The technical staff of our Planning Commission is now the planning staff of the Council of Governments. Again, it is my own belief that these full-time professionals were never happier. I doubt that any sincere and well-motivated individual enjoys developing plans which may get no farther than inclusion in an unwanted and unread report. It is vastly different to know that the real decision makers in the region are deeply interested and involved in the planning process and that they fully intend to be guided by findings and recommendations which now come from their own staff.

Others who delay in accepting the council of governments approach are those who believe that it represents some loss of local autonomy, that it is some kind of step in the direction of eliminating grass roots participation in governmental matters.

In my opinion, nothing could be farther from the truth. Councils of governments, as a matter of fact, will restore local autonomy which has already been lost and will prevent the further erosion of this invaluable characteristic of American government. Let me cite a few examples of what I mean by this.

What recourse does a taxpayer now have under present metropolitan conditions if the wind carries toxic fumes from a factory in a neighboring community into his home? None, at the local level. There may be a state or a federal level agency which would step in to grant relief under certain conditions. Or he might be able to take civil action in the courts under certain conditions. But as far as local government having some kind of ability to help him, there is none. In this case, a council of governments might help — it certainly would not detract from local authority.

What advantages of self-government does a taxpayer have if an upstream community dumps untreated sewage into a river from which his own water supply comes or which should serve him as a recreational facility? Does he really have local self-determination, or is he forced to turn to a higher level of government to step in and to set standards and to enforce its own regulations? Is it not true that when the communities which share the use of the river fail to meet together and fail to develop their own standards, it is really a case of discarding — rather than safeguarding — local autonomy?

And what rights does an individual have if on his way to church or to go shopping or to see a movie he gets a ticket from a police officer for doing something which is perfectly legal and proper in the community in which he resides? Would it be a loss of self-determination or would it be a benefit to all of us if some regional organization were interested not in taking over the law enforcement function, but in seeing to it that traffic signs and signals are uniform and that parking regulations are consistent and that an officer's hand motions mean the same thing in all of the communities in which we have to travel daily.

And perhaps most serious of all to many of us, where is our "government of the people" when a community in which we work but do not vote can tax our income? We have no say in how these taxes are spent. Where is our "government of the people" when one community can make a unilateral decision on an airport which adversely affects all the people of a region merely because the airport is located in that community? Do we have any ability to be heard at all in these cases? Of course we do not. A council of governments would not take anything from us in cases such as these. Rather, it would give us a forum and a voice which we do not now have and which would actually enhance the spirit of demoratic government. It would permit many decisions which are not now being made locally or which are being made by only one of the many affected local jurisdictions to be considered by the region as a whole.

For, after all, there can be no argument to the conclusion that many urban problems do affect an entire region and that no single jurisdiction can or should cope with these problems on its own. These problems are of such a nature that the affected community does not control their source — as in a polluted lake. They are of such a nature that only an area-wide effort can have a beneficial effect, and again a polluted lake is a good example. They are of such a nature that the monetary cost is always too high for any one community to bear on its own. And they are of such a nature that the interests of economy as well as of effectiveness are served by joint action.

Now I believe that it might be well for me to turn from the matter of the potential of councils of governments and to deal with some of the practical problems which they do produce. I am indeed a strong proponent of the council concept, but I am realistic enough to realize that they are not without their own brand of difficulties.

Fortunately, I do not have to include the subject of financing under this listing of problems. Not only are federal funds available to support many of a council of governments' activities, as I have mentioned before, but the fact that operating costs are shared between the member units makes them one of the few governmental agencies which are relatively easy to support.

This has been true since the beginning of the council movement. The first council was limited to county membership and was known as the Supervisors' Inter-County Committee. It was the forerunner of our own Southeastern Michigan Council of Governments. I have spoken with individuals who have been associated with this pioneer organization since its inception and they agree that it has always been seen as being worthy of support by its member units.

The same is true of the first of the nation's current type of councils, the Willamette Valley Council of Governments in Oregon, which I had the honor of organizing. (Councils today do not restrict themselves to one type of local government, such as counties or cities, but insist on both. In addition, there is developing an ever-increasing interest in including school districts and other substantial recipients of local revenues as full-fledged members of councils of governments.) Without exception, as far as I have been able to determine, no one has ever quit a council on the grounds that benefits received did not exceed the pro rata share of the cost.

The selection of functions has not been a problem of councils of governments either. Of course, one region may select some functions and not others, depending on local attitudes and conditions. Flexibility in this respect is one of the advantages of the council concept. For the most part, however, there is a considerable degree of unanimity.

First of all, councils perform the planning function as required by the federal grant-in-aid legislation to which I have referred earlier. They are usually involved in planning for transportation, land use, water treatment and distribution, sewage facilities, open space, hospitals, airports, libraries, etc. Since the Partnership for Health Act of 1966, some have also been involved in comprehensive public health planning.

Planning, of course, usually includes the so-called Section 204 review-and-comment function. This refers to the Demonstration Cities and Metropolitan Development Act which requires that all local government applications for federal grants for the planning or construction of the type of facilities which I have just mentioned be submitted for review and comment by any "area-wide agency which is designated to perform metropolitan or regional planning for the area in which the assistance is to be used . . . " This means that the councils must review applications for the federal aid and must comment as to the consistency or lack of consistency of the proposed project with over-all regional plans.

In addition to planning, most councils also provide a variety of other services. Technical assistance in a variety of activities, including the preparation of applications for federal aid, is one type. Purchasing of various types of supplies, equipment and other commodities is another. Compilation and dissemination of news of interest to units of government within the region is a third.

Some councils also operate certain types of facilities or action programs. Police academies and firefighter training programs would be one such example. Electronic data processing installations is another. Operation of an ambulance service is a third. Recruitment and examination programs for governmental personnel is still another.

Other councils perform a research function on behalf of their constituent units. For example, they have inventoried housing needs within a region. They have developed uniform building codes. They have evaluated land use ordinances with a view toward identifying conflicts and inconsistencies. They have developed plans for interjurisdictional police cooperation in times of emergency.

Possibly most important, the councils of governments have served as a vehicle for facing a great many other urban problems. Quite apart from any need for planning, there is the fundamental need to get local officials from numerous jurisdictions to recognize a problem as a regional problem and to sit down face-to-face to discuss means of overcoming it. Councils have been doing this, and while it is too early to evaluate the success of the many councils which have come into being within the past year and a half, there is every reason to believe that the record will be an extraordinarily good one. Councils are providing a focal point for political and administrative attention and they are producing a sense of common purpose.

Finally, it also appears to me that councils of governments have not been faced with particularly difficult problems of organizational structure. While there are variations, the consensus appears to be for a governing body composed of representatives of the member units and an executive committee selected by that body which oversees operations during the period between meetings of the Council. Voting systems, representation formulas, dues assessments, veto provisions, requirements for admission and for withdrawal — these and other contents of the by-laws appear to be rather easily determined and do not seem to cause significant operational difficulties. In other words, the mechanics of setting up and running a council of governments is not a significant problem so far as we can tell at present.

Now, as to the problems of councils which are significant, I would say that there are three, and I would warn you to be on constant alert for each of them in the case of your own Mid-America Council. Any one of them can wreck your organization in a hurry.

The first of these is the unwillingness, the inability, or the fear of moving ahead with meaningful activity once the council has been established. This, I fear, is going to occur in far too many instances.

The fact is that the creation of a council of governments is no guarantee that action will be taken on regional problems. On the contrary, discussion of such problems within the council and failure to arrive at acceptable conclusions could lead to total inaction. The very existence of a council prevents other organizations from applying the regional approach which it, ostensibly, had been created to provide. In other words, no other agency in a region in which there is a council can hold itself out as being responsible for and authorized to deal with such area-wide concerns as pollution and traffic, land use and transportation. A council of governments coopts these matters and if it does not deal with them, no one else can. The formal recognition and designation of a council as the single agency representative of regional interests within an area by the federal government itself makes it particularly difficult for any other organization to step in.

This sort of inaction could possibly be deliberate on the part of some council members who want to prevent anything but localized and independent action, regardless of the issues involved. They could raise any number of fanciful objections. They could continue to ask for more and more studies. They could continue to employ parliamentary techniques to avoid a final tabulation of views. They could persist in disagreeing on the definition of a problem or the best alternative toward a solution or on the role of each of the local units of government involved. They could simply keep specific matters off the agenda.

But whether the delay and indecision of an inoperative council is attributable to the understandable fact that so many of our urban problems are most difficult and seem to defy tactics of solution, or whether it is due to deliberate tactics of delay, the result is the same. A council will not long maintain the interest of its members or the respect of the citizens it seeks to serve if it becomes a "meet and eat" society. Action is essential, even if the action is no more than success in making everyone fully familiar with the problems, of giving them an opportunity to express their views and their priorities, and of laying a firm groundwork for future progress of a more tangible sort.

The second problem which I have reason to fear so far as the future of councils of governments is concerned is that of inadequate citizen involvement. Very few of the existing councils seem to understand the essentiality of involving the "grass roots" citizens in their planning and deliberations.

One criticism — perhaps the major criticism — of special authorities in past years has been that they are neither responsive nor responsible to the citizens. They function much as their directors want them to function, and the private citizen has no means whatever of expressing his dissatisfaction or displeasure if their activities injure or displease him. He is burdened, either through the payment of fees of taxes, with the cost of supporting the authority, and he is governed, in one way or another, by its policies and procedures. But he has virtually no voice in what the authority does.

Much the same criticism might eventually be leveled against councils of governments if they continue as many of them have begun; that is, if they continue to ignore the public. Council members are elected public officials with but a relatively few exceptions, but they are elected as officials of a single jurisdiction and not of the region as a whole. As a result, the individual taxpayer who feels the need to provide the council with his own views on some matter which appears on its agenda cannot be certain that he can do so effectively by conferring with the elected official of just one of what might be more than a hundred constituent units. By the same token, the citizen who feels the need to react against an action or decision of a council of governments cannot and should not hold a locally elected official responsible for such action or decision.

There are several roads open whereby councils of governments can provide regional citizens with access to a council of governments, and of permitting them to be truly involved to the limit of their own interests. One such technique would be to allow regional citizens to appoint or to elect several lay citizens to council membership, and perhaps, even to the position of council president. Some of these "grass roots" members might even be permitted to serve on the executive committee as "ex officio" members.

I do not want to suggest what kind of person these public representatives might be. The experience of the Office of Economic Opportunity and its Citizen Action Committees is that there is something to be gained by including the region's economically disadvantaged on policy boards which deal with the region's social and physical welfare. On the other hand, we in southeastern Michigan have adopted the "regional statesman" concept in selecting citizen representatives for our own council. They are likely to be college presidents or labor union officials or heads of utility companies or others in highly prestigious positions. Either type of public representative — or other — or several types — might do most for holding the council accountable to the public. This is a matter for local decision.

Another way of achieving this same end of citizen participation would be for council members, officials and staff, to make a very deliberate effort to actively solicit the involvement of a great many lay citizens as members of advisory committees, or by asking them to provide technical advice and assistance. This could also be done by the frequent holding of conferences, workshops, hearings, and other events in which the public would not only come to know of the work of the council, but would also feel that it has a real opportunity to become a part of its activities.

Another possibility is for the council to publish regularly the nature of its deliberations, its budget, its annual report, and to invite written comment. It could then hold public meetings on matters which arouse unusual response and concern, and could provide the opportunity for questions and comments.

Councils should also maintain a formal program of keeping civic associations and professional societies and other formal organizations aware of their efforts to find solutions to specific problems. These organizations should also be requested to prepare briefs on position papers for council consideration. Again, public meetings and audience participation could follow.

But whatever techniques are employed, the effort should not slacken. Public support is important, principally, because councils are voluntary organizations, which have no mandated authority. They depend on persuasion, and persuasion depends on knowledge, understanding, and trust. The council which is viewed with doubt by the regional public will not do great things, for its members will have no sense of direction or support from the citizens who have elected them to office.

Third, and finally, I am concerned that there is the possibility that Councils of Governments will restrict themselves, entirely, to consideration of the physical problems of a region. This, too, could be disastrous, for there is no longer any doubt whatever but that the physical characteristics of a region are inextricably bound up with the social, the political, and the economic. It may be that the comparative lack of success of many of our nation's Regional Planning Commissions in the past stems from this failure to look beyond the physical elements of the maps and drawing boards.

For it is neither wise nor practical to say that an airport should be constructed at point x in a region because such factors as soil condition and highway access and proximity to rail lines makes it the most suitable location. We ought to be sophisticated enough by now — particularly after our unfortunate experience in urban renewal and public housing programs — to know that there is more to it than that.

We ought to worry also about how many families will be displaced as a result of situating the airport at that point and whether there are other homes available to them which they can afford. We ought to worry about what the so-called "best" location will do to established patterns of church membership, to the business clientele of established stores and shops, to the ability of a school district to continue to function, to factories which provide jobs, to the traffic patterns of neighboring communities, to the tax base of the jurisdiction directly affected, to the value of adjoining land, to a great variety of matters which affect people.

Most elected officials can and do think in social and political and economic terms almost every time they make a decision. They must continue to do so when they act as members of the councils of governments. Even though they may feel no direct effect in the form of voter reaction when they determine that a given site in some distant community would be a good place for a new airport, they must act as though they do.

This requirement for a sense of social, economic and political, as well as physical needs, of the region also means that the members of many councils of governments must concern themselves with some of the problems which have long — though mistakenly — been considered as problems of their neighbors. Downtown slums are not the exclusive problem of the core city, for they affect every suburb, despite the independence of their civic authority. The disease and the crime, the poverty and the unrest spawned by those downtown slums affect every resident of every region both directly and indirectly. A distressed core city school district, for example, produces inferior students which in turn produces higher unemployment rates which in time produces crime, higher taxes and many other unescapable difficulties for residents of school districts which do have adequately financed programs.

At the other end of the region, racial discrimination in some suburban communities affects the inner city by producing ghettos and a sense of alienation and bitterness and a rejection of law and order and, as we have seen, riots and other civil disturbances.

Now these three concerns I have mentioned — the possibility that councils of governments may maintain the status quo, that they may fail to be properly responsive and responsible to the public, and that they may limit themselves to physical development only — are the problems which worry me the most. Time will tell whether or not my concern is well founded. But I would leave this thought with you in conclusion.

You have the opportunity to confront the problems of the communities in your region with a new institution which shows great promise and whose pitfalls have been identified. You will need some courage and a great amount of effort to get your program underway and to keep it moving in the direction of a truly democratic system of self government.

But you really have no alternative. To fail to make the attempt is to lose without trying, for there is no alternative way of coping with urban problems which shows any evidence of promise at this time. Nor will the problems of the cities and counties cure themselves. They can only get worse, and that may lead not only to the complete loss of our right to govern ourselves but also to a kind of urban existence which we surely do not wish for the generations which will follow us.

It used to be that we talked about only two things being certain . . . death and taxes. It is time to recognize the third certainty . . . that of change. Change, too, is inevitable. It is no longer a question of "will there be change?" it is now a more practical question of "how will the change occur?"

We no longer have the power . . . you or I . . . to deny the dynamics of change. Our counties and cities are changing, our technological alternatives change almost daily, our needs change as citizens, as leaders, and as people.

Someone must shape the change in this region . . . you are fortunate to have an on-going Council of Governments — with much untapped potential.

The shaping of that change must be done now, and . . . again . . . you are fortunate because "now" is when your area's Council of Governments is ready to embark on the adventure.

It will be a long, tough road. But never lose sight of the alternatives this region faces otherwise . . . the uncharted, unplanned chaos of every town for itself.

I would suggest to you, that the alternatives become simply these: If not a Council of Governments, who? If not now, when?

Discussion

Question: Would you please amplify a point that you just raised? My concern is with the question of fear, a certain degree of threat. The councils of governments idea is seen as a challenge to the existing framework. We can recognize it, we can state it, now how do we get a handle on it? Do something about it? Get busy with it? I am sure you do not have any quick and ready answer, but would you comment on this problem?

Mathewson: There is one sound answer and I think it is one that everybody in the room has. I think each person in this room could give an answer to your question and I suspect that what he would say is first, we know that any organizational effort depends on leadership and staff and obviously you have the leadership here in Kansas City. This is apparent from the things that we have heard. My understanding is that the present planning commission has provided staff to the Council of Governments which is something I think that you would want to examine. As I indicated to you in the Council of Governments that's closest to me, we continued the planning commission with the planning director as a division of the Council of Goernments but a nationwide search was instituted to employ a person as the director of the Council of Governments. I think you would be interested to know the salary that was offered and paid for this is higher than any other public official in the Detroit metropolitan area, including the mayor of Detroit. Whether they got their money's worth or not in the person, I won't say, but this is the indication of the commitment on the type of person they were looking for. When you are staffed and your leadership has a staff to rely upon, then obviously you've got to get moving. You've got to develop something for the membership to chew on, and something for the public to react to.

I wouldn't attempt to suggest your priority of metropolitan issues, but I am sure you have them. You may be going to build a freeway through an area that will displace a lot of citizens, you may have a pollution problem of one sort or another, or you may have crime in the streets that spills over into several other jurisdictions. How are the law enforcement officers relating to one another? You could name the list of things that you could address yourself to and then incorporate the practical things that the council could immediately engage in, such things as developing a joint purchasing program which can save very substantial sums of money for each of the jurisdictions with no loss of authority of autonomy on their part. And you could develop a regional electronic data processing bank. You know the things that are your issues; it simply takes leadership and staff and enthusiasm and determination to get them going.

Question: I wonder if you ever had your state highway department tell you that it didn't know an airport was coming? How do you solve a problem of communication that fundamental?

Mathewson: I think this is the name of the game council of governments and I suspect that your question is rhetorical. If the council of governments does not do the job then it shouldn't be in being. You would be interested to know that in relating to the council in the Detroit area, we do have a representative of the governor's office who sits with the council of governments and regularly attends;

he is an ex officio member of the executive committee, a nonvoting member. Also, the federal government has a representative that sits with the Council of Governments. So we do attempt to provide a liaison in relationship to the state and the federal government as well as one another in the metropolitan area.

Question: You mentioned three problem areas, one of which is the matter of providing adequate citizens' involvement on the "grass roots" level. You mentioned a number of devices. In your own experience, have local universities provided any assistance on these matters?

Mathewson: Yes, I think that as you recall, one of the things the Council of Governments could do would be to provide a research component for the governments of these areas. You have a number of excellent research resources here in the Kansas City area: the University, or any other relevant organization, such as Community Studies, Inc. I think that the Council of Governments could and should relate to these and any other research resources in bringing the problem to them, providing liaison with researchers to be sure that the problem is clearly understood by them and interpreting their findings back to the various governmental jurisdictions.

Question: I am concerned particularly about the attitude of the state legislature. Have you experienced an anti-urban feeling from your legislature?

Mathewson: Yes, in fact we have a double-barrel situation. We have a part of our state that is quite rural, all upstate and in the upper peninsula. Metropolitan Detroit is suspect often and we feel discriminated against in many instances by some people in the state legislature. Of course, this is one of the purposes of the Council of Governments, in unity there is strength and we feel the more effectively we can take our cause to the state legislature through our League of Municipalities and through our county association, the better off we are. We do not attempt to lobby, per se, but we can present them our position because after all they are state-wide organizations.

We can stand in a much better position to present our situations to the legislature if we as a group have met and agreed that the legislature knows this is a united position on the part of the six counties in the southeast of Michigan. We have another factor that you may not have experienced here and that is we have a governor who is quite sincere in his belief that the state government should play an ever increasing leadership role in the resolution of urban and metropolitan problems. And while certainly this is to be commended, to be applauded, while it is good on one hand, it has caused us some problems at the local level. And I wouldn't go into the details of the problems, I think you can imagine what some of them are. But it again makes it all the more important that the local units in a metropolitan area join together so that they can present a united front to the state administrators as well as the state legislature in furthering their views and their needs. I think you are going to see this coming in the next four years.

Question: Would you comment on the inclusion of school districts in the area Council of Governments?

Mathewson: I am so glad you asked that question. This is one of my pet interests. And I am going to try to be restrained in my comments because I know from reading your by-laws that you do not include school districts here. I really cannot understand it. I suspect that in the Kansas City area, like most other places in the United States, that nearly if not more than half of the total tax resource goes to the schools. To sit down and talk about discussing metropolitan problems and to exclude from that discussion table or bargaining table, whatever you folks call it, the jurisdictions that consume or utilize approximately half of the total local resources is hard for me to understand. Especially since we know that finances are perhaps the biggest single problem that faces all our local governments. I do know that in the formation of councils of governments this has not been the practice of the cities and counties. Well, first of all the counties started getting together rather carelessly and then the cities started getting together, now the counties and cities are getting together.

I think it is very important that the schools be invited in. This is being done more and more around the United States as I mentioned in my paper. They are full-fledged members in the Southeast Michigan Council of Governments. The first mixed jurisdiction Council of Governments to be formed in the United States was the one in Oregon and they included school districts. All of the Texas Councils of Governments included the school districts. The Wichita Council of Governments includes them. The Cleveland, Ohio, Council of Governments includes them. The Toledo, Ohio, Council of Governments includes them, etc. It is definitely a strength. We find in our Council of Governments that they are among the most enthusiastic and dedicated members of the council and of course the interrelationship of the problems that they have and the cities and counties have is now a legend. This whole business of poverty and transportation and job training and any of the social matters that concern local communities certainly involve the schools to a large degree. I would agree if you suggest school districts be included as full participating members of the Council of Governments.

Question: Isn't there one stage in the game where you get to be so big that you are a pretty unwieldy group?

Mathewson: This is a problem, no question about it.

Question: For instance, there are seventeen school districts in the city of Kansas City alone.

Mathewson: We have one hundred school districts in the Detroit Metropolitan area.

Question: Does each one have a representative?

Mathewson: Yes. Our Council of Governments has a potential of over three hundred and fifty members. And the executive committee has thirty-five members even after cutting it down through a very complicated formula of representation which is partially on a population basis. The council itself has representation on a jurisdiction, one vote basis regardless of whether it's a city of a thousand people or the city of Detroit. Within the executive committee, however, there is some recognition of population or size of the jurisdictions but not as the one man, one vote principle. There is some recognition of this. The thirty-five members on the executive committee are selected through a system of caucusing within each county by each type of jurisdition. Interestingly enough, we give full membership and inclusion to townships in our Council of Governments, because they are a full municipal corporation in Michigan. So we have four local governments: townships, schools, cities, and counties. They caucus each year at the annual meeting and select their representatives within their county from their particular type of government to the executive committee. And to date it has worked satisfactorily. I think in terms of numbers ours is the largest Council of Governments in the country although there are some quite large councils.

Question: I would like to go back to the question of the school districts. We did a study of the thirty-nine councils and the hundred largest commissions that existed eighteen months ago and it seemed to me that having school districts included was only the first step, because outside of Texas and California, where state legislation required some actual work between school districts and the Council and other organizations, even those councils that had school districts within them actually don't do anything in education other than maybe say to the school districts, "You should plan." Nothing was actually happening that we could see. I would like to ask what specific steps have been taken to coordinate withn the system, among the school districts or between the school districts and your other members?

Mathewson: The Council in the Detroit area has functional committees and these committees are carefully selected to include representatives from each of the types of governments so that at the committee level, functional committee level, the school people will be working with city people and town people and the township people and so forth. Each of the four types of governments elects a vice chairman of the Council of Governments so that you have four vice chairmen in addition to the overall chairman that is selected.

In the matter of joint purchasing it was found that the schools were able to provide a good deal of expertise and assistance to the counties, cities, and townships. Their purchasing practices were more advanced than the other governmental units. Also it was found that the schools purchased some commodities in very great quantities; for example, typewriters or paper or pencils, things like this, and that the other jurisdictions can ride on their very low unit prices they had established. In turn, some things the other jurisdictions purchased in large quantities and the school districts were able to benefit from this.

The committee was studying financing of local governments and of course school people are very much involved with this. This is a problem that draws no distinctions. It is a common problem for all the units. Quite frankly, I think one reason the schools now are so much interested in participating is that once upon a time they had things going their way, they had a corner on the local revenues and they were pretty smug about it, but that's not the case any more. They are really up against it like all the other governmental jurisdictions are and they are glad to sit down and discuss their financial problems with the other jurisdictions.

This may give you some further insight as to the relationship between the schools and the other jurisdictions.

Question: Are you approving sites that are suggested for new schools?

Mathewson: Yes, this of course goes through the physical planning division of the Council of Governments. Incidentally, I should say there are six divisions in that particular Council of Governments, each with a regional leader or regional director; there's the general government division which handles all such things as electronic data processing studies and developments on a regional basis, joint purchasing which we have talked about, uniform tax collection, anything of a general government nature comes under that division; there is the education division which obviously relates to the schools. Incidentally, the junior colleges are members of the Council of Governments and they have full voting rights as well as the other schools; the public works division; the public safety division; the planning division, of course, is the largest and most important, it not only does the physical planning for the area and sends along a review, but it also does the transportation planning, it has a continuing comprehensive transportation planning responsibility for the Council; and the health and welfare division. Those are the six divisions.

Question: There are perhaps alternatives to the approach you just suggested. You might have, for example, a federation approach or a county federation or you might have an urban county which extends services to your unincorporated areas and to your municipalities such as in Los Angeles or even an area-wide single function district. I was just wondering, in view of the fact that these other more formal structures which have been tried for example in Canada, the Toronto or the Ottawa system of incorporating the formal council's structure with powers to act for the counties and municipalities, do you believe that the approach the Council of Governments is taking is the practical one and that it will ultimately develop into one of these forms of structural metropolitan government or do you believe that your voluntary form is sufficient for the present?

Mathewson: You have touched a number of points. Although I accept the inevitability of change, it would be foolhardy on my part to predict how the councils will develop or change. I would quickly add, however, that I would not at this juncture change from a voluntary association of governments into a metro form of government, even though you suggest that this would bring about consolidation of all the local units of government into one large unit of government. I happen to be old-fashioned enough to believe that a Council of Governments enables us to best govern by having the input of citizens and of the several governments. Even though it may lead to some inefficiency, I think that the value far outweighs the cost of any such inefficiency. I would say further with regard to your question when you cite Toronto, Canada, or Dade County, Florida, that these are governments which have been established within one county. They are not multi-county governments. In fact, Toronto is only part of one county with only some dozen jurisdictions which through consolidation have been reduced somewhat. There are relatively few jurisdictions and less than one county. When you are talking about six or seven counties, this obviously would be no answer. Parenthetically, I would say that there is nothing incompatible or inconsistent between strong county home rule or strong county government and a Council of Governments. In fact, they are quite compatible and quite desirable. The stronger and more efficient your county government, the more effective partner it is in a council of governments. Dade County is really little more than a strong county government. Again, it is confined to one county and I think some approximately twenty-four jurisdictions. When you come to an area such as ours with over three hundred and fifty jurisdictions, four million people in six counties, to talk about amalgamation into one county government is completely beyond my comprehension. To say they did it in Toronto or they did it in Dade County doesn't answer the question at all for me. I don't think it's relevant.

Now, as for single purpose authorities, I think that the regional single purpose authority most likely will be the answer within areas that attempt the council of governments' approach. When you decide to handle transit on a regional basis you undoubtedly will set up a transit authority. Most likely you will have taxing authority throughout the whole region. If you decide to cure air pollution on a regional basis you will most likely have some sort of air pollution authority with a large charge back against the government or general taxing power. However you finance it there will be some powers of sanction. I think the essence of your question is how do you keep from Balkanizing your area into a whole group of single purpose districts?

In other words, don't you just trade one type of fragmentation for another type of fragmentation? I think the way you do it is to have the regional authorities or districts, whatever they are as set up, become for planning purposes and some measure of control, creatures of the Council of Governments. What do I mean by that? I simply mean that I think their members should be appointed by and responsible to the Council of Governments and that their budget and bonding proposals and their financial reports be submitted to the council of governments for their public review and comment. In this way the federal government is already saying that if the money authorities asked for federal funds, the request must be reviewed from the federal standpoint through your Council of Governments. I think that in these several ways you can make fragmented units responsive to an overall planning agency, namely the Council of Governments, which is responsive to the public and can look at things on a multi-functional viewpoint for review.

Question: I would like to comment a little bit and then ask a question. It is interesting to note that when the Bureau of Public Roads started putting a little pressure on our metropolitan area to form a regional operation, they considered a Council of Governments at the beginning. But because the Kansas City metropolitan area is possibly even more fragmented than the Detroit area, since there are two states involved, all they could form at that time was an area-wide metropolitan commission, even though at that time there were additional federal funds if there was a Council of Governments. They did form a twenty-eight man planning commission. And they no sooner started in December, 1966, than by the very next summer support was developed for an area-wide Council of Governments. Some planning commission members felt that this could possibly lead to the end of the Metropolitan Planning Commission because it took so long for this area to form a metropolitan planning commission; that to come along immediately with the Council of Governments would weaken the efforts of the metropolitan planning. They did see the need to have one staff for both the planning commission and the Council of Governments. This gave us sort of a pulling together. One of the problems members of the planning commission pointed out was that these heads of government are always so busy.

The Council of Governments has been officially kicked-off as of October, 1967, and has been meeting regularly. We did find it a little hard to get quorums. This contrasts with our experience with a planning commission made up of some elected officials, but the majority of nonelected people.

This ties in with your comment about school districts and why they aren't included. It was hard enough to get the seven counties and the four largest cities and then representation from the small cities; sure it's not one man and one vote, and sure it's not school districts at this time, although they were considered. There is no reason, as you pointed out, why this thing couldn't evolve and reformat. For instance, not too long ago they finally agreed that there ought to be some ex officio members of the two legislatures on the commission. I think the answer to the problem is that it is an evolving thing and it's not cut and dried.

What I would like to ask is really a twofold question. How do we get a regional orientation with citizen awareness of regional problems? You say it must come in some way, eventually. How, by crises? Or is there a tremendous communications and public relations program that can get people interested? You pointed out the relationship of the intercity to people living in the suburbs who have probably fled to the suburbs because of intercity problems or possibly other reasons, like evasion of taxes, but really, how do we get this kind of interest?

The second question concerns money. The two deficiencies in the growth and control of this area are the problems of the lack of an area-wide land policy and the absence of an equitable tax policy. Supposedly to arrive at policy of this nature would require state concern involving state legislation from the two states. How do you get state awareness and interest? How do you get two-state cooperation?

Mathewson: Let me by way of a prelude say that the nice thing about going out of town to talk is you can make things look real rosy and real easy and say, what's the matter with you guys, why are you moving so slowly, and so forth and so on. Truthfully, five long hard years of solid work went into developing the Southeast Michigan Council of Governments and it was only six months ago that they hired their director. There were several hundreds of thousands of dollars of private monies that went into the development of the council. The interim staff was paid from private foundations. Even before that, as I mentioned, there were ten years of experience with county supervisors in their county committee in which at least the six county governments were working together with a paid staff. So there are fifteen years of hard work in the history of the Council of Governments in Michigan and it's really not as far down the road as I would portray here today. So much for being honest and setting the record straight.

Also, with the business of the two states we anticipate, and there are provisions in our enabling legislation for, the inclusion of Windsor, Ontario, across the river from Detroit in the council. This has not been attempted yet because of the obvious complications. We feel that we've got enough problems to get three hundred and fifty jurisdictions together here on the United States side without making it an international problem. So we understand and appreciate the problems.

Now talking about your question of communications. This is the heart of the whole Councils of Governments' movement, or the whole regional planning movement, or the whole intergovernmental relations movement regardless of what variety or shape it takes. Until we develop a regional constituency, until the citizens understand that they indeed are economically and socially and politically interdependent within the metropolitan area, the finest planners in the world and most dedicated of council officials and staff in the world are not going to be able to achieve very much.

For this reason, our foundation, Metropolitan Fund, is investing substantial sums of monies each year in trying to bring about this regional constituency. Speakers are continually going out and speaking on all the issues that relate to the total region that show the interdependence of the suburbs and core city and vice versa, to the interrelationship of all the various parts of the six county region. We have a newsletter that endeavors to do this. It is put out each month. We have developed films for this purpose and so forth.

I do think that you may well discover that you will find regional people. I brought up the point, that several councils have appointed regional representatives. In addition there may well be regional people elected to the council or it may be that the Chairman of the Council of Governments might well be elected and in this sense he would become a metropolitan mayor. This would put tremendous public visibility into the council because he would be running on and debating the regional issues — whether we should clean up air pollution that affects the whole region, or whether we should change the river, or whether we should put a freeway here or should put an airport there or whatever.

Short of that, I mentioned that you have a number of other things that the council could and should do to relate to the public. This is certainly very important. If some outside agency such as a foundation can invest some money in trying to help develop regional constituency, it is much more believable than if you are trying to do it alone because the council by itself is seen as trying to better its own end. I think foundations are in an excellent position to help, in that with the combination of the two a regional constituency can be developed. It must be if they are going to succeed.

Now, with regard to your question about state awareness. I think with the Nixon administration, that there is going to be state awareness with a vengeance.

With the leadership coming from Washington, all that we've got to do in the metropolitan area is be sure that it's not misapplied. We need to see that we are organized so that we can take advantage of it and help direct it so it won't be crammed down our throats.

Question: On the issue of leadership and visibility, you talked about developing a regional constituency and mentioned the possibility of electing a chairman at large from a region. In areas where this may not be politically feasible, do you see any evidence that those who become involved with the Council of Governments can develop some vested interests in providing real leadership because of the kinds of newspaper publicity or other political capital they can get out of it? In other words, you can't get real leadership unless somebody has a vested interest in seeing the thing work. How do you find a basis for such a vested interest?

Mathewson: It's so new that I couldn't give you a whole lot of examples but the few things that I have seen and heard lead me to believe that this may be coming. One elected official recently indicated that the political outcome of the election was very important to him because of the potential impact on who would be his government's representative to the Council of Governments.

Question: Since there are no Black colleagues here that might ask the question, I will ask it. How have you responded to the arguments that people find it suspicious that the movement is toward shifting decision making powers from the cities to the regions?

Mathewson: I have anticipated the question. I think what you are trying to say goes rather like this: "In the core city at long last we Negroes, we Black people, appear to be coming into our own. We're going to have political power. In fact, in some cities, we now are in the majority and have our elected Black mayors, such as Cleveland, and it's expected in Detroit if not in the next election, certainly the one after this one. So now what you're going about is you're going to set up a Council of Governments which diffuses this power of ours again. It does that by bringing in suburbs." This, I think, is the import of your question.

We get this thrown at us every day in Detroit because, as you know, Black Power is a significant political factor in the Detroit area, and we simply say to those who ask us questions about it that if you don't go to the Council of Governments' approach, one of two things is going to happen. Either the governments of the metropolitan area are going to be taken to Lansing, the state capital, or to Washington. And certainly if you go to Lansing you know how much of a voice the Black man is going to have there in the state legislature — very little. The other thing that could happen, if it stays at home, it will go into the form of a metropolitan government. I think this is highly unlikely but this is the other alternative. Again, you are really going to lose your power because you will indeed be diffused. Your vote will be diffused into a metropolitan all-purpose government. So your best bet is to support the Council of Governments strongly because this does include the city of Detroit where your present political power lies. It keeps Detroit intact and keeps it with its voting representation on the Council of Governments. You do have an undiluted input into the Council of Governments through the city council. We don't always get acceptance to this argument.

Question: You have to have some acceptance, a fairly good acceptance with that approach.

Mathewson: No, I wouldn't say so. I wish I could say so. They listen and they nod their heads and they go away unconvinced. I don't know that they go away unconvinced intellectually, it's just that they are very, very suspicious.

Question: How many Black representatives do you have on the three hundred fifty member Southeast Michigan Council of Governments?

Mathewson: Our representation is proportionate to the degree to which they are elected to their local government body.

Question: There are some Black people within your structure?

Mathewson: Yes, but they are certainly in the minority because there are a minority elected.

Question: Kansas City has a regional planning commission and they now have a Council of Governments and we recently established an urban coalition. I wonder if you might comment on what you think that the leadership potential is for each of the three approaches.

Mathewson: I think I made it abundantly clear that I thought you had no business having both a regional planning commission and a Council of Governments. You should have a Council of Governments in which a regional planning commission is the planning arm. I will be glad to go into that further if you want me to but that's my view and I tried to give a good deal of support and background in my paper.

Now for the urban coalition, I am familiar with the Urban Coalition in Detroit, which is called the New Detroit Committee, because again my foundation was responsible for forming it. It didn't take us five years, it took us five days because the town was burning down. That's what we have covered as of July 23rd, 1967. We formed an urban coalition and it was staffed and funded and housed in our headquarters. A year later, about fourteen months, it spun off and is now a separately incorporated organization still sharing the same quarters with us but with their own funding, their own staff, and their own committee, board of trustees and so forth. I see no conflict at all and there need be no duplications with an urban coalition and a Council of Governments. I can see a great deal of compatibility between the two. An urban coalition is essentially a private sector operation. There certainly should be public representation on it and it should be a regional organization although it will inevitably focus its major attention on the core city and more specifically the core of the core, the disadvantaged area, of the core city and its problems.

I think that some of the comments that I have made in my prepared paper about Councils of Governments calling for attention to the social issues of the day as well as physical planning, would certainly relate to the urban coalition. A good deal of the program policies that would be developed in and by the urban coalition should be referred to the Council of Governments for their review and recommendations. The members of the Council of Governments are the jurisdictions that will have to implement these findings.

Essentially an urban coalition is going to deal with the matters of jobs, housing, education, but this doesn't provide an attitudinal change which relates to this regional constituency that I talked about. It doesn't come to grips with the problem of the suburbs being able to relate to the inner-city and vice versa. I think that an urban coalition can serve a fine purpose for a community such as Kansas City by doing both. It's an extremely frustrating job. There are no awards passed out in an urban coalition, but nevertheless, it is a very necessary undertaking and there can be a very complementary relationship between a Council of Governments and an urban coalition.

Question: This is a long question on the equity and inequities of taxes in a metropolitan area. Many metropolitan areas do have certain areas that are fairly wealthy. Take Clay County, Missouri, for example, they have a city hall in North Kansas City. I think the daytime population is 60,000 and the nighttime population is about 6000. Their school district is loaded. They have one of the best school systems in the area because they have the money. Yet there are other dormitory areas or other city areas that are hurting. Or take Platte County, Missouri, where within the next two years a major new airport is going to create all kinds of industries. Platte County will probably have the biggest source of income in the whole metropolitan area. Yet 30% of the people who are going to be using the airport live in Johnson County, Kansas, in another state, in another county, in a whole covey of cities which are of the true suburban type. Now, how can we tackle allocation of resources so that we can really knit the area together in respect to schools in the right places, sewers more at the right time, highways to handle the people, when we really can't mix funds. The Council of Governments by its very nature means that even if you develop a plan that says you need this road in the next two years, this park next year, or this fire station at that time, but they fall in particular jurisdictions that don't have wherewithal to buy these things, how can we ever get the funds out on a regional level to implement whatever plans the Council of Governments agrees to?

Mathewson: This is really a tough question. Our foundation, several years ago, came to the conclusion that there were three things that would have to be done if the metropolitan "problems" would be solved in our region. One, we felt we had to have an institution, a governmental instrumentality that we would be able to work on a regional basis, hence the establishment of the council. And we looked at all of the alternatives and felt this was the best one both operationally and politically. We said, second, and not in order of priority, we've got to develop a regional constituency to back up this institution so the council will have somebody to relate to and vice versa. We are spending considerable sums of money trying to develop this regional constituency. We have a full time regional citizenry information staff within the foundation and the program is building. Third, we said to get the institution and to get the citizens thinking about regional problems, we somehow are going to have to be able to finance the regional program. The new programs undoubtedly will cost more than existing programs. We want the funding shared on a regional basis so that there won't be inequities. We are going to have to spread the financial resources across the region and we do not have the answers to this. We employed one national firm to examine this problem for us, quite frankly they didn't come up with any answers that we thought were real answers. They published a report. We paid many thousands of dollars for it with few answers. We are continuing our study of this problem and trying to develop the ways and means for financing on a regional basis. So, I guess all I am saying is that you are right and I agree with you. We don't have an answer to it. We are working on it, but we don't have an answer yet.

Question: One of the answers to that problem which has been successfully explored to some degree is the method by which the state allocates aid to school districts. For example, in some eastern states, the state furnishes state aid in inverse proportion to the wealth of the district. So for example, an industrial area will get little state aid while an area with very high residential population and low per capita assessment will get very strong state aid. I know for example in New York there are some suggestions that the basis for financing school districts be eliminated from the locality and be borne 11% by the state which will then return the funds to the localities in that proportion. New York state is now furnishing approximately 50 to 55% of all the aid to school districts. The task is to eliminate the property tax and put financing on a more statewide income tax basis. That can be done on a statewide level. Is there any reason why it cannot be done on a regional level through a Council of Governments if you obtain constitutional statutory change?

Mathewson: Well, I understand that your mayor joined several other mayors in the state and petitioned the governor to make a very substantial allocation of state funds available to the cities and most interestingly, in the inverse ratio to the population; that is, the larger the city the larger the percentage funds go to them, not on a straight line basis, but on an ascending basis. It can be interesting to see what reaction this will get. We can imagine what reaction this may get from rural members of the legislature, in any event. But again, for the people in my very wealthy suburban community of Bloomfield Hills, to be willing to accept that is difficult to achieve. Look at Bloomfield High School for example. You can't believe it. It is carpeted. It has a private lake. It has teaching machines, fifteen students to a classroom. It's the ultimate. Downtown Detroit in the inner-city, there are buildings that were built at the turn of the century still in use and fifty students in a classroom and the quality of teaching is visibly poor. I doubt if you are saying that we are going to raise those schools in the inner-city up to the level of that school in Bloomfield Hills with a private lake and fifteen students to a classroom. What you are really saying is that we are going to meet somewhere in between by spreading the wealth and instead of one having fifty students and another having fifteen, we are going to end up with a medium of hopefully twenty or twenty-five students per classroom. Now it takes an awfully lot of understanding and dedication to the regional concept, to the regional constituency, to bring those sorts of things about. It's got to come, there is no question about it. But what you are talking about is an attitudinal change on the part of the citizens.

Question: Have you made much progress in this area you call attitudinal change?

Mathewson: We didn't have a riot this summer [1968].

Question: That's progress, I will agree. Would you want to elaborate any more? We didn't have one this summer either. We had one in April but it was small and we didn't have any more.

Mathewson: There is no question that the avenues of communication have been opened that never existed before and the level of understanding between the inner-city and the suburbs is at a much higher point than it ever was before. And this is the result of tremendous effort on the part of the media and television every night and publications, and newsletters, and mild newspaper copy and thousands and thousands of man and woman hours and speakers' bureaus and so forth and so on, not all of which we have done certainly, but we have had a very big part in it. Now whether understanding has increased sufficiently, I cannot judge. I know it has increased, but not as much as it should.

Question: You mean it is a positive thing and hasn't caused negative polarization?

Mathewson: There has been some polarization. There has been a counterforce that has come into being too. But I would say that the positive outweighs the negative.

Question: Could you comment on the New Detroit Committee in this situation?

Mathewson: This is the urban coalition that I have talked about and with which we have been so closely associated. When we set up the New Detroit Committee, the first thing we did was to turn our entire citizen information program and staff over to the New Detroit Committee to carry on the dialogue that I am talking about. Housing, education, and jobs are three of the things that you want to immediately think about, do something about. But you will be hedging if you do not give prime attention to trying to bring about an attitudinal change within the community. You can put the disadvantaged in excellent homes and give them excellent educational facilities and give them all jobs; there is still going to be trouble in your town if alienation continues. At least from our experiences. Maybe not here.

Question: The implication I get and I don't think you want to leave this impression in talking about your Detroit experiences is that a lot of these things might not have happened or didn't happen until there was private money placed with the seed money. I think that there are places around the country where in the formation of Councils of Governments and to a certain extent in formation of urban coalitions, that there wasn't substantial outlay of philanthropic money. Should we sit back and wait for the Kansas City area until there is grant money available to help these things get started? Or is there something that can be done right now?

Mathewson: Obviously don't wait. Go to it any way that you can. I will say, however, that my experience has been that a private input can be extremely helpful and beneficial to a Council of Governments. The original one that I was associated with in Oregon was brought about by a private study. It was initiated from city hall in the principal city of that area, but interestingly enough it was done through private contributions and private citizens' committees were set up to review the study and to then call all the governments to form a Council of Governments. Admittedly, there was a little bit of role-playing there; we were getting somebody to tell us to do something that some of us wanted to do. But this was the way of involving the citizens and giving them regional awareness that is so very important. So, however, you do it, yes, try to involve the private sector. That is your first step in developing regional constituency. Second, if you can get the private money, it gives you an opportunity to do things much more quickly than you would be able to do otherwise.

While it's not particularly related to the comment itself, I have been intending to get on the record, although I have talked about the Council of Governments in a community of four million people, with three hundred and fifty jurisdictions and so forth, by no means should anyone believe that Councils of Governments can only be developed or are only useful in huge metropolitan areas. They are very appropriate for communities the size of metropolitan Kansas City. Where you are straddling the state line they become all the more important. There are many communities around the United States that have growing Councils of Governments that are much smaller than Kansas City and they are fulfilling a very worthwhile role.

11

The Decentralization of Urban Government: A Systems Approach

Guy Black

It has long been obvious that a city is a system in the nontechnical sense that a system is an assemblage or combination of things forming a complex or unitary whole. Cities have survived and grown for a variety of reasons and are characterized by differences in their economic bases and functional compositions. Some cities are principally administrative centers of government, while others have grown as centers for trade and industry. Whatever their origins, most cities are now complex organizations serving a multiplicity of functions. [1]

It has become increasingly evident that one can neither understand cities nor solve their problems by focusing on limited and specific problems. To date, however, systems analysis applied to cities has been partial in scope, and generally oriented toward limited problem areas rather than the city as a whole. It is not clear that this pattern can change very quickly, given the analytical difficulties involved.

What, in fact, are the potentials for the systems approach in urban affairs? Can the results justify the effort? Are hardware-oriented aerospace systems approaches, dealing with elaborate, technological systems, directed at fairly limited purposes, and applied by a strongly hierarchical organization also suitable for systems of people who are motivated by complex, conflicting and perhaps undefinable purposes, and loosely coordinated by the diffused power embodied in constitutionally limited urban government? The purpose of this paper is to suggest systems approaches which appear to be promising. Particular attention will be paid to the interaction of governmental organization with the systems approach.

System Concepts

In view of the diversity assigned to "system" and "systems approach," it is helpful to define the terms as used here. [2] A system is a representation of reality in which the scope is determined by where a systems analyst decides to define system boundaries. A system concept is, to some extent, an arbitrary analytical convention, as any complex of activity is characterized by a continuum of interactions. The system model explicitly identifies only those attributes which are relevant to the analyst's purposes, ignoring many details judged to be irrelevant. A system concept is usually structured as a set of subsystems. Subsystems in turn have their own subsystems, and the process can be carried down several levels.

A system concept may become the subject matter for a systems approach.

This has come to mean an integrated analytical and managerial effort. Analysis of a system may take a number of forms. The most common approach follows well-defined methodological lines, starting with identifying objectives, defining a system model, establishing functional relationships between the elements of the model and between system-wide inputs and outputs, and selecting levels of the inputs and outputs which will yield an optimum result by some criteria, such as a cost-benefit ratio.[3]

Management is part of the system approach, and a distinction can be made between operating and implementation system management. Operating system management is that of a system in being, as where the management of an electric power system seeks to supply needs by its various power plants. The managerial task is to meet a fluctuating demand for electricity in the most efficient way at all times. An operating system manager has limited opportunities to make any major alterations in the physical equipment at his disposal, and he concentrates on means to obtain the best result with the system at his disposal.

Implementation system management is concerned with the choice and design of the capital equipment of a system, either by the creation of an entirely new complex of hardware, or by modifying or replacing the old. This is the type of system management which is well-known in the aerospace industry; it is the means by which a new airplane is added to the weapons inventory, or a high-speed interurban rail system might be created. As investment decisions usually result in construction of facilities, or procurement of equipment which cannot be altered or replaced until fully depreciated, the incentive for a high quality of analytical support of these decisions is indeed great. Implementation systems analysis does indeed focus on alternative capital equipment configurations, and indeed much of systems analysis is especially tailored to identify the optimum capital equipment configurations.

**Purposes that Systems Approaches to
Urban Problems Might Serve**

Among the possible reasons for taking a systems approach to the city, one is to improve existing operations, and another is to identify desirable changes in the fabric of the city. Each has some appeal, and one does not preclude the other. That financial constraints impose severe limits on rapid major changes in the fabric of the city suggests, however, that improvement of existing operations will have much practical appeal. The concepts of operating systems management may be particularly attractive. A system management plan might also provide for immediate improvement in operating and gradual adoption of a new capital plant.

It is perhaps premature to make capital investment decisions until the manner in which capital will be used is well understood. That is, an investment in public housing is likely to be premature until some decision is reached as to whether to rebuild the ghettos in their present sites, or to disperse the present residents. Analyses which will shed light on such questions are, principally, analyses of operating cities, and hence operating systems analyses. Indeed, they must combine analysis of the operation of existing cities, given the present pattern of investment in homes, roads, and publicly owned facilities, and alternative patterns, taking into account the costs and problems associated with achieving the alternative patterns.

To justify a systems approach, it should be clear that something is gained by a combined analysis of many activities. This is likely to be so wherever the interactions between activities are sufficiently strong that an effective program for one cannot be well designed without taking the other into account. Possibly the educational system, the employment services, and the public transportation system interact so that something can be gained by considering them as a single combined system. That a system approach should be preferred might be concluded at the point where analysts, examining individual problems separately, find that they need to make assumptions as to the other programs. A case of this occurred in New York City several years ago, where a new air pollution regulation intended to reduce burning of solid waste in apartment house incinerators created a disposal problem with which the City Department of Sanitation was not prepared to cope.[4] Obviously, the solid waste and the air pollution problem needed to be considered jointly in a systems approach.

Organizational Criteria for System and Subsystem Concepts

Clearly, systems concepts of the urban situation must be comprised of a set of integrated subsystems. But these subsystems can be structured in several ways. One subsystem might be transportation, taking into account the capital equipment supplied by government (roads), by individuals (automobiles), and by companies (mass transit and automotive service). This could be paralleled by subsystems concepts of other activities, so that in total they would encompass the whole fabric of urban life.

An alternative subsystem structuring might take as distinct subsystems the functions of government, of industry, trade, commercial transportation, and residents as consumers, which also could integrate into a total system.

The choice should be conditioned by the practical possibility of relating the various subsystem concepts as developed under alternative approaches to subsystem structuring, to decision-making bodies. If the span of subsystems corresponds to the span of control of organization, the possibility of a better understanding of operations through uses of systems analyses will be greatly enhanced. Yet the existing structure of authority need not be considered as fixed. The span of organizational authority can be taken as a variable.

That the fractionation of governmental functions has reduced the attractiveness of urban system concepts has been noted many times. If there are no mechanisms by which joint management of air pollution control and solid waste control could be obtained, an overall approach would serve as a management guide to no organization. Ergo, the natural locus for a systems approach in urban government is that level of administrative authority in which span of authority and scope of the problem match.

If it were always the case that the mayor or city manager exercised line managerial authority over all functions of government, such a locus could be found for any activity of government by moving up the hierarchical structure. Unfortunately, city governments are not structured in this way. There is considerable decentralization of authority in American cities. School systems are usually autonomous; sanitation districts, public utility districts, bridge and highway authorities, and the like, are also frequently autonomous, so that systems concepts which depend for implementation on managerial authority cutting across such agencies encounter numerous obstacles.

Further, the action potential of higher echelons with a sufficient span may be quite limited even where ostensibly there is line authority. The available option is frequently coordination by committee and consent. The system concept on which agreement is possible under these circumstances is likely to be one that confers no substantial disadvantage on any existing administrative entity of government. If the impasse cannot be resolved, the only available options may be charter/constitutional reform, which recasts organizational structure, or suboptimizing. An example of suboptimizing that resulted from organizational autonomy was cited by a National League of Cities panel which noted that New York City and Washington, D.C. were considering the widening of bridge approaches at $21 to $23 thousand for every additional vehicle that could enter the city and were not prepared to widen the streets to accommodate the extra traffic.[5] An overall transportation system analysis should have been the basis for combined bridge, city street, and public transportation system concepts.

In any event, the diffusion of authority within the structure of government is only part of the problem. Private actions limit the span of authority. Commuters cannot be forced to use public transportation, though they may be influenced by taxation. It has not been easy to force apartment house owners to install smoke abatement devices. Assuming that such devices were identified as elements of the optimum environmental control subsystem, it would perhaps be a concept that could not be implemented. In short, system concepts must be couched with reference to the structure of decision-making authority among units of government and among government and private sectors, in which each decision-making unit will be motivated by self-interests that in some degree are likely to be inconsistent with the system-wide optimum.

A viable system concept may, however, be based not on system-wide direct control, but a combination of direct control within a certain sphere, and of influence within a wider sphere.[6] Among available influences are, of course, the direct economic impacts of taxes, fees for various services, licenses for various activities, permits in line with zoning and other public policies.

Some Alternative Administrative Structures
for Objective-Oriented Government

To speak of the systems approach and objective orientation at once is a redundancy. The systems approach is objective-oriented by definition, although objective orientation is not the exclusive property of the systems approach. It has been stressed as the critical element in newer styles of management by Drucker,[7] and by Simon,[8] whose book on *Administrative Behavior* draws heavily on the problem of city government for its illustrations.

Objective orientation is not sufficient to identify a single structure for government. Functional organization, exemplified by vertical lines of authority for functions such as police, fire, welfare, education, is one possible objective-oriented structure. This is the common pattern in most government. Some authors have attributed its wide usage to an enthusiasm, often stressed in the movement for council-manager government, for business methods. Functional organization is well-adapted to tight financial and cost control, and heightens incentives for efficient resource use by functional supervisors.

The functional approach places a critically important coordinating burden on top management wherever organizational performance is materially affected by interfunctional coordination. Measures of effectiveness tend to emerge within functional organizations, which in fact place a premium on suboptimizing performance by functional hierarchies. Many-layered functional hierarchies severely reduce the ability of top management to communicate with lower-echelon operating managers. The latter, in time, tend to operate in conflict with overall organizational objectives in ways which are often subtle, unexpected, not easily detected, nor easily changed. A functional organization also has vested interests in an area of activity and organizational form which may in time become obsolete.

Functionalism has often been a significant advance in administrative efficiency. Reorganization along clearer functional lines has often been a significant step forward and many organizations — industrial and governmental — continue to suffer from irrational structuring of functional responsibilities.

Starting several decades ago, a trend in industrial organization started to gain momentum toward what Drucker has called federal decentralization. This amounted to the creation of operating divisions under a general (nonfunctional) manager to whom subordinate functional hierarchies reported. Typically such divisions were organized around a particular product — for example, one brand of automobile in a company with many, or serving a geographic area. Divisional general managers in charge of decentralized units then became a principal means for interfunctional coordination within a limited portion of the entire enterprise, which they were able to implement by direct managerial authority, through shortened lines of communication. With decentralization of this type, top management tended to divest itself of detailed interest in functional performance within divisions, retaining as specialized staff activities generalized coordination through such means as standard practices, advice to management at all levels, and broad policy guidance. Functional organization did not disappear, but operated within the framework of a hierarchy of general managers.

The strong resemblance between "federal" decentralization in industry and the systems approach of the aerospace industry is worth stressing. The essence of the aerospace systems management approach is the focusing of managerial control over all activities that pertain to a particular task, regardless of their functional differentiation, or the a priori existence of organizations structured along functional lines. The results of either federal decentralization or system manager approach are many and interacting. One is a shortening of lines of communication from the operation level to a decision-maker with multi--functional authority. Another is that the work assignment and objectives become restricted to a limited sphere.

For example, in a functional — not system — research and development (R & D) organization in industry whose personnel worked on many projects in combination with other functional performers, the director of R & D would be faced with continuing problems of allocating personnel among projects, arbitrating among competing demands by project managers. A project manager would negotiate for the services of R & D, production, and other functional groups, and would seek to advance his project smoothly and effectively through use of the type, level and schedule of services he could obtain from each functional manager. On the other hand, in the systems management approach, project managers would have direct control over all personnel employed on their system; they would promote their systems even though it affected adversely the efficiency with which particular functions were performed.

Under a system manager approach with its high premium on the system schedule, the system manager would tend to make decisions that advanced the project smoothly and expeditiously, even if this meant that some R & D personnel might be temporarily idle; under a functional organization the R & D manager would strive to keep his personnel effectively employed at all times even though this meant temporary delays in some systems.

The sources of the trend toward federal decentralization in industry should not be oversimplified. Clearly one factor was the growth in overall size and complexity of organizations; another was an element of fad in organizational style; another, a highly dynamic economic environment which placed a premium on responsiveness to changing conditions. The trend toward functional decen-tralization which first developed in large industrial complexes has been widely considered to have been an effective response to organizational difficulties arising in large-scale organizations.

Government has rarely participated in this kind of experimentation and state-urban government less than the federal government. To some extent, governmental structures are much more difficult to change than industry structures, given the constitutional and legal basis of their organizational structure. Yet innovation in urban government structure is not entirely unknown, as is exemplified by the widespread adoption of the council-manager form of government. Only recently has there been any tendency, however, toward experimentation with federal decentralization.

It is in many respects a misinterpretation to speak of the systems approach as a unique attribute of the aerospace experience. In a broader perspective, it is a manifestation of a more general pattern of the evolution of organizational structures. Indeed, since federal decentralization is particularly oriented at operating efficiency in industry while the aerospace approach focuses more on the procurement of capital equipment, there may be a different relevance in the two types to operating management and capital budgeting management of urban government.

Program Packaging as an Approach to
Restructuring Urban Government

The Planning, Programming, and Budgeting System (PPBS) is, to a considerable extent, directed at creation of a more rationalized objective structure, taking the congruence of objectives as the basis for rationalization. Program packaging is, of course, principally functional in its orientation. As Steiner has noted,[9] PPBS tends to be end-product oriented as well as functional in structure. As such, it is in some ways intermediate between planning and budgeting structured by resource types organized around functions, and that organized by objectives. In PPBS the packages are so broadly defined that they correspond rather well both to function and to related groups of objectives. Indeed, in the Department of Defense, products which have been created by the systems approach almost invariably fall within a single "package."

As in federal PPBS, interest at the urban level focuses on the consolidation of the budgeting exercise along objectives-oriented lines. Hatry has suggested an object-oriented PPBS structure for a city government consisting of the following packages: personal safety, health, intellectual development and personal enrichment, environment, economic opportunity, leisure time opportunity, and transportation-communication.[10] In urban government as in federal, the contents of any one package can be evaluated in terms of a simpler objective structure than for government as a whole. The availability of a common set of objectives and criteria for the elements integral to each package simplifies decisions as to the mix and level of various activities within the package, and then between packages.

PPBS focuses on a rationalization of the budgetary structure without necessarily requiring an administrative reorganization along functional lines. The unit of government performing public safety functions might not have full control over its vehicles, for example, but the budget decision as to the number of police vehicles might be made as part of a public safety program package, with trade-offs between vehicular patrol, etc.

In view of the difficulties in changing the organizational structure, the quick payoff potential in PPBS is attractive. But as long as PPBS is not ultimately followed by reorganization along functional lines there are some major obstacles to obtaining that payoff. The potential impact on day-to-day operations within functions is definitely limited. The quality of the PPBS exercise itself is likely to be seriously degraded. Program managers are likely to encounter many difficulties in obtaining insights into activities not under direct control. If the director of public safety wishes to make cost-benefit trade-offs between foot patrol and vehicular patrol, he will need data from the municipal garage, which in the first instance may have limited incentives to collect the data, and may be very conscious of the implications of the data for the garage's interests. The existence of program budgeting thus argues for adjusting the managerial structure to conform with the budget structure.

The federal experience suggests that the hoped-for potential for PPBS may not be realized without reorganization along package lines. The slowness with which package concepts in the federal program have broadened to cross the jurisdictions of major departments seems to be attributable in part to the failure to restructure organizations along package lines.

Some caution should be exercised in proposing reorganization of government along package lines. Urban government might be decentralized, not on a functional basis but on a geographic basis. But program packaging and geographic decentralization are not mutually exclusive, and indeed geographic decentralization might simplify combining of functions into packages corresponding to administrative units within geographically decentralized governmental units. In short, it might make possible the interfunctional program evaluation that has eluded the federal government.

Simon has specified two conditions for decentralization — whether functional or geographic — to be successful:

(1) It must be technologically feasible to split the work activity, as well as the objectives.
(2) Segregated work activities must not affect, to a substantial degree, values extraneous to the specified organizational entities.[11]

These conditions leave room for alternative approaches to organization of the functions of city government. For example, New York City has created a service center for business in which the functions of government which interface directly with the businessman are combined. Gordon reports that metropolitan New York highway contractors have to go through as many as 187 procedural steps before they get highway specifications approved by every governmental body involved.[12] Consolidation in a business center should lead to lower bids for highway work, perhaps also an increase in the number of bidders, and opportunities for economies in administration.

Geographic decentralization of urban government may, at first blush, appear to be a medicine with more problems than the disease. One of the problems of modern government has been the multiplicity of jurisdictions imposed upon an ever-changing and growing metropolis. Often it has inhibited the rational performance of functions, for example, where there are economies of scale in a public function such as sanitation service. If jurisdictions operate service departments independently, the services will be performed less efficiently than they might be, where the least cost scale is larger than the requirement of any jurisdiction.

Simon's second condition is impinged upon where jurisdictional boundaries are drawn so that operations servicing particular areas seriously affect other jurisdictions. There are clearly many functions for which the appropriate area is the entire metropolitan area; it may even be larger — as is expressed in the idea that the airshed is the appropriate jurisdiction for abatement of air pollution.

Geographic patterns of economic and social activity in metropolises are not always conducive to delineation of areas which encompass the principal activities of most residents. The separation of residential, entertainment, and employment into large specialized districts means that it will often be impossible to define areas to which the principal activities of large groups of persons are confined. A governmental unit based on place of residence cannot perform functions which relate both to social life and employment of its residents.

Nonetheless, there is probably a spectrum of governmental functions for which area structuring might be useful and meaningful. The possibilities have been most explored with reference to poverty areas. There seems to be real differences in the mix and quality of services that residents of such areas desire, as compared with middle class neighborhoods. Areal decentralization of urban government would mean a substantial change in how functions were performed. The line of authority from the city-wide general manager (or mayor) to the general manager of a geographic entity less than the whole city would be strong, as would the line between functional personnel within the small area to the area manager, but functional personnel would relate less strongly to the functional staff which reports directly to the mayor.

There will also be potent reasons for relating the area manager to his constituency as well as to the central city government, since it has been clear that a more direct personal contact between citizen and official will be critical in offsetting the malaise of modern city government. While areal organization tends to add to the complexity of the urban system, the possibilities in areal decentralization are certainly worth some exploration.

Criteria for the Structure of Urban Systems

Area decentralization of decision-making authority must involve forms of interaction and administrative arrangement between areal government and central government which are not clear. Identifying the mix might itself legitimately be considered a system problem. Part of the system would be the central government, part of it areal government. Account might be taken of the different functions of parts of the city, including some in which the principal activities are associated with place of residence, while others focus on industrial, recreational or other specialized functions. These concepts can form the basis for a system concept of a decentralized metropolitan area government. Such a concept — and the system model which it implies — including both geographic and functional decentralization, include real challenges. The possible variations in organizational structure are great, not merely as presented in the formality of the organization chart, but with respect to decision rules and constraints on the decisions. Budgetary constraints — perhaps distinct for operating and investment budgets — and procedural constraints are quite different things. To conceptualize a viable system concept in these terms will require a spectrum of alternatives. There are few tools in systems analysis for deriving this spectrum; what analysis can do is to evaluate whatever alternatives analysts — or others — have the wit to conceive.

Organizational arrangements that combine administrative autonomy for geographically decentralized units with the efficiencies of large scale have been shown to be feasible many times. It should be possible for subject-matter knowledge of urban government to make a selection of organizational forms, functions and activities that can be decentralized by area under suitable constraints.

The administrative structure of General Motors is illustrative of the process in industry. Divisions making bodies, engines, and electrical equipment have substantial autonomy; by supplying each of the automotive divisions, they achieve economies which would not be available within the automotive divisions. However, the terms under which these component divisions supply the automotive divisions are negotiated between them and most divisions may, if satisfactory terms cannot be reached, seek customers elsewhere, as the automotive divisions can seek outside suppliers.

Arrangements might be used in city government in which inter-unit ground rules, though differing in form, produced the results for government which GM obtained for itself. A critical survey might be undertaken of specific functions for which intergovernmental contracting for services would be a useful part of a system concept. Arrangements might be developed by combined purchasing, or by joint sponsorship of research and development into urban problems.

Indeed, independent governments have shown themselves to be cognizant of the advantages that might be obtained. A recent example was the banding together of a number of California school administrations to create an incentive for the building industry to research new materials and construction concepts.[13]

The preceding sections have suggested that two polarizations for system structures are possible. One follows functional decentralization, organized by program packages, with hierarchies of administrative control within each function. The other is geographic decentralization, in which police, welfare, sanitation, and other functions would report to an area general manager, who in turn reported to a city-wide general manager. Because operationally viable system concepts must follow organizational lines, the appropriate system models for these alternative concepts would differ substantially.

That these alternatives should correspond to real differences in system performance would seem to flow from the inevitability of suboptimization by the managers of subsystems. If, in fact, subsystem objective functions were entirely consistent with the objective function for the city as a whole, structure might be unimportant. But inconsistent suboptimization is an inevitable fact of life, arising from the complexity of the city as a system, the impossibility of understanding the whole city, the impenetrability of the "real" objective functions and the political nature of government. The perfect object structure would, for example, reflect fully the different value structures held by persons with different occupational, ethnic, and other characteristics.

Government must respond according to certain gross characteristics of groups, and in ways which are consistent with our concepts of equality and democratic procedures. The result is inevitably some degree of suboptimization. The practical objective is an organizational and system concept which results in the least amount of suboptimization — and it would appear that the choice of functional versus geographic decentralization rests on this point.

If there were no significant differences in the characteristics of population in various parts of a city, the case would be relatively weak for geographic decentralization. On the other hand, where some areas of a city are ghettos, and others are middle class or upper class neighborhoods, or differ in ethnic composition, there may well be distinct possibilities that with appropriately drawn boundaries, geographic decentralization would result in a lessened degree or suboptimization. It is reasonably clear that functional structure has served particularly to decrease the quality and relevance of government for poor neighborhoods. The breadth of nonresponsiveness is adequately documented.[14] Means must be found by which functional administrators can be more responsive to the objectives peculiar to a particular geographic area and particular groups. The challenge in functional reorganization, including PPBS, is to do this without losing sight of objectives for the city as a whole. It is entirely possible that the practical limits of responsiveness of functional organization to area differences will be inadequate for the problems of the modern city. Geographic decentralization may be a better alternative regardless of possible improvements in functional organization.

To carry conjecture forward systematically, Table 11 — 1 has been prepared. In a systems approach, an objective structure is a logical basis for allocating responsibilities between area-based units of government and functionally based ones. The left hand column structures what might be considered the objectives of urban life, whether or not the direct responsibility of government. This listing is loosely derived from several objective structures such as that of the Eisenhower Commission on National Goals, and the PPBS program package structure developed by Harry P. Hatry.[15]

Across the top of the table are listed characteristics of activities judged to bear on how the effectiveness of urban government, with respect to the objective on the left, is affected by areal or functional decentralization. These were derived from the work of Professor Zenon S. Zannetos.[16]

At the intersections, personal judgments as to the relative advantages of areal decentralization versus functional decentralization have been entered. The table is principally illustrative; the objective structure would need to be elaborated, as would the characteristics.

In the right hand column a score for each objective area equal to the number of pluses less the number of minuses, indicates whether or not the case for decentralization by area is strong; a high negative score indicates that geographically centralized, albeit functionally decentralized, government seems most favorable to attainment of the objective. Intermediate scores suggest objectives for which responsibility should be split between area and central units of government, or performed by areal government, subject to constraints, imposed by a central administrative authority.

The large number of low positive and negative scores suggests that there are few functions of government that should be entirely centralized or decentralized by area. The picture that emerges is one in which small area government would be the primary administrator of public order functions, health services, programs directed at esthetic quality, control of land use, juvenile education, and that local government can best encourage direct social participation and moral/ethical performance. Its activities in these areas would be conditioned moderately by constraints or control by central government. It would share responsibility more equally with central government in encouragement of health-enhancing behavior by private persons (e.g., health education and cigarette smoking), pollution control, social equality, cultural enrichment, adult vocational education, and transportation. Governmental units centralized by function would be the principal units seeking objectives in economic performance, mass media communication, natural resources, utilization of capital, and technology.

An additional requirement for a system concept is unity and relatedness in the elements which comprise the system and subsystem. While there are indeed interactions between the objectives and related activities suggested for area government, too little is known about these at the present time. It is not merely academic that the responsibility of an areal administrator correspond to a well-conceived subsystem, since the cohesiveness of his task depends on it. The issue is perhaps most critical for operating systems management, but the integration of capital budgeting with operating systems is also part of the problem of a viable system concept.

If a system model for the city includes small area administrative units as subsystems, it must also include city-wide system units which relate to the area subsystems. The interrelationships will depend in the first instance on how area boundaries are drawn, and second, on the scope of functions assigned to small area administrators. Some services might be provided by centralized department, in effect contracting to provide the type of service desired, as determined by small area managers. Other activities might retain a functional status with strengthened line authority under a city manager, perhaps consolidated into program packages. Such arrangements might be chosen for any of a number of reasons, perhaps because they were only weakly related to other functions

Table 11-1

Implications of Decentralization by
Area or Function, Taken as
Alternatives, On Ability of Urban
Government to Perform According
to Certain Objectives

(+) means area decentralization
favorable

(−) means functional decentralization
favorable

(0) means neutral

ACTIVITY CHARACTERISTICS

OBJECTIVE CATEGORY	Neighborhoods have distinctive objective structures	Attainment enhanced by city-wide coordination	Attainment enhanced by neighborhood coordination	Significant efficiencies in large-scale operation	Information in hands of officials
Public Order					
Protection of Property − Theft	+	−	+	0	+
Protection of Property − Fire	0	0	0	0	+
Protection of Persons	−	−	+	+	+
Maintenance of Social Discipline	+	0	+	+	+
Health					
Health-Enhancing Behavior By Private Persons	−	0	+	−	+
Health Services − Preventive	−	0	0	0	+
Health Services − Curative	−	0	0	−	+

ACTIVITY CHARACTERISTICS

Instability or uncertainty in needed activity	Motivation of citizens and officials	Reaction time requirements	Relevant Characteristics of activities	Number of pluses less number of minuses
+	+	+	+	6
+	+	+	+	5
+	+	+	+	5
+	+	+	+	8
−	+	−	−	−2
+	+	+	+	4
+	+	+	+	3

Table 11-1 (Continued)

ACTIVITY CHARACTERISTICS

OBJECTIVE CATEGORY	Neighborhoods have distinctive objective structures	Attainment enhanced by city-wide coordination	Attainment enhanced by neigh-borhood coordination	Significant efficiencies in large-scale operation	Information in hands of officials
Environmental Quality					
Esthetic Quality	+	+	+	+	+
Pollution Abatement	−	−	+	−	+
Efficient Resource Use					
Land Use	+	0	+	−	+
Labor (Productivity)	+	0	−	−	−
Capital	+	−	−	−	−
Technology	+	−	−	−	−
Quality of Life					
Moral/Ethical Performance	+	+	+	+	+
Social Participation	+	+	+	+	+
Standard of Living	−	−	−	−	+
Leisure Time Performance	+	+	+	+	+
Equality of Persons — Social	−	0	−	0	+
Equality of Persons — Political	−	−	−	−	+
Equality of Persons — Economic	−	−	−	−	+
Cultural Enrichment	+	−	+	−	+

ACTIVITY CHARACTERISTICS

Instability or uncertainty in needed activity	Motivation of citizens and officials	Reaction time requirements	Relevant characteristics of activities	Number of pluses less number of minuses
0	+	+	+	8
+	+	+	−	1
0	−	+	+	3
0	−	−	−	−5
0	−	−	−	−6
0	−	−	−	−6
0	+	−	+	6
+	+	+	+	9
0	0	0	−	−4
+	+	0	+	8
+	−	0	0	−1
+	−	0	−	−4
0	−	0	−	−5
0	0	0	+	2

Table 11-1 (Continued)

ACTIVITY CHARACTERISTICS

OBJECTIVE CATEGORY	Neighborhoods have distinctive objective structures	Attainment enhanced by city-wide coordination	Attainment enhanced by neighborhood coordination	Significant efficiencies in large-scale operation	Information in hands of officials
Resource Development					
Education — Juvenile	+	+	+	0	0
Education — Vocational (Adult)	+	0	—	—	+
Natural Resources	—	—	—	—	—
Physical Capital — Public	+	0	+	—	0
Physical Capital — Private	+	—	—	—	—
Economic Life					
Conditions of Employment	—	—	—	—	+
Income Maintenance	—	—	—	—	0
Economic Security	—	—	—	—	+
Social Economic Infrastructure					
Transportation — Scheduled	—	—	0	—	—
Transportation — Nonscheduled	—	—	—	—	+
Communication — One Way (Mass Media)	—	—	—	—	—
Communication — Two Way (Private)	—	—	0	—	0
Number of pluses less number of minuses	−2	−13	−2	−16	15

ACTIVITY CHARACTERISTICS

Instability or uncertainty in needed activity	Motivation of citizens and officials	Reaction time requirements	Relevant Characteristics of activities	Number of pluses less number of minuses
0	0	0	+	4
+	0	0	+	2
−	−	+	−	−7
+	+	+	−	3
+	0	0	−	−3
0	−	0	0	−4
−	−	0	−	−7
−	−	0	−	−6
+	0	+	+	−1
+	0	+	+	0
−	−	−	−	−9
+	0	−	−	−4
12	1	7	1	

assigned to small area managers. Other functions could only be effectively managed on a city-wide basis, or constitutional or legal difficulties might prevent a consolidation, and so on.

City-wide officials would provide leadership, define city-wide programs, deal with interarea and multi-area problems. An advisory and coordinative staff, organized by functions, would promulgate standards and criteria for performance within small area units, and perform reviews. This staff would be entirely advisory to area and city-wide officials, without line authority. One important group of standards would be in personnel administration, as it would remain essential to provide attractive civil service career opportunities within a city-wide bureaucracy, and to deal with employee organizations on a city-wide basis.

Means would be needed to control tendencies of area governments to suboptimize vis-à-vis other areas or the city as a whole, or to fail to capitalize on economics of scale. The use of constraints on the course of action which area governments might take was a key element in the recent proposal for decentralizing the New York schools.[17] As the areas would have no independent taxing power, a powerful control by the central government would exist through its control over funds.

An example of a system of constraints upon autonomous units is operative in the British policy system. As reported by Sir Harold Scott, there are 155 different police forces in England, each a separate independent body administered by its own local standing committee of borough councilors and justices of the peace.[11] The Home Secretary is responsible for seeing that the police forces are efficient, which he does by regulations governing pay and conditions of service, and through an inspectorate. The training of recruits, for instance, is on a common plan in schools maintained by the Home Office.

Perspective and Conclusions

Of course the functions of urban governments are not generally organized by objective structure. Further, there are significant interactions between objectives as, for example, personal liberty and public order. Objectives such as scheduled transportation, are often advanced by private firms, and others, such as moral/ethical performance, are advanced by private and public means – churches, schools, the family and law enforcement agencies. The limitations of coordination that result from adherence to a private enterprise system are very real, and it is clearly necessary to conceive of systems that are consistent with a division of objective seeking behavior between government and private enterprise.

Local areas are not likely to be permitted to pursue local objectives entirely as seen in their own light, even when immediate external effects are minimal. Educational objectives are affected markedly by income, ethnicity, and parents' occupations. Even if all areas desire quality schools, parents' concepts of quality differ. The aspirations of parents in some ethnic districts may be low, and it is not in the interests of society that such parents be unchallenged.

Given the present state of data, urban system models will be severely limited for many years. Many models such as the one discussed above are abstract concept and it is difficult to ascertain their structural validity. How soon these limitations will be overcome depends on the success of efforts to identify and develop meaningful data. Data can be one of the more important long-term results of the model city program, if concerted, well-designed methods for measurement are incorporated into the programs.

The complexity of model building may also be an impediment to application of systems analysis to urban problems; there has not yet been sufficient experience with urban models to appreciate fully the potential difficulties. Systems management concepts are potentially useful in urban affairs. Change is definitely needed in urban government, it is expensive to obtain, and the success of producing change and the costs of producing it are dependent on adequately powerful and well-conceived managerial plans, and on relevance to some unit of government.

The systems approach was adopted by the military largely under the crisis pressure of the missile race. Difficulties in achieving efficient performance arose partly from the size and complexity of missile efforts that were beyond the scope of a preexisting functionally structured organization. It is not clear that the urban crisis has yet generated pressure for organizational reform comparable in degree to the missile race, but the evidence that we are at least on the way to that point is persuasive.

Experiences with poorly conceived federal decentralization are not a case against benefits in all such decentralization. The fractionated governments typical of metropolitan areas are not valid examples of the Simon-Drucker concept. These authors both stress the critical role of the chief executive in a federal system, a function which no one is empowered to perform (unless the state governer) in a typical metropolitan area, and must be performed effectively in any federally decentralized structure of urban government.

Proposals such as the neighborhood service center idea or the neighborhood corporation have placed considerable emphasis on mechanism by which the area government might be made responsive to residents. But the responsiveness under current proposals is likely to be limited by the continued status of service sources in a preexisting functional hierarchy controlling and performing that service, and with city-wide interests and responsibilities.

The complexity of the objective function in urban government has often been cited as a basic reason as to why the techniques of defense-oriented systems analysis are inapplicable to the city. While defense objective functions are by no means as simple as many critics have assumed, the objection is not without merit. It is not so much that objectives of the citizen are complex, but that there are many citizens with different patterns of objectives. No one has yet put a list of possible long-range objectives for city government on the ballot and asked voters to rank them.

Discussion

Question: For better or for worse we are talking about more citizen involvement. One of the big problems with the administrative structure is that we would be eroding the political process. How do you work this back into your systems approach? We've talked about functioning — how about processes?

Black: The systems approach is the part of the problem I was particularly interested in, but your point is well taken. This is a question, is it not, of power and human relations? There is a positive contribution in citizen involvement to the effectiveness of government. It is obtained from a sense of participation, which can be obtained more effectively by a unit of government which is more accessible to people in their communities. A panel operating out of Department of Health, Education and Welfare has been looking into the general question of social indicators. One member whom I know has been looking for a social indicator of Effective Participation. Part of his task is, first of all, to define what is meant by effective participation, then to figure out how to measure it. I suspect that what they will propose is the sort of thing which would be enhanced by a small area of government. If you increased the participation of the people in an area and could measure it by a social indicator, then it is pretty clear that the result could be incorporated into a formal systems analysis, as there would be a functional relationship between effective participation and some characteristics of government.

Question: My concern again would be creating the basis for the people in that neighborhood to really decide what they want. How would they be able to compete with another neighborhood for their share of the city's taxes. If the administrative structure divides the pie, it isn't going to be divided very rationally in terms of how the people will be served. If it is reasonable to break the thing down into small units administratively, how can you insure legitimacy and support for the local manager?

Black: This is a very difficult matter, but I believe that it can be done. Alternative approaches are possible. One structure might be a simple city manager who wouldn't appoint neighborhood managers out of hand, but with the advice of elected neighborhood groups. The kind of cohesion needed in a metropolitan area might require the coordinated strength that comes from neighborhood managers being picked in this way. Another alternative might be independently elected district councils which would pick a neighborhood manager who would automatically be in a strong, independent position, vis-a-vis the city manager, but more responsive to the neighborhood. This is comparable to what now exists in many metropolitan areas. The fact that locally elected people derive their authority directly from the elected council gives them a tremendous amount of independence. Too much may be inconsistent with the kind of coordination which you need in order to make work the concept I am talking about. But the autonomy of locally elected persons can be circumscribed in a number of ways.

Question: It seems we have two big options — to maintain present structure or to change it. If we change it we should strive in the direction of decentralization while at least maintaining some city-wide budgets. Don't some of these functions have to be broadened beyond the city to cover the whole metropolitan area? When doing this you automatically face political questions because of existing political units which must be dealt with. Do you think your approach could be used on functions that went beyond the city? Or will metropolitan governments be able to provide region-wide services incrementally, justifying each one as they evolve?

Black: I see no real difficulties with the evolutionary structure, although there are several arguments against it. One is the political point that through evolution you would gradually dissipate the pressure for a really substantial change. In the process of making gradual adjustments you may even block the possibility of further change. If you build a two-lane road where you really need a four-lane road you make it a good deal more expensive ultimately to get a four-lane road, and this is a question of strategy.

Question: It seems to me in terms of delivery of services that decentralization is hard to support in those terms. The crisis of cities isn't that cities are doing poorly in pumping water into the houses or those kinds of services — the crisis is that the people feel powerless and don't command control of their own destiny. In these terms, I think that decentralization offers a way of letting an individual get involved with a manageable area he can understand and actually try to control his own destiny. So I think that political aspects of decentralization are really the important ones that have to be figured out.

Black: If government remains no more effective than it is at present, will people be happier if they feel involved? Supposing that a government was really inadequate, and the people who were affected by the inadequacies recognized that they were responsible because they participated. I question whether or not people would be satisfied with inadequate government merely because they had participated in the process. Dissatisfaction with present government exists to a large extent because it is not doing the job very well, and that a change in the structure which increases participation without also improving the quality of government isn't really going to fill the bill.

Question: Yes, but I believe that decentralization by getting citizens to participate will improve the quality of the results. Then it is a means to an end. I think that there are a lot of people who talk as if participation is an end in itself. While there are, in fact, positive social benefits in the process of participation, I must confess that personally I look upon it principally as being a means to an end.

Black: I don't see participation as an end in itself but participation, with meaningful results.

Question: Then evaluating it as a means, you would be willing to look at a number of alternative means to participation? And go on to judge one objectively against the other and put them in context. But I think I would go so far as to say that participation is to some extent an end in itself in our society. As long as it produces results it is a means. It is just a facade if you participate and have no power. The revolt that it going on today — whether it is on the campus or in the inner-city or in the suburbs or in Vietnam — comes about because people want to have some say about their immediate environment. It is a world-wide revolution that goes from East Europe to Berkeley.

Black: There are also episodes in history where people revolted against government that was doing very well. People don't necessarily like very efficient government if it is not their government, and directed at what they want from government. The British Empire was extremely efficient, but it wasn't helping the people of India.

Question: I wonder what it would do to your particular concept if instead of complete functional decentralization you tried a modified Lakewood plan, where the decentralized head is less a manager than a coordinator? He would work primarily with a budget in renting services, or buying certain levels of service from a central agency. Let's say he would rent carry-back trash collection and a swimming pool because the residents of the area want that as opposed to something else. Does this change your concept or is this also the kind of thing you have been talking about?

Black: Yes, though I didn't specifically refer to Lakewood. I do not propose complete functional decentralization. Some things can be highly decentralized, but there are some other things which cannot be. And there are some things which can only be decentralized under certain conditions. The economies of scale can be obtained, and desired characteristics of services retained by the areas under the kind of trucking arrangement for trash collection which is typified by the Lakewood plan.

Question: This gets into the political phase of it, but I wonder how you handle an issue where the mores of the suburbia are in large part different from the community at large? Let's say they demand legal policy rackets, or horse racing, or whatever it may be. Would this local area have that kind of autonomy to allow this activity? There seem to be differences of opinion as to basic mores of the suburbs and the ghettos which probably rest in their respective socio-economic roots. Perhaps a better example is district A establishing bars and taverns along its border where they really serve the residents of adjoining district B. A particular district may decide that it wants to be the vice capital of the city for fun and profit.

Black: I will go back to talking like an economist and use the well-worn word *externalities.* It would depend upon the extent to which the decisions made within a particular area did in fact affect the welfare of another area. In this particular example you would have to put the question in these terms — does the existence of the vice center in Area A substantially affect the well-being of Area B? If your conclusion is that it does, then the central administration needs to impose some constraint.

Question: One of the major things we are getting into today is that much of our services lie within a comprehensive framework. Family services, for example, relate here and there but do not have any common ties, with the result that we often undo with one program what we have done with another. Does this mean, to refer back to the report on schools in New York, that we ought to throw out all our present governmental services? Then the new structure could uniformly affect city government, county government, and the county as a total service package, abolishing these various horizontal tiers too? First you would have to abolish absolutely the whole comprehensive set of services that we really haven't been able to come to grips with.

Black: Many urban services interact strongly with each other. For example, welfare, sanitation, public safety, education, and health functions are increasingly being brought together for this reason. There are certain obvious things that we generally can agree upon should be brought together. Let's explore the viable limits of such combinations. Consider one at a time the things that might be added to core packages. If someone is on welfare it makes a lot of sense to think about some kind of coordination between the employment service function and the welfare function. Then consider transportation facilities. In Watts and a few other places it turns out that the unavailability of public transportation had a great deal to do with people being on relief and not having jobs. So there is a need for coordination there. An employment service might know where the jobs were that the people in a particular district might be able to fill and they might in coordination with the transportation system serve these people and make the jobs more accessible. Eventually you might come to consider other functions such as fire protection where there did not seem to be much interaction with the strongly related group of functions.

Question: I think that is where I probably part company with you. I take the position that if I can write a program at City Hall then I don't need a thousand employees to get the program moving. If I can basically have control of the information system, design and write the program, I will then turn it over to the delivery people. The program will run the way I programmed it. So the program working with citizen organizations becomes the key here. Also working with a limited number of staff people. You can then decentralize on a very modest basis — you don't have to take 500 or 1000 people out of that 50,000 member community — you can do with three people. Citizen organizations can do the job but an information system has to be developed so the people will get the kind of inputs of information so that they can begin to feed a program back to the key decision makers. That to me makes more sense than the kind of thing that you are suggesting. You would have to pick and choose, while I am saying you don't have to pick and choose but rather throw it all in the pot. If I am going to be the area administrator give me the opportunity to look at everything, not just the functions you want to let me look at. We are going to look at the whole spectrum but I want to be able to pick and choose and to write my own program. I don't want to send it back up there. Granted, the central authority may have to consider my program with other area administrator programs, and then the real political decisions have to be made at the top level. In the meantime, I can be working on my community organization people and keep pushing at the area level. That makes more sense to me and it is going to be easier to work than trying to decentralize this part of the police department and not this part of the fire department. Frankly, I think you are going to run into some real problems in decentralizing several of the functions you talk about. I think the computers make it very difficult to decentralize police operations because the work load changes by the minute. You would have to deploy your people on the same basis and it can't be done of a fixed areal basis. And that may be true of some other functions.

Black: That is a very interesting point and I don't want to rebut it in an argumentative way but there are some things which occur to me. I should stress the need for working out details. In the small towns around the Washington area, we have a lot of independent volunteer fire departments. Their continued existence fascinates me, as they are a kind of archaic holdover, and yet they do the job. Small fire departments have had cooperative arrangements for a long time. Each town runs its own fire department. If they have a big fire in Falls Church, a call goes out to the Arlington or Fairfax Fire Departments. This ability to shift resources among areas is consistent with considerable local control, because Falls Church still decides how many firemen it will have, what kind of fire trucks, when it will buy new equipment, and where in Falls Church to locate any new stations. Even so, these various cities have been able to work out administrative arrangements by which they can support each other. Perhaps something of this sort could be done with the police function although we haven't had as much experience with it.

Question: I think it is worth noting that the model cities programs did not develop at least up to this point on this theory.

Black: It will be interesting to see how the interactions between model cities areas and the parts outside the model cities area are worked out. A recent study proposal for a model city neighborhood specifically wanted the study team to look into this question.

Question: In the police case there are some real difficulties not only because of communications but also in deploying mobile tactical squads. They must work across jurisdictional boundaries. In the Kansas City metro squad which is deployed in cases of major crime you've got five counties in two states cooperating. They seem to have found some way to do it. If, however, we are talking about the Lakewood plan, really the guy out in the area has to work with a budget and he wants a certain level of services. What does he do in terms of traffic control? I happened to live in an area which has one of the main highways through it, now do I put my budget which I want to use for patrol work in my neighborhood into controlling traffic for you guys who live in the suburbs? No, that is their problem and I am going to protect my neighborhood. So there you come back to needing a city-wide perspective. Obviously you can't have each of these areas running its own police training academy, we need that perhaps above the city level. The Lakewood manager has options since he can contract with the county of Los Angeles for service, or he can set up his own city department to perform particular services. We can run cost comparisons since he has got twenty-eight other cities out there contracting for this service. It is a kind of self-correcting system but you can't contract police services in the same way though.

Black: I think your highway example, specifically the super highway through the neighborhood, presents a genuine dilemma. It is clear that many super highways do not serve the people of the neighborhood in which they are located. There are places even now where the super highways are patrolled by the state police rather than the city police. Hasn't it been true for decades that when a highway runs through the middle of some small town that the state police patrol it and the city police concentrate their efforts elsewhere?

Question: Any good systems analysis has to take into account the realities of the situation. Some of the bones of contention that have been mentioned here such as too many jurisdictions or lack of responsiveness to the residents are realities that any good systems analyst must take into account. So it doesn't become a matter of programming alternatives. For example, it seems to me that in the case of too many jurisdictions, there has been a presupposition that you have to change the structure in order to do anything. This strikes me as simply one alternative out of many in any good systems approach. As far as the neighborhood commitment is concerned this is a problem, but can you not program it recognizing it as a problem? Explore various alternatives. For example, I don't think that we can accept as gospel truth that residents in the neighborhood want to control local government that much. The ones we hear from want to, but you cannot really divorce this from the quality of service and this depends upon how you define service. It is said that one of the problems of residents in the ghetto that seems to have led to a lot of the push for neighborhood centers is the notion that services are not being delivered to them. The ghetto resident cannot easily find his way to the Jackson County Welfare Office. Moving that office down into the ghetto may not make a bit of difference if the services continue to be provided the way they are now, that is, where the individual has to publicly confess that he is poor and has to go through all these tests. If the service was reoriented to treat this individual with dignity the results might change rapidly. It's a question of responsiveness to programming of the service. Good systems analysis sees these particular things as realities and tries to program around them.

Black: That statement points out one of the critical phases in a systems approach. It is important that a systems analyst be a creative person with the ability to develop a number of concepts which can then be analyzed. While the mechanics of systems analysis are very useful in making comparisons between concepts, and evaluating one against the other, the analytical methods are not techniques for coming up with new and original concepts. Until you have those concepts there is nothing to analyze. The people who understand urban government must participate in coming up with creative concepts of alternative structures. Once this has been done well, the systems analyst, with his analytical machinery, is in a position to go to work.

12 Intergovernmental Management of Urban Problems

Thomas P. Murphy

The foregoing presentations, while different in perspective and content, have a unifying theme. They call for application of the new technologies to the problems of urban America within the broad context of the institutional, administrative, and political deficiencies which characterize our present governmental system. This theme assumes that adaptations must be made region by region and so differs markedly from the traditional approach of cataloging specific physical and social problems along rigid functional lines on the assumption that there are clear layers of responsibility by governmental level.

The typical urban government faces the following problems: it lacks a broad enough jurisdiction to deal with its many physical problems; it lacks the resources to make a meaningful assault on its social problems; it is unable to apply a long-term perspective because of the urgency of the immediate needs; and, in many cases, it is constrained by outmoded organizational forms or constitutional limitations on its powers, placing the governmental unit in the position of attempting to operate with one arm tied behind its back.

Senator Muskie has provided an overview of the first problem, namely, the difficulty of bringing about effective intergovernmental cooperation as a result of outmoded governmental structures at the town, city, county and state levels. Professor Grant has focused attention upon one particular kind of structural reorganization which has been tried in several different contexts — that is, a form of metropolitan-wide government. The difficulties of achieving long-term planning in an environment disrupted by recurrent daily crises was viewed from the systems analysis standpoint by Dr. Black from a technological perspective and by Dr. Lakshmanan from the standpoint of social applications of the new technology.

Five major aspects of the problem faced by urban governments were discussed. Intergovernmental relations or coordination problems, planning problems, internal structural problems, financial problems, and managerial problems have all been considered in their theoretical and practical respects. If there has been one overriding message from the papers, it is that general capability levels and general models are needed to enable each region and area to develop its own particular programs to meet its own unique set of needs. In providing the conceptual framework for urban management, Professor Grundstein said, "Every problem exists only in relation to a bundle of specific decision-makers."[1] Senator Muskie covered some of the same ground when he said:

I think it would be a mistake to try to create a blueprint for metropolitan government that we try to apply to every metropolitan area in the country . . . . In some cases it may result in a formal structure of metropolitan government. In other areas it may not go beyond the level of interlocal planning. The test is whether it works.[2]

The purpose of this paper is to focus upon the Kansas City metropolitan area as an example and consider how the new technologies and new approaches either are, or may yet be, received within a specific governmental context. To do this, we will first isolate the unique characteristics of the seven-county Kansas City area setting it apart from other areas and then, in some measure, define the area's particular needs.

Government in the Kansas City Metropolis

Metropolitan Kansas City contains seven counties, over one hundred independent municipalities, and an aggregate population of just under one and one-half million people. Originally, settlements grew on both banks of the Missouri and Kansas rivers which became part of the state line, creating a Kansas City in each of two states — one in Missouri and the other in Kansas. Kansas City, Missouri, with a population of approximately 600,000 in 1969, is the core city and the dominant municipal unit. Kansas City, Kansas, has a population of 180,000 with its own inner-city urban area, large minority population, and all of the problems of urban America.

In the post World War II years, the population has expanded outward to the counties. Johnson County, Kansas, has become the most preferred site for the white, upper and middle class "bedroom" communities which typically grow up in any metropolitan area. It serves as a suburban county for Kansas City, Kansas, as well as for Kansas City, Missouri. Wyandotte County, Kansas, and four Missouri counties — Jackson, Clay, Platte, and Cass — have been similarly affected in varying degrees.

Perhaps the most unusual feature reflected in the map of Greater Kansas City is that Kansas City, Missouri, is located in parts of three counties. This is a relatively recent development traceable to 1940 when Kansas City started its annexations north of the Missouri River. A major annexation effort resulted in inclusion of parts of Clay and Platte counties within Kansas City, which now has a total land area of 316 square miles, fourth largest in the nation behind Jacksonville-Duval, Los Angeles, and Oklahoma City. The annexation program carried out by Kansas City also resulted in the enclave phenomenon. That is,

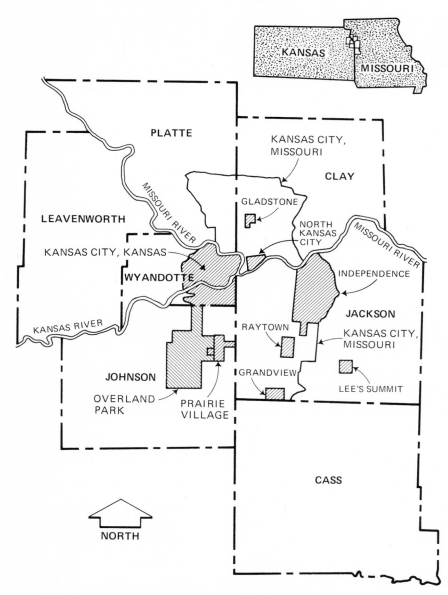

SEVEN COUNTY METROPOLITAN PLANNING REGION

(Source: Kansas City Metropolitan Planning Commission, Kansas City Region.)

there are several Missouri cities surrounded on three or all sides by Kansas City which are not part of Kansas City. These include the cities of North Kansas City and Gladstone in Clay County and the cities of Raytown and Grandview in Jackson County. The annexation movement has left bad feelings in these areas. For example, the problem of extending sewers to the fringe areas of Kansas City has been insurmountable. As a consequence, Kansas Citians in the different counties have received different levels of municipal service, while paying the same municipal tax rates.

Fifty-two per cent of the land area and eighty-four per cent of Kansas City's population is located in Jackson County, Missouri. Looked at in relation to Jackson County alone, Kansas City comprises sixty per cent of the county population. Independence, Missouri, has a population of 113,000, about fifteen per cent of the county total. Lee's Summit, Raytown, and Independence have blocked eastward expansion of Kansas City by their own annexations. In fact, Lee's Summit with a 1968 population of only 16,000 has the second largest land area in the state, larger than that of St. Louis, whose population is fifty times larger.

The only other city in the seven county area with a population over 50,000 is Overland Park in Johnson County, Kansas. Fifteen smaller cities dot the northeast corner of Johnson County, the area favored by most of those who work in the two Kansas Cities. Kansas City, Kansas, has an interesting relationship to Wyandotte County in which it is located. With only forty per cent of the land area of the county, Kansas City has ninety per cent of its population. There are only two other cities in the county — the largest having 3600 residents.

Some key socioeconomic factors relating to the seven counties are contained in Table: 12-1

Superimposed upon the normal problems of intergovernmental coordination and intercity rivalries and jealousies, is the fact that two different states are involved in any major attempts at cooperation in the Kansas City metropolitan area. At the state level, legislation permitting local action for either Kansas City has been most difficult to obtain. Obtaining parallel legislation in the same legislative session has been almost impossible.

Historically, Kansas has been a Republican State and Missouri, Democratic. The difference in parties, philosophy and control in the two states may have been a larger factor than is generally appreciated in making it difficult to obtain coordination in metropolitan Kansas City. In terms of internal state politics, Kansas City, Missouri, has taken a back set in influence to the St. Louis area, while Kansas City, Kansas, must defer to Wichita, which is the largest and most politically powerful area in Kansas. This means that the Kansas City region has often received less than its proportionate share of state aid — an increasingly important factor in local government financing.

Although this metropolitan area has only three-quarters of one per cent of the national population, four per cent of the United States Senate should be

Table 12-1

Comparative Socioeconomic Data[3]

County	State	Per Capita Income	Non-White Population
Cass	Missouri	$1997	2%
Clay	Missouri	2779	1%
Jackson	Missouri	2606	16%
Platte	Missouri	2455	1%
Johnson	Kansas	3736	1%
Wyandotte	Kansas	2265	15%
Leavenworth	Kansas	1907	10%

responsive to its needs. However, the potential of this political leverage has generally been unrealized because of the failure of the states and of the region to develop coordinated plans and programs. With these background considerations in mind, let us proceed now to look at some of the specific problem areas, and the emerging new approaches which might hold promise for more successful intergovernmental coordination in metropolitan Kansas City.

Intergovernmental Coordination of Services

In his systems approach to the decentralization of urban government, Professor Guy Black proposed criteria which could be used in attempting to define which services might be best administered on a decentralized basis. He concluded that decentralization of services would likely contribute to improved services, decreased delivery cost, or both in some cases; but that these beneficial effects would be unlikely to occur with respect to some other governmental services. A study of several key functional areas in the Kansas City region reflects that it is these latter functions which are most likely to be the subject of intergovernmental contacts and crises. Black stated:

Governmental units centralized by function would be the principal units seeking objectives in economic performance, mass media communication, natural resources, utilization of capital, and technology.[4]

Most summaries of urban services include some functions which are exclusively or partially privately administered as well as those administered by government. For example, at most local levels the question of economic development tends to be a problem for the local economic power structure and the chamber of commerce unless it is intrinsically related to some governmental problem or crisis such as unemployment or welfare. In some instances the local government cooperates with local industry to draw upon federal or state programs for depressed areas. In the absence of these conditions, the governmental actions which tend to encourage or discourage economic growth — such as zoning plans, urban renewal, and extension of sewers and roads — are triggered at the initiative of private entrepreneurs, builders, and developers who make investments, request variances, and ultimately create the need for governmental services in newly developed areas.

On the other hand, Black's summary also includes natural resources and technology which together constitute much of the physical ecology of the total metropolitan area and so are less related to a need for governmental decentralization. In fact, although his classification of implications did not specifically attempt to set quantitative criteria, Black suggests that these functions may require an areal jurisdiction transcending the boundaries of any particular city or county government.[5]

The theses of this paper are that first, functions requiring areal jurisdiction are more likely to be found in metropolitan areas where there are a multiplicity of governments and second, in interstate metropolitan areas it is more difficult to properly organize appropriate adaptive institutions to deal with such matters. Additionally, it will be suggested that these efforts are not limited to aspects of governmental servicing which relate primarily to the physical environment, but rather include also questions related directly to the social environment. Therefore, consideration will be given not only to air pollution, water pollution, planning, and transportation but also to police services, fire protection, and miscellaneous social services.

Air Pollution

Beyond the technological problems, the control of air pollution involves finding a governmental jurisdiction broad enough in scope to issue and enforce appropriate regulations. As is obvious from the description of the multiplicity of governments in the Kansas City area, no such single governmental entity exists. Various experts estimate that air pollution costs the nation $65 per capita annually in terms of lost work capacity and destruction to property. However, the harmful effects of air pollution are not traumatic and sudden, but rather the result of an accretion process over time. For this reason, it has tended to pale in comparison with more pressing urban problems. As may be deduced from

Professor Grant's paper, governments in general, and metropolitan areas composed of multiple governments in particular, are extremely unlikely to take any action involving structural changes in the absence of a universally obvious service crisis.

From an ecological standpoint, Kansas City's air pollution problems are less severe than those of other cities. The four major sources of air pollution are the internal combustion engine, industry, power production, and refuse disposal. Because of unique geographic and meterological factors, the motor car and other engines are not significant contributors to air pollution in the Kansas City area. It is not surprising therefore that until 1965 when Kansas City, Kansas, and Wyandotte County jointly entered into a contract with Midwest Research Institute for a study of air pollution, neither of the states and none of the counties or cities in the area had done anything tangible about the problem.

Nonetheless, the conclusions of the Midwest Research Institute study were:[6]

1. the industrial area had a monthly dust fall rate of 132 tons per square mile;
2. it had 125 micrograms of suspended particles per meter;
3. the wider urban area had a monthly dust fall rate of 50 tons per square mile; and,
4. 79 micrograms of suspended particles per meter; and
5. a 40% reduction in pollution was necessary to remove threats to public health.

The study was undertaken partly as a result of complaints to the Federal Aviation Agency by pilots flying into Municipal and Fairfax airports, located in Missouri and Kansas, respectively, at the confluence of the Missouri and Kansas rivers. Furthermore, a 1966 United States Public Health Service study concluded that within a three-mile area of the two airports twenty-one sources caused eighty-five per cent of the total estimated annual particulate emissions from all sources. These sources are generally distributed in the river valley area and some are so located as to have a specific and marked effect upon airport operations. "Permissible flight patterns at Fairfax Airport, for example, are such that each of three major sources of visibility-obstructing emissions will, at one time or another, be between the control tower and an aircraft following its flight pattern."[7]

Although the Kansas City problem clearly called for interstate action to obtain common standards and coordinated enforcement, to date efforts to obtain an interstate compact agreement have failed. Missouri passed legislation for the compact in June, 1967, but the final bill was so watered down that even if Kansas had followed suit, the results would have been negligible. For instance, the bill required proof of health damage from pollution before sanctions could be invoked; it also would have required public officials to obtain search warrants prior to entering plants suspected of causing pollution. These encumbrances to effective enforcement were cited by Kansas legislators as a primary reason for their failure to enact the legislation.[8]

The influence of industry upon the final form of the Missouri legislation was also considerable. In 1965 Missouri had established a state Air Pollution Control Commission under the Missouri Air Conservation Law.[9] This seven-man commission has limited authority to force compliance with its regulations, primarily through court proceedings. However, the act specifically exempts political subdivisions which have established their own pollution codes, if these codes meet the minimal standards of the state body. In effect, this meant that any code passed in Kansas City, Missouri, would not be subject to state approval.

A similar group, the Kansas Air Quality Conservation Committee, was established in 1967 but the legislature gave it no enforcement powers.[10] The result is that at the state level, both the standards and enforcement in the two states vary widely. Since the majority of the industrial pollutants in the area are located in Kansas, it is reasonable to expect that at least some Kansas legislators had more pragmatic reasons for withholding support for even this relatively innocuous bill. The position of local industry is that the admittedly high cost of anti-pollution measures, which in some cases entail substantial changes in industrial processes, would place them at a competitive disadvantage with similar industries in non-regulated areas.

By terms of the Federal Clean Air Act of 1963, a local, state, or regional area can receive matching federal funds on a one-to-one, two-to-one, or three-to-one basis, depending on the level of government and degree of compliance with federal standards. Since November, 1966, Kansas City, Missouri, has received federal funds on a two-to-one basis to assist in establishing a comprehensive pollution control office.[11] Although the local agency has thus been established with federal help, it was not until April, 1969, that Kansas City, Missouri, passed a pollution ordinance.[12] The recommendation of the city's health department for a reasonably stiff law was opposed by industry, acting through the chamber of commerce. The chamber proposed an alternative bill which would concentrate mainly upon restricting residential burning. This was a power struggle which demonstrated that local industry was not yet willing to face up to its responsibilities. However, the approved ordinance set maximum emission requirements on both industrial and residential burning in accordance with the State of Missouri Air Conservation Commission regulations. It should be recognized that it was state and federal pressures that ultimately forced the city's action. The city prohibited residential trash burning although it did not provide a city-wide trash collection program. This anomaly had its greatest effect in the inner-city areas and led to pressure for the establishment of a city trash collection service.

In contrast, Wyandotte County enacted emission regulations for Kansas City, Kansas, early in 1967. While generally acknowledged to have been ineffective when initiated, in 1968 more serious efforts to enforce the regulations led to improvement in the quality of the air. Thus, Missouri has tougher state laws than

Kansas but Kansas City, Kansas, is taking the lead in anti-pollution ordinances. Kansas City, Missouri — the primary victim of all the area pollution, including that emanating in Kansas — did not enact ordinances until there was substantial state and federal pressure.

Tentative cooperative steps have been taken between the Kansas City, Missouri and Kansas City, Kansas which give some hope that an interstate agency will eventually develop. The cities have established a common laboratory for evaluation of pollution data, with Kansas providing the equipment and Missouri providing the plant and personnel. If this beginning is to blossom into a regional pollution control mechanism, several steps seem to be indicated. Kansas City, Missouri, must resolve its own political problems and pass additional effective control ordinances; the State of Kansas must give its commission enforcement power; and the two states must come together on a formula for a mutually agreeable and effective interstate compact for the metropolitan area. Perhaps, the availability of additional federal funds, which could be increased from two-to-one up to three-to-one if an interstate agency is established will provide the necessary incentive.

In January, 1967, the director of the National Center for Air Pollution Control stated that, "although most of our severe pollution problems involve more than one state jurisdiction, there is not a single effective interstate program in the nation."[13] As described above, the Kansas City region is unfortunately no exception to this rule. The effects of inaction have not been sufficiently obvious to stimulate appropriate state and local intergovernmental coordination. The interstate question has clearly served to complicate solution of the matter still further.

Water Pollution

Water pollution, like air pollution, is a regional problem. The Kansas City area is trisected by the Kansas River which flows through Kansas City, Kansas; the Big Blue River which flows from the southeast part of Kansas into the Missouri at Kansas City; and the Missouri River, the major artery which flows from northwest of Kansas City but then turns east and bounds the northern edge of the city's central business district. The natural drainage of the entire area is into the Missouri River. Wastes from the industrial districts from the Kansas City in each state, the added dumping from the smaller communities in the surrounding area, plus material traceable to sources as distant as the stockyards at Omaha, Nebraska, have turned the mighty Missouri into a flowing sewage system. The situation is so bad that a responsible official has suggested seriously that the river be maintained as a polluted waterway serving as the main instrument for disposal of waste. Since removal and disposal of waste is presently the river's chief economic function, he argues that it would be cheaper to maintain this function and find alternate means of providing freight transportation and recreation for area citizens.[14]

Water pollution problems came to public attention in the 1950's, largely through efforts of the United States Government. As a result, both Missouri and Kansas have established Water Pollution Control Boards which meet minimal federal standards. The two boards have sufficient powers to enforce pollution regulations, and so the variance in state standards and enforcement noticed in air pollution is not present in water pollution. Although Missouri has met the minimum federal requirements of water quality and is receiving federal grant money for completed programs, there is a possibility that new legislation might cut off further federal aid. A revision of federal standards which is presently being debated would allow only those states financing secondary water treatment systems to be eligible for federal aid. Because Missouri has over eighty million dollars worth of priority programs to fund and cannot finance a secondary treatment program, if this revision is adopted, the state may no longer qualify for federal funding.

The main trunk sewers of Kansas City, Missouri, cross the Kansas line in a number of places, and the city has working agreements with adjacent jurisdictions in both states to tie into the lines on a fee basis. An injunction filed by Kansas City, Missouri, preventing additional home building in a large area of Raytown was upheld in 1967. As a result, a joint sewer plan was agreed upon. Raytown was thus enabled to sell bonds for the necessary sewer work and construction was allowed to continue. By April of 1970, Raytown will be connected with the city and there should be a substantial reduction of pollution in the Little Blue River, a major source of water for Kansas City. Enforcement questions at the local level become both political and emotional footballs since they involve the setting of standards, taxation, and land values. The small municipalities cannot in themselves take advantage of economies of scale, so when they act independently their costs tend to rise out of proportion to those of the largest cities. There is now a dual need in the metropolitan area for better planning facilities, and some mechanism, such as an area-wide agency, to enforce uniform standards.

The facilities problem is easily demonstrable. There is a mathematical relationship between the size of a sewage plant and its cost such that after a certain point, more sewage can be processed at less cost in a larger facility. That is, hypothetically, a $1,000,000 plant can process 1,000,000 tons of sewage, but by increasing the cost of the plant $500,000 to $1,500,000, 2,000,000 tons of sewage can be processed. In 1966 Kansas City, Kansas, and Kansas City, Missouri, were in the process of building separate new plants on the Big Blue River which crosses both states. Efforts were made to negotiate a joint-use agreement. A consulting engineering study, sponsored jointly by the two cities, confirmed the possibility of savings of approximately $2,000,000 in the cost of construction, maintenance and operation. Nevertheless, Kansas City, Kansas, refused to participate in the joint endeavor. Both cities now have their own separate plants located about one-half mile apart on opposite sides of the state line. Likewise, no single authority yet exists to enforce standards.[15]

Planning Regional Facilities

The 1961 Federal Housing Act provided for one-third federal matching funds on regional park projects which were approved by a regional planning commission. This led to the rapid establishment of the bi-state KA-MO-PAR group. Representatives from three counties met with delegates from fifteen towns and cities to establish the organization in November of 1964. The primary motivation was not to guarantee planning coordination but rather to establish a paper organization sufficient to satisfy criteria for interstate cooperation to insure that federal money would be forthcoming. The stated purposes of the group were to form a better means of communication, promote cooperation in the development of plans to assist the Johnson-Wyandotte Regional Planning Commission and the Transportation Planning Commission of Kansas City by providing park data, and to serve as a review or coordinating committee in park and recreational matters for the metropolitan area. Later, the planning function of the KA-MO-PAR group was merged into the Metropolitan Planning Commission. Its key members are now on the advisory board of the Metropolitan Planning Commission which provides technical advice on parks and recreational facilities.

The current national interest in providing vest pocket parks in urban areas, along with the concerted efforts to build up the National Park System, constitute a good example of a function with different aspects, some of which should be locally organized but others of which require a regional or national perspective. Since funding of this function is usually the responsibility of the level of government operating the facility, the intergovernmental relationship emphasizes the planning and coordination aspects. As a practical matter, in the Kansas City area the counties have tended to take the leadership in establishing regional park systems. Jackson County, particularly, succeeded in developing several large parks which service residents of the surrounding counties. Lake Jacomo, for example, involves 994 acres of lake on a total reservation of 4300 acres and serves five hundred thousand visitors per year. Kansas City also has a strong parks program and has operated all park facilities within the city borders. Yet it was Jackson County that took advantage of the vest pocket parks program and installed them within the cities of the county.[16]

In this context of regional-wide facilities and accessibility of federal money, it is noteworthy that Jackson County created a Sports Authority under state law in 1966 to consider the question of new facilities for professional football and baseball in the metropolitan area. The old stadium used by the Kansas City Royals baseball team and the Kansas City Chiefs football team is no longer adequate for the region, yet the city of Kansas City was financially unable to undertake construction of a new facility. Any governmental organization attempting to raise the funds for such a stadium would do so on the assumption that it would serve the entire region, otherwise it would not be economically viable. Jackson County put together a proposal for two stadia on one site with a movable roof to provide an all-weather environment. The total cost of the two stadia came to $43,000,000 and bonds for this purpose were approved in a special election in June, 1967. Escalating labor costs resulted in revision of stadia plans since the bond funds voted were inadequate to include the movable roof. This problem of obtaining extra funds has not been resolved.

Even if any other governmental entity in the area had wished to challenge Jackson County in making the sports stadium decision, it would have been unable to do so. Jackson County had undergone an extended period of dormant government and thus was the only unit of government in the region which had available the bonded indebtedness necessary to undertake such a large project. There is no evidence that representatives of any of the other potential users in the region were consulted regarding plans for the stadium, including its location. None were represented on the Sports Authority which is appointed by the governor of Missouri. Yet, in 1967 the Kansas City Chiefs sold one-half of their season tickets to residents of Kansas. Functionally, one area governmental unit took upon itself a community decision which it could back up with its own finances. The situation might have been considerably different if stadia were eligible for federal funding subject to a regional coordination.

Similarly, Kansas City decided that since existing runways are not adequate for the new high performance aircraft, and because the location of the Missouri River made it impossible to extend the runways of Municipal Airport, a new airport was needed. Because of the extensive annexation program which Kansas City had already carried out, it had large areas of acreage within the city boundaries north of the river in Platte County where the Kansas City Council decided to establish the airport. Ultimately, the city's voters were called upon to approve a revenue bond issue. That is, the bonds required for construction of this supersonic airport would be paid off by rental fees and user fees paid by the airlines. Additional monies are forthcoming from the Federal Aviation Administration for the runways, towers, and electronic equipment associated with this facility.

In this case, the decision as to who would build the regional airport was influenced by the existing contracts between the airlines and Kansas City for the existing airport facility. No claim was made by Kansas City that the Platte County location was the most central location for the entire region necessary to support such a vast facility, and no other government was represented on the body which drew up the proposals. In fact, in 1963 an effort was made by some Jackson County leaders to have the state set up a metropolitan airport authority. Since the airport was a profitable venture, the city of Kansas City opposed the move and thus maintained control of the airport.

Perhaps because the decision to establish the new airport was not a regional decision, the necessary highway access was not planned. The airport is scheduled to open in 1970 but decisions as to routes and funding of highways is not expected to be complete until early 1970. As envisioned by highway engineers of both states, the expected traffic generated by the airport travelers and workers will be of such magnitude that at least three major routes of limited access must be constructed to handle it adequately. These routes will require an integrated highway program involving five counties on both sides of the state line. If these requirements had been foreseen and planned as part of the Interstate Highway system, there would have been no problem. However, both Kansas and Missouri have five-year plans for highways and securing revision of those interstate route plans is very difficult since it means disappointing other areas whose projects would have to be deferred. In the 1968 campaign both incumbent governors up for reelection discovered the answer — more federal aid.

In this category of regional facilities there is an interesting mix of decentralized and metropolitan-wide decision-making. In the Black matrix, the airport and the stadium would seem to fall into the objective category of "Resource Development — Physical Capital — Public." The most relevant activity characteristics would seem to be "Significant efficiencies in large scale operation" and "Motivation of citizens and officials." Black found the first of these two to be factors tending against decentralization and the second a feature arguing for decentralization.[17]

As it happened, the scope of these two public service facilities was such that a major city or county was the lowest level at which consideration could be given to accomplishing the project. Clearly there were also other factors present — the total cost and the fact that the whole region rather than any one jurisdiction was the market goal — which would suggest that the planning, financing, and operational control could reasonably have been a multijurisdictional concern. However, there was no effective operating mechanism to accomplish this cooperation. If there had been no city or county with the power to take the appropriate unilateral steps, a crisis would have emerged which probably would have led to the establishment of a metropolitan mechanism to respond to the metropolitan need. Professor Grant's paper showed that it was just such inability of the existing structure to meet community needs that led to the success of the metropolitan reform movements in Dade County, Florida, and Nashville-Davidson County, Tennessee.[18]

As for the "Motivation of citizens and officials" activity characteristic, there again the Black matrix works out well. Since the officials of Kansas City and of Jackson County were willing to undertake the airport and stadium projects, the decision-making could be decentralized from the Kansas City metropolis to a single jurisdiction within it. These decisions, however, would have been insufficient without the "Motivation of citizens" and of private interests — the airlines, the Kansas City Chiefs, the Chamber of Commerce, the construction unions, and the Kansas City *Star* — to finance and work for a successful vote of the body politic. Under Missouri law, revenue bond issues require a vote of the people and the airport bonds were approved by a vote of 25 to 1. Since the Sports Complex involved general obligation bonds, state law required a two-thirds favorable vote by the county citizens. The issue passed with a favorable vote of 68.2 per cent.[19]

A negative vote on either issue could have triggered a "metropolitan crisis" of inaction — possibly leading to a push for some metropolitan structure to fill the void. As Professor Grant points out, successful suboptimizing on issues such as these serves to shore up the existing institutional structure and so delays the formulation of new metropolitan mechanisms. In a sense, federal aid may occasionally have the same effect. The anticipation of state and federal aid caused Kansas City to fail to make adequate provisions for roads to the new facility and to secure the necessary intergovernmental planning that was required. In this case a substantial need existed for interstate coordination as well. Ironically, as the construction costs of the Jackson County Sports Complex escalated, it became obvious that the only way to build the facility within the dollar limits of the bond issue would be to have the expanded road system needed to serve the facility paid for out of highway bonds. Here again, the answer was ultimately found in federal road funds obtained through the state government.

Law Enforcement

In the Black matrix the "Public Order" category had a relatively high positive score, suggesting a need for heavy decentralization of law enforcement. This is generally consistent with the existing traditional patterns of local autonomy in law enforcement. In the seven county Kansas City metropolitan region there are approximately fifty-four police departments. The total number of law enforcement officers in the area exceeds 1700. These departments include the Missouri Highway Patrol, Kansas Highway Patrol, seven county sheriff organizations, and forty-five city departments. The impact of the automobile, special problems resulting from the enclave situation, and the historical presence of organized crime in Kansas City has made the organization of the law enforcement function an inherently complex problem with inefficient results. The President's Crime Task Force recently cited Kansas City as a city suitable for high intensity study.[20]

There are a total of three crime laboratories of varying quality, which means that fifty-one police organizations have no laboratory facilities at their immediate disposal and can do little more than take latent fingerprints. Laboratory services are obtained from the Missouri Highway Patrol at Jefferson City, the Kansas Bureau of Investigation at Topeka, and the FBI in Washington. Kansas City, Missouri, has some ballistics and chemical analysis capability, latent fingerprinting comparison, and photography equipment available. In 1968, over one hundred requests from other departments in the area were serviced by the Kansas City department. To date, no fee has been charged by the city to the other agencies, as excess capacity exists in Kansas City and the number of requests is not too large to handle. The existence of two state laboratories has tended to reduce the pressure to develop a well staffed, effectively trained, and adequately equipped area crime laboratory in Kansas City. At one point it was suggested that a neutral agency such as the Midwest Research Institute be designated as the area crime laboratory contractor with payments on a fee basis, payable by the various police departments using the service. However, Midwest Research Institute was not interested in taking on this operating role.

Of the fifty-four police departments in the region, only five have a permanent training department and only ten have formal training programs. Kansas City, Missouri, has the greatest resources, but conducts a formal training program with only two permanent instructors. The 1968 budget did not include substantial additions to the force and so eliminated the "Police academy," although limited funds were obtained to allow refresher courses to officers already on duty. However, when the budgetary crisis passed, funds were allocated for the hiring and training of new recruits as well.

Major crimes are reported by both city and county police departments to the state police at Topeka and Jefferson City. Although effectively involving the two states, this nevertheless means there is no complete record in the metropolitan area. The Kansas City, Missouri, Police Department has a computer with extra terminal capacity and is connected to the FBI computer in Washington, providing rapid access to information on major cases. However, there are many types of police information which are not reported to the FBI or the states which would be useful for a local intelligence file.

Similar problems exist in development of a centralized communications network. In some jurisdictions within the area, local police and local fire departments are not on the same frequencies and men in the field cannot communicate directly with each other without going back through the headquarters unit. The two state highway patrols, three county sheriffs and five city police departments are on the same teletype service but this system needs to be extended to include other departments.

The seven county area has a total of eight jails. Virtually all of these are outmoded facilities holding more inmates than contemplated by their original design. They also afford numerous opportunities for entrepreneurial activities. One sheriff whose official salary was $12,000 per year, reportedly made as much as $77,000 from running vending concessions in the jails and retaining the differential between the per diem paid by the federal government for boarding prisoners and the actual county cost.[21] The continued existence of such plums is one of the major factors inhibiting not only metropolitan restructuring, such as Professor Grant described, but reorganization of existing county governments.

Professor Black stated that "the large number of low positive and negative scores suggests that there are few functions of government that should be entirely centralized or decentralized by area."[22] Black footnotes his matrix with the observation that "the table is principally illustrative; the objective structure would need to be elaborated, as would the characteristics."[23] More detailed definition of the elements related to his "Public Order" category would demonstrate the wisdom of both of these statements.

In assigning values to the "activity characteristics" related to "Protection of Property-Theft" and "Protection of Persons," Black has correctly emphasized such factors as the "Neighborhoods have distinctive objective structures," and "Attainment enhanced by neighborhood coordination" as reasons supporting decentralization. He reaches the same conclusion with regard to "Reaction time requirements" and "Information in hands of officials" but credits "Attainment enhanced by city-wide coordination" with area-wide tendencies.[24]

Actually, depending upon the kind of crime involved and the nature of the criminal, all three of these characteristics could tend toward centralization. The Black opinions on these particular characteristics are compatible with neighborhood crimes by neighborhood youths, for example. They are less appropriate to the activities of more mobile criminals whose targets are spread over a broad area and who use more subtle techniques so that neighborhood cooperation becomes less important than the availability of specially trained squads of police capable of dealing with narcotics violators, extortionists, gamblers, and vice overlords. In addition, only the economy of scale characteristic reflects the increasing need for expensive facility investments and new technology such as the increased use of computers. Many of these very factors account for some of the innovations introduced into law enforcement in metropolitan Kansas City.

For example, the Metro Squad was organized in 1964 by area police departments in five of the seven counties, most of which had no detectives. This was de facto recognition by some of the departments that they were incapable of providing professional investigative services in situations involving serious crimes. The Metro Squad is composed of 165 officers from thirty-nine separate law enforcement departments. Some departments have only one member on the Metro Squad whereas Kansas City, Missouri has thirty-five. Metro Squad is available to any area police department which requests its assistance. This enables the local police department confronted with a major crime to continue its routine work.

The executive director of the Metro Squad is an officer in the Kansas City Police Department. Officers assigned to it generally have at least some background in investigative work and receive a forty-hour training program at the Kansas City Police Academy in which local FBI officers participate. To avoid legal problems of unauthorized police officials operating in various jurisdictions, a reciprocal arrangement has been worked out for deputizing all members of the Metro Squad to operate throughout the metropolitan area.

Another example of area cooperation in law enforcement is Operation Barrier. Criminals apparently assume that they derive some added protection by making use of the intergovernmental overlay of which law enforcement agencies in the area are a part. They therefore frequently skip from one jurisdiction to another after committing a crime. To counter this potentially serious fugitive problem, police agencies have worked out a cooperative master plan of strategic positions which are manned by the participating departments on a signal from the executive director. In the four-year period 1964 — 68, Operation Barrier was employed one hundred twenty-three times and on nineteen occasions contributed to the arrest of an escaping suspect.

A special consideration which seemingly inhibits coordination in the area concerns the status of the largest and best equipped police department — Kansas City, Missouri. Corruption in the city government while the Pendergast machine was in power resulted in control of the police department passing to the state of Missouri. The police department of Kansas City has been controlled by a police board appointed by the governor since 1939. Although the city of Kansas City must pay all police costs, the state legislature, rather than the city, controls the salaries and working conditions of the police. In recent years it has taken as long as two years for the city to obtain passage of state legislation for a change in the salary scale and retirement plan for city poliemen. Such difficulties among the city, the state legislature, and the governor are not calculated to fill other law enforcement agencies with the confidence necessary to turn over all their records, training programs and intelligence data to a centralized metropolitan agency which would necessarily be dominated by the Kansas City Police Department — although organization of such a metropolitan force would possibly include as one of its conditions the dissolution of state control of the police.

Ultimately, it would seem apparent that some broadened law enforcement unit will be necessary, although it need not mean that local departments should be abolished. It is conceivable that a metropolitan jurisdiction could be initiated to provide an area-wide attack on major criminal activities, operate a crime laboratory and a communication system, maintain central files, and provide a police academy for all police in the area. Local police departments could continue to handle such matters as traffic control and local patrol work.

In working out the split of metropolitan and local police functions all of the activity characteristics used by Professor Black would be relevant and would have to be applied in a systems analysis framework to all the objective categories of law enforcement. In general those aspects in which large capital investments, long training periods, or special mobility and skill requirements are key elements would tend to fall into the metropolitan wide agency's jurisdiction and those which depend for successful implementation on detailed knowledge of the social and physical relationships of neighborhoods would tend to be decentralized on an area basis. This kind of split would seem very appropriate for the police function which traditionally uses areas or precincts for the local work and city-wide squads or task forces for the specialized functions. The major change, then, would require broadening of the total area of coverage for the specialists and introduction of a new, broader-based top administration to coordinate the operations of the areas as well as those of the functional specialists.

Fire Prevention

As might be expected, few outlying areas in the Kansas City metropolitan area have full time fire departments. The full time departments have reached intergovernmental agreements to assist each other. Formerly state lines constituted a problem in that insurance policies of the departments did not cover other department activities in their area. This situation has been negotiated by current contracts requiring the assisting department to be responsible for its own acts of negligence or injury when operating in another area, provided these acts are within the coverage of the insurance policies.

By definition, fire fighting is a localized activity since geographical proximity is essential to effective fire control. The Kansas City, Missouri, Fire Department has 866 firemen, while Kansas City, Kansas, has 360. There are necessary differences in the training requirements for a fireman. For instance, Kansas City, Missouri, has a substantial number of high-rise buildings; Kansas City, Kansas, has only three buildings over twelve stories high; and Independence has none over five stories.

The training problems facing the police also affect the fire departments. Kansas City, Missouri, has a new $1,200,000 training academy with a ninety-foot tower and a training staff of five firemen. New firemen spend thirty days at the academy before being assigned to a station house. Firemen from outside Kansas City, Missouri, are occasionally trained on request but this is strictly on an *ad hoc* basis. The fire departments do not trade information on building codes or materials problems which develop. They rely exclusively on a national communications network, which omits potentially valuable local interchange.

None of the departments has an arson expert. The Kansas City, Missouri, fire department relies upon a man from the police laboratory with arson investigation experience. The total relationship between fire prevention and arson is apparently heavily influenced by the fire insurance companies, who have their own motives for pressing for reform in these areas and provide some of these services to the fire departments in the insurance companies' own interest. On the other hand, a metropolitan-wide police force with an adequately equipped crime laboratory could provide arson investigation service to all departments in the area.

With the exception of these functions — training, information exchange, and arson investigation — the state line represents a minimal impediment to effective fire fighting, because of its inherently local nature. This evaluation is generally consistent with the Black matrix which indicated a high value for area decentralization of fire department functions.[25]

Social Services

Dr. Black rated education and health services as functions which needed a high degree of decentralization. On the other hand, other social welfare functions would seem to be included under his "Quality of Life" category in which he considers "Equality of Persons — Social, Political, Economic." All three of these categories were given ratings indicating a need for a predominance of area-wide administrative control.[26] Detailed consideration of some of these functions indicates that the Black analysis has some validity but, here again, a more detailed definition might lead to different conclusions.

In any attempt to consider the problems of poverty and unemployment, the important question is whether or not job vacancies are being made known to potential workers and whether appropriate training has been given to those who need it. In interstate areas, it is clear that often opportunities will be on one side of the state line and the availability of manpower on the other side. The primary governmental agencies involved are the state employment services. The Office of Economic Opportunity has found it necessary to spend much time attempting to create truly responsive employment referral services for those in the poverty areas. There is reason to wonder whether state employment services established on two sides of the state line and run by organizations based in the state capitals are coordinating sufficiently to help the hard core unemployed who do not know how to demand this kind of service.

In the Kansas City area, some placement officers in the employment services trade vacancy information on a satisfactory basis. However, evaluation of the effectiveness of these organizations is done by persons not part of the poverty-fighting organizations and often not living in the metropolitan area. The temptation of the employment field office is to skim the cream off the top and thereby improve its performance figures, while not really engaging in any innovative approaches to reach those generally classified as the hard core unemployed. This is a problem in rural areas as well as in urban areas in many states. It is more serious in an urban area which has two separate offices, one run by the State of Missouri and one by the State of Kansas.

In the end we have a federal program operated by two states to solve a local problem — but with inadequate cooperation with another federal-local funded program being operated by a nonprofit community action delegate agency. After much jockeying and negotiating it was finally agreed that the state employment offices would put placement officers directly into the neighborhood centers of the community action program. In this specific problem area there is need for both area-wide coordination of vacancy information and neighborhood implementation to relate vacancies to the hard-core unemployed.

Welfare administration problems are now being resolved by federal instigation. Prior to July 1, 1969, Kansas and Missouri had a wide differential in eligibility for welfare recipients. Significantly, the disparities existing within the Kansas City areas were not resolved on a local or state level, but on the federal level. Federal action promoted removal of length of residency requirements, making persons eligible to receive benefits by stating their residency and intention to remain a resident of that state. Yet differences in payments continues to confuse the much discussed welfare problem.

Education is another of our traditionally local functions. However, the higher one moves in the educational sphere, the more likely it is to become a regional function. The Kansas City region has responded to this need. Although the University of Missouri (Kansas City) is the only graduate school in the metropolitan area, there are twenty-three undergraduate institutions within the region, most of them private, denominational institutions of relatively small size. In 1963 a group called the Kansas City Regional Council for Higher Education was organized to attempt to help these institutions turn their regional involvement into an asset. Starting from a local seed grant this organization now receives substantial federal funding. Recent ties established between the University of Kansas, thirty miles west of Kansas City, and the University of Missouri (Kansas City), for dual participation in the Department of Housing and Urban Development's Urban Observatory program has laid groundwork for further partnership in urban problem solving. The Kansas City Urban Observatory is one of the first six to be established under subcontract from the National League of Cities.

At the junior college level there has been much controversy. Kansas City, Missouri, has long had a quality junior college system. The Metropolitan Junior College District includes parts of several counties and therefore many suburban communities. The need to provide inner-city students with vocational education threatened the very existence of the system in 1967. Attempts were made to establish new academic facilities in the suburbs, threatening to turn the old facilities into a ghetto institution. After public acrimony, court fights, and a report by consultants, the new campus will be located within Kansas City near enough to the inner-city to serve those needs. Two additional suburban campuses are being built as part of the deal which resolved the stalemate over a new site.

The Kansas City, Kansas Community Junior College system is also having growing pains. Construction has begun on a new suburban site which should be operational by fall 1971, accommodating 2000 new students in addition to those served by its downtown structures. In 1967 the voters of Johnson County, Kansas, voted to establish their own junior college in response to suburban demands and geared toward a pre-college program. On the Kansas side, therefore, the inner-city and suburban programs are to a large extent separated, creating the possibility of one emphasizing vocational education and the other aiming at a high quality pre-college academic program.

The first of what hopefully will become a series of cooperative junior college arrangements has recently been established. Selected students from the Johnson County program may enroll in the dental assistant curriculum of the Metropolitan Junior College system. This cooperative breakthrough hopefully will set a pattern for greater metropolitan cooperation.[27]

This existence of separated junior colleges on the Kansas side of the state line is not encouraging to those who now believe that the only effective way to upgrade the education received by ghetto students is to intermix such students with suburban students. In education, the convenience feature of neighborhood schools which presumably accounted for the high decentralization rating supplied by Professor Black is now being challenged as a result of the studies of poverty and its effect on education, minority groups and interracial relations.

Metropolitan Institutional Responses

The previous discussion strongly suggests a need for application of some systems approaches to not only questions of physical planning but also to social services where the values supporting the programs may be undergoing revision as a result of improved understanding of urban stresses and strains. Area officials are aware of the unique problems presented by the state line and have taken some actions to minimize problems. However, the greatest incentive for such arrangements was to qualify for federal funds.

The police Metro Squad and Operation Barrier were the only regional mechanisms initiated by local authorities without the actual or potential inducement of federal funding. Even so, the mechanism adopted is essentially an ad hoc mutual coordination device. The one major and enduring functional institution that has been established is the Kansas City Area Transportation Authority, a bi-state special district dealing with a physical and technological problem.

Coordination for physical planning in the metropolitan area has also had a rocky past. In 1957 the Kansas legislature passed the so-called Mo-Kan Metropolitan Development Compact bill which would have established a comprehensive bi-state planning and development agency with full corporate powers, including the right of eminent domain, but without taxing authority. The compact died with rejection by the Missouri legislature. The same thing happened again in 1965. Since the dominant urban center in the area is located in Missouri, one would logically have expected the Missouri legislature to pass the bill. One observer concluded that the compact failed in Missouri because Kansas City, Missouri, failed to push it. He theorized that this was because its aggressive annexation policy which had relieved a great deal of Kansas City's land pressure and blunted the perceived immediate need for intercommunity urban cooperation.[28]

Given this unpromising background, it is not surprising that problems arose in meeting the terms of the Federal Highway Act of 1962. Road projects in an urban area had to fit within the context of an area-wide planned development to qualify for federal money. Missouri and Kansas legislative restrictions did not permit the formation of an interstate planning commission without new legislation. Two separate agencies were established in 1964 with the expectation of meeting the new federal requirements. The Johnson-Wyandotte Planning

Commission was established on the Kansas side of the line, and the Transportation Planning Commission of Greater Kansas City was organized on the Missouri side. Shortly after their formation, the two agencies applied for federal grants, but were rejected as grant recipients on the grounds that such funds could go only to a single *region-wide* planning agency. Subsequently, counties and municipalities in the bi-state region had federal road money withheld and then other money for federal programs was also denied when federal legislation required evidence of regional coordination as a precondition to grants. The state and local governments involved finally took two concrete actions that satisfied federal authorities.

The Kansas City Area Transportation Authority

The Kansas City Area Transportation Authority was established in 1965 as a special district authority for passenger transportation in the seven county region. Since the formation was accomplished through the interstate compact formula, enabling legislation had to be obtained concurrently in the Missouri and Kansas legislatures, and Congressional approval had to be obtained. Although this was accomplished, any additional powers that KCTA might deem necessary in the future would likewise require dual legislative and congressional approval.

For example, the first major step of KCTA was the purchase of all private transit lines in the bi-state metropolitan region. To facilitate this action, new legislation was needed to allow KCTA to negotiate labor contracts and service existing pension funds of the companies. Such actions by a public body were prohibited by Missouri law. Enabling legislation to this effect was passed in both states in 1967, and by Congress in 1968. This is a cumbersome process inhibiting effective administration.

The ten commissioners of the KCTA are now elected by the members of the Mid-America Council of Governments (MACOG), with the chairmanship rotating between the states annually, and five members of the commission drawn from each state. A built-in malapportionment exists between both the two states and among the individual counties since most of the citizens and area served are in Missouri.

The original financial support for KCTA came from the State of Missouri ($50,000); Kansas City, Missouri ($30,000); and Kansas City, Kansas ($15,000). Kansas City, Missouri, contributed an additional $30,000 for fiscal year 1967 to KCTA and despite enormous budgetary problems within the overall framework of city programs, it approved $40,000 additional funds for KCTA in fiscal 1968. The State of Missouri has contributed nothing further. Kansas City, Kansas, contributed an additional $30,000 in fiscal 1968. It should be emphasized that, like the formation of the agency, monetary support for KCTA at present is totally voluntary. Nevertheless, the absence of support from the State of Kansas affords evidence of the ambivalent support the agency has received.[29]

Because of the specialized nature of its duties, and the technical nature of its planning, the KCTA relies on outside consultants with experience in transportation systems in other cities. KCTA does not consider the Metropolitan Planning Commission (Metroplan) its planning arm, although it "coordinates" with Metroplan. The view from Metroplan is somewhat different; officials there see themselves as the rightful planning agency for all transportation. The restrictive weakness of KCTA is that it has jurisdiction only over passenger rather than commercial or freight transportation. This means that KCTA cannot plan or implement a comprehensive transport program. For instance, KCTA originally had responsibility for planning passenger access to the new supersonic airport, Kansas City International, to be located in the Platte County portion of Kansas City, while responsibility for freight transportation to and from KCI fell outside its purview. Some of the differences between the Metroplan and KCTA seem to be derived directly from the fragmented manner in which they were formally created. However, there is now a technical advisory committee for airport planning which includes the joint membership of Kansas City, Metropolitan Planning Commission — Kansas City Region, and representatives from Clay, Platte and Leavenworth counties.

Metropolitan Planning Commission — Kansas City Region

Despite the success of founding the KCTA, there was still doubt about the willingness of the states to approve a broad-scope metropolitan planning compact. Transportation was functional, limited, and a pressing and obvious need. Necessity being the mother of invention, it was determined in 1964 that counties in Missouri could enter into planning agreements with adjacent jurisdictions in other states. Some based this reasoning on legislation dating from 1947, and others on powers deemed to be inherent in the state constitution. In any case, this opinion removed the need for specific new legislation in Missouri, which the Mo-Kan Compact had been unable to secure. With the tacit cooperation of Missouri thus assured, the Kansas legislature in 1965 granted counties and cities authority to enter into planning agreements across the state boundary. Under the laws of both Kansas and Missouri, such planning agreements do not qualify as interstate compacts, and therefore, neither Congressional nor state legislative approval was necessary for implementation of the planning agreement.

Metroplan was officially born in December, 1966, by virtue of a voluntary pact among the four Missouri counties — Jackson, Clay, Platte, and Cass; and the three Kansas counties — Johnson, Wyandotte, and Leavenworth; plus three of the four cities of more than 50,000 population — Kansas City, Kansas; Kansas City, Missouri and Independence. Overland Park, Kansas, the fourth city, did not join until July, 1969. These bodies are the voting members of Metroplan and provide one-third of the operating funds; the other two-thirds is paid by the federal government.[30]

The Metropolitan Planning Commission is made up of twenty-eight members, fourteen from each state. The commission oversees the entire operation of the agency and its staff. The Missouri participants accepted a Kansas demand for equal distribution between the two states so that, as in the case of the KCTA, there is malapportionment.

Virtually all federally funded projects for the region go through Metroplan. It is the local agency that must indicate local coordination has taken place, and almost all federal programs now require such evidence. Not all planning initiates with the commission, but plans made at the local governmental level must eventually pass through its review and obtain approval of the commission before they are given federal consideration. The legitimacy and authority of Metroplan stems solely from its position as the regional agent for certifying projects to the federal government.

The key points of the first five-year plan developed by the commission are in two areas: (1) a comprehensive land use study including the cataloging of 600,000 parcels of land in the seven county area; and (2) a comprehensive study of transportation in the region with recommendations for implementation. In collecting land use data, the commission drew up a uniform data collection system which it had to convince the counties to adopt. One of the initial problems in setting up a central data bank was that the data being collected differed in each county, and that different computer systems were in use and tapes were not compatible. While each of the local governments will continue to keep its own separate records, they are now able to supply compatible tapes to the central data bank at Metroplan.

Once the transportation study passed its initial stages, administration was complicated by the jurisdictional questions involving the Kansas City Area Transportation Authority which was set up specifically for passenger transportation. The ambiguous aspects of this relationship may eventually be operationally defined by MACOG.

Mid-America Council of Governments

In October, 1967, the evolution of metropolitan institutions moved a step further with the creation of the Mid-America Council of Governments.[31] Metroplan's relationship to MACOG is still in the process of being defined, since MACOG has yet to assert its full role in the region. In principle, Metroplan's jurisdiction is that of planning and coordination. There is no requirement that the member governments disband Metroplan. On the other hand, since member organizations fund both organizations, area governments could transfer all of their functions to the Council of Governments and obtain federal recognition of MACOG as the regional coordination certifying agent. At this moment Metroplan by virtue of its link to the federal government is the substantial on-going agency and is serving as the staff of MACOG.

In the case of Metroplan the control of the elected officials is less directly obvious but just as real. MACOG is composed exclusively of elected officials from the seven-county area. It is a voluntary organization which can serve as the metropolitan planning coordinator or take on any other role its membership agrees upon. It would seem apparent that MACOG will eventually have to select one issue or function to demonstrate its capacity to act effectively as a region-wide body. Its legitimacy and support will be in jeopardy until it pragmatically demonstrates its ability to execute some operational programs.

At present MACOG is serving as a forum and meeting place for regional officials and joint use of the staff of Metroplan is a reasonable procedure. The assumption is that at some point MACOG will assume some operating roles and may eventually absorb the Metroplan staff as its planning staff with additional staff for newer roles. The Metroplan board could be retained to serve as a functional planning advisor to the broader scope MACOG.

Effect of the State Line

Having now taken a detailed look at the general planning agency for the region (Metroplan), the special district agency created for passenger transportation coordination in the region (KCTA), and having attempted to delineate the relationships between these institutions, the new MACOG, and the various jurisdictions serviced by them all, it remains to assess the positive or negative effects of the state line in the operation of the agencies.

Officials of both MACOG and Metroplan emphasize that their greatest problems of coordination stem from the traditional interplay of self-interest groups in the various political subdivisions — that is, municipal and county governments. Working with, and where possible, reconciling these conflicting interest positions is the business of government in either an intra- or interstate situation. Thus, the conflicting interest of two Missouri counties such as Jackson and Clay might present more problems than, say, those of Jackson and Wyandotte counties in Missouri and Kansas, respectively. There is no reason to assume that the conflicts between counties in two states need necessarily be any greater than those involving counties within the same state. In this sense the state line seems to present no additional problems.

Nevertheless, we have noted that the various attempts at intergovernmental cooperation have involved legal or technical barriers to interstate cooperation. This circumstance may explain why the director of Metroplan insists that *below the state level* of government there are no unique problems posed for his agency because of the state line. At the higher level, as we have already seen, the problems are twofold — revenue and enabling legislation. Speaker Unruh, Supervisor Roos, and County Administrator Kelly presented some specific aspects of those problems.

Further evidence of the actual stresses that still exist because of the lack of bi-state coordination can be found in the Model Cities applications which were channelled through Metroplan. To enhance the attractiveness of the proposal, the applications of Kansas City Kansas, and Kansas City Missouri, were sent to the Department of Housing and Urban Development under one covering letter from the mayors of both cities. In fact, the plans were drawn up independently and were to be implemented totally independent from one another. As things worked out, the Missouri application was approved in the first round and the Kansas application was not approved until October, 1968. Today, implementation of the two plans is proceeding in independent directions — which is not unreasonable since the poverty areas are not contiguous.

As previously described, the chief problem encountered by KCTA, and one that may crop up again, is the necessity to obtain legislative sanction from both states for any additional powers. At this point KCTA has finally moved into the operational stage since acquiring area transit lines. With the right of eminent domain, and the ability to issue revenue bonds, KCTA has a good deal more actual authority within its limited sphere than any other region-wide agency. However, it still needs additional sources of funds in addition to fare-box revenue from the bus system. It is the only special district agency functioning in the area besides the normal ones of education, fire, sewage, and water.

Conclusion

One of the keys to speculation about the future of interstate and inter-governmental relations in the metropolitan area must lie in an examination of the past and present state of affairs. By examining both the program areas and the more general institutions for the implementation of planning, one can gain a better idea as to whether the announced future projections are realistic — or whether they are either overly ambitious or overly cautious. Clearly any progress is contingent upon improved mechanisms of intergovernmental coordination.

There is mounting evidence that at least within Jackson County there is a willingness to take active steps to obtain regional cooperation. In January, 1968, the city government of Kansas City created a new position of Assistant City Manager for Intergovernmental Relations. Within a matter of days the county government, following suit, initiated plans for a Department of Inter-governmental Relations. This Department announced purposes of (1) main-taining relations with state and federal governmental units, and (2) promoting interregion cooperation through close work with such administrative bodies as the Mid-America Council of Governments. The establishment of these positions should enhance intergovernmental cooperation in the metropolitan area.

In assessing the Kansas City region and looking toward its future prospects for area-wide governmental coordination, some definite patterns emerge based upon comparison with the experiences of other metropolitan regions. Since the Kansas City region contains seven counties, the merging of city and county functions on a regional basis appears most unlikely. Both the consolidation model of Nashville-Davidson County and the federation model of Miami-Dade County about which Professor Grant spoke, are generally conceded to be feasible only when a metropolitan area is contained wholly within one county.

Similarly, city-county separation represented by the experience of St. Louis County is not a practical alternative since Kansas City spans three counties. Annexation is responsible for not only this spread but also the resultant enclave phenomenon. Kansas City, Missouri, Independence, Lee's Summit, and Raytown have all accomplished annexations of such wide scope that the primary momentum for this alternative has now passed on the Missouri side of the metropolitan area.

However, Kansas City, Kansas, has just completed a major annexation and it is conceivable that it may continue to pursue this course. Since there are only three municipalities in Wyandotte County — Kansas City, Kansas, and two smaller municipalities with a combined population of only 4200 — there is an excellent opportunity for city-county consolidation within the criteria suggested by the Nashville experience.

There remain only a few potentially practical alternatives for the region. The first would be establishment of numerous metropolitan-wide special districts, including multi-purpose districts to provide services to the seven county area. The local model exists in the KCTA. If this alternative is implemented, local relationships would eventually become even more complicated than they already are.

A second logical mechanism could be found through extension of the Mid-America Council of Governments. Robert Williams and Kent Mathewson provided some information on ABAG and Detroit which could provide guidelines. The functional areas currently being considered as appropriate for metropolitan-wide consideration under MACOG are air pollution, health planning, water pollution, and police services. MACOG is currently attempting to secure designation as the regional health planning coordinator for federal fund applications. If the council is able to develop successfully one or more of these functional areas, the wisdom of using the special district approach might become questionable. The flaw in this analysis lies in the voluntary nature of the COG. If any elements of the seven county area object to participation in any of these functional restructurings, the voluntary fiscal as well as power base of COG could be eroded. Additionally, the Mid-America Council of Governments has no present authority to impose a tax on any of the residents of the seven counties or hundred cities. The financial question cannot help but become important if operations in some of the functional areas are undertaken.

The alternative of encouraging a gradualist approach to expanding area intergovernmental cooperation has as much appeal as any other. The number and history of some of the cities and counties in the area and the occasional indications of distrust of the largest single unit — the City of Kansas City — make it unlikely that all of these governmental units would be willing to give up their sovereignty to a metropolitan government. On the other hand, the use of limited approaches such as identifying specific functions which are especially adaptable to region-wide treatment may prove adequate to meet the most urgent needs of the metropolitan area. To organize such functions under MACOG rather than as independent special districts would avoid some of the drawbacks of special districts which, when set up independently of the local governments, tend to undermine overall regional planning.

The test for the Council of Governments will occur during the next few years when an attempt is made to move from a voluntary discussion group to an operational organization carrying out the functions delegated to it by constituent counties and cities. This model has the advantage that even if some cities do not care to go along, a contract basis could be established to provide for payment for services rendered by the Council. Participating governments could then pay their pro rata share and governments desiring to stay outside the cooperative effort could continue to run their operations.

There is mounting evidence that specific efforts will be made to improve cooperation of smaller cities with their own counties and to establish a seven county organization capable of undertaking some significant service functions. The MACOG mechanism is potentially capable of filling what is now a very serious vacuum of services in the area. Judging by the philosophies traditionally held in the state capitals of Kansas and Missouri, the Kansas City metropolis seems to qualify as one of the areas of the nation least likely to be affected by the Toronto approach. Professor Grant described how the province took the initiative in providing a new framework for local government. The leadership for new metropolitan mechanisms in the Kansas City area must come from political and governmental leaders in local government on both sides of the Kansas -Missouri line. There is encouraging evidence this leadership will be forthcoming and, if so, it is hoped the governors will take a supportive attitude.

Notes to Chapters

Notes to Chapter One

1. See David McClelland, *The Achieving Society* (New York: Free Press, 1967).
2. Raymond Bauer, ed., *Social Indicators* (Cambridge, Mass.: MIT Press, 1966).
3. March and Cyert, *A Behavioral Theory of the Firm* (Englewood Cliffs, N.J.: Prentice Hall, 1964).
4. James G. March and Herbert A. Simon, *Organizations* (New York: John Wiley and Sons, Inc., 1958).

Notes to Chapter Three

1. Research by League of California Cities which led to creation of their "New Mayors and Councilmen's Biannual Institution," a decade ago. The National League of Cities is commencing a similar program in 1970 for the same reason, based upon their research.
2. Nathan Glazer writing in the New York Times, *Magazine,* October 22, 1967, quoting from "Compendium of Statistics On The Social and Economic Conditions of the Negro," Bureau of Labor Statistics and Bureau of the Census, Washington, October, 1967.
3. Lincoln Steffins, *The Shame of the Cities,* (New York: 1904), p. 31.
4. Speech, Annual Conference, American Institute of Planners, Seattle, Washington, 1967.
5. According to the Bureau of the Census, 40% of the population is now under 21. In 1970, the median age (half the population is older and half younger) will be 27.3:

	Median Age
1940	29.1
1950	30.2
1960	27.8
1966	27.3
1980	27.8
1990	28.7

6. Federal Trade Commission, "Second Report on Low-income Buyers in the District of Columbia," *The New York Times,* July 9, 1968, p. 22.
7. *Report of the National Advisory Commission on Civil Disorders,* Bantam Books, (New York: March, 1968), p. 206.

Notes to Chapter Four

1. Max Ways, "O Say Can You See? The Crisis in Our National Perception," *Fortune,* Vol. LXXVIII (October, 1968), p. 121.

2. The Intergovernmental Cooperation Act, formerly S 698, became PL 90-577, effective October 16, 1968. The final bill did not include provisions to federal grant-in-aid programs and did not establish uniform federal relocation and land acquisition assistance.

There were five main titles to the Intergovernmental Cooperation Act. The Act:

Provided for improved administration of grant-in-aid to the states.

Authorized federal departments and agencies to provide specialized or technical services on a reimbursable basis to state and local governments.

Directed the President to establish a federal intergovernmental coordination policy with respect to grant administration.

Provided for periodic Congressional review of federal grant-in-aid programs.

Required the Federal Government to consider local land use plans when acquiring or disposing of federal land within local jurisdictions.

3. Tom Wicker, *J.F.K. and L.B.J.; The Influence of Personality upon Politics* (New York: Morrow, 1968).

Notes to Chapter Eight

1. The concept of the capability level of urban management, which is introduced in this article as a criterion for urban management manpower development, is elaborated at some length in a subsequent publication. See the author's, "The Quality of Urban Management," in Schmandt, H.J. and Bloomberg, W. Jr. (eds.) — *The Quality of Urban Life,* (Beverly Hills: Sage, 1969), pp. 395—419.

2. The reference to the municipal engineers are based on the research paper by Larry A. Wernette, *The Municipal Engineer 1894—1914* (1968), prepared as a part of the Urban Management Science Project of the Graduate Program in Public Management Science.

Notes to Chapter Nine

1. John Friedman, *The Spatial Structure of Economic Development in the Tennessee Valley* (Chicago: University of Chicago Press, 1955).

2. Jan Tinbergen, *On the Theory of Economic Policy* (Amsterdam, Netherlands: North Holland Publishing Co., 1952).

3. Charles E. Lindblom, "The Science of 'Muddling Through'," *Public Administration Review,* Vol. XIX, Spring, 1959.

4. Raymond Vernon, *The Myth and Reality of our Urban Problems* (Cambridge, Mass.: Harvard University Press, 1966).

5. Robert Presthus, *Men at the Top, a Study in Community Power* (New York: Oxford University Press, 1967).

Notes to Chapter Eleven

1. G.M. Kneedler, "Functional Types of Cities," *Public Management,* Vol. XXVII (1945), pp. 197–203.

2. J.S. Gilmore, J.J. Ryan, and W.S. Gould, *Defense Systems Resources in the Civil Sector: An Evolving Approach, An Uncertain Market* (Washington, D.C.: U.S. Government Printing Office, 1967), Appendix A, "Definitions."

3. G. Black, *The Application of Systems Analysis to Government Operations,* New York: Frederick A. Praeger, 1968.

4. Richard Myrick and Barbara S. Marx, "The Control of Incinerator-Caused Air Pollution in New York City: 1964–65," Staff Discussion Paper 202 (Washington, D.C.: The George Washington University, Program of Policy Studies in Science and Technology, March 1968), p. 15.

5. National League of Cities, "What Kind of Cities Do We Want?" Report of special panel chaired by John F. Collins, *Nation's Cities,* Vol. V (April 1967), p. 34.

6. E.C. Banfield and J.Q. Wilson, *City Politics,* Vintage ed. (New York: Random House, 1963), Chapter 8, "The Centralization of Influence."

7. P.F. Drucker, "Building the Structure." *The Practice of Management* (New York: Harper & Brothers, 1954), Chapter 17.

8. H.A. Simon, *Administrative Behavior: A Study of Decision-Making Processes in Administrative Organization* (New York: Macmillan, 1961).

9. G.A. Steiner, "Program Budgeting, Business Contribution to Government Management," *Business Horizons,* Spring, 1965, p. 45.

10. H.P. Hatry, "Criteria for Evaluation in Planning State and Local Programs." State-Local Finances Project, The George Washington University, Washington, D.C., May 1967 (also published as Committee Print of U.S. Senate Committee on Government Operations, 90th Congress, 1st Session, July 21, 1967).

11. Simon, *op. cit.,* p. 192.

12. M. Gordon, "Too Many Governments," *Sick Cities: Psychology and Pathology of American Urban Life,* (Baltimore: Penguin Books, 1963), Chapter 12.

13. D.S. Schon, *Testimony Before the Subcommittee on Scientific Manpower Utilization of the Senate Labor and Public Welfare Committee, January 26, 1967* (Washington, D.C.: U.S. Government Printing Office, 1967).

14. U.S. Commission on Civil Rights, *A Time to Listen – A Time to Act: Voice from the Ghettos of the Nation's Cities* (Washington, D.C.: U.S. Government Printing Office, 1967).

15. Hatry, *op. cit.*

16. Z. S. Zannetos, "On the Theory of Divisional Structures: Some Aspects of Centralization and Decentralization of Control and Decision-Making," *Management Science,* Vol. 12 (December 1965), pp. B49—B68.

17. Mayor's Advisory Panel on Decentralization of the New York City Schools, *Reconstruction for Learning: A Community School System for New York City* (New York: November 9, 1967).

18. Sir Harold Scott, "The British Policy System," *The Concise Encyclopedia of Crime and Criminals* (New York: Hawthorn Books, Inc., 1961), pp. 28—30.

Notes to Chapter Twelve

1. Grundstein.

2. Senator Muskie, pp. 88—89, above.

3. Metropolitan Planning Commission, *Population Projections — Kansas City Metropolitan Region:* March, 1968.

4. Guy Black, p. 233, above.

5. *Ibid.*

6. U.S. Public Health Service (HEW), *Air Pollution — A National Sample,* Washington, 1966 and Midwest Research Institute, *Kansas City, Kansas, Air Pollution Survey,* 1966.

7. U.S. Public Health Service, (National Center for Air Pollution Control), *Kansas City, Kansas; Kansas City, Missouri, Air Pollution Abatement Activity: Visibility at Municipal and Fairfax Airports,* (Washington, D.C.: U.S. Government Printing Office), January, 1967.

8. Missouri, Seventy-fourth General Assembly, *Kansas-Missouri Air Quality Compact,* Senate Bill No. 428, 1967, and *Interview* with Norman Goar, Kansas State Senate, Westwood, Kansas, January, 1968.

9. Missouri, *Revised Statutes, Cumulative Supplement* (1967), Chapter 203 "Air Conservation."

10. Kansas, *Statutes Annotated* (1968), Chapter 65 "Air Pollution."

11. *United States Code Annotated* 1968. Public Law 88—206, Dec. 17, 1963, 77 Stat. 392 (Title 42, 1859 — 18571).

12. City of Kansas City, Missouri *Ordinance No. 365359,* April 6, 1969.

13. John Middleton, *The Federal Role in Air Pollution Control,* U.S. Public Health Service (HEW), 1967.

14. Glen J. Hopkins, *Kansas City's Pollution Abatement Program,* paper presented at Thirty-ninth Annual Conference Water Pollution Control Federation, September 28, 1966.

15. *Ibid.*

16. Kansas City *Star,* November 3, 1968. County Manager James Kunde received the "Manager of the Year" award at the 1968 Conference of the International City Managers Association based in part on the vest pocket parks program.

17. Black, *op. cit.,* pp. 231—232.

281

18. Daniel R. Grant.

19. Kansas City *Times*, June 28, 1967.

20. William Reddig, *Tom's Town*, (Lippincott: Philadelphia, 1947) and Lear B. Reed, *Human Wolves: Seventeen Years of War on Crime*, (Brown, White-Lowell Press: Kansas City, Missouri, 1941).

21. Kansas City *Star*, December 27, 1967.

22. Black, *op. cit.*, p. 233.

23. *Ibid.*, p. 232.

24. *Ibid.*, pp. 234—235.

25. *Ibid.*

26. *Ibid.*

27. Kansas City *Star*, August 29, 1969.

28. Howard Neighbor, "Problems of Bi-State Metropolitan Organization — Kansas City Area," *Midwest Review of Public Administration*, Vol. 1, No. 1, February, 1967, p. 20.

29. Kansas City *Star*, October 23, 24, 25, 26, 1968, and the *Annual Budgets* fiscal year 1968—69, Kansas City, Kansas, and Kansas City, Missouri.

30. U.S. Code Annotated, *Federal Housing Act of 1954 as Amended*, Title 40, Section 701, 1962.

31. Kansas City *Times*, October 13, 1967.

F. Gerald Brown

Gerald Brown is Assistant Professor of Public Administration and Program Coordinator, Center for Management Development, School of Administration, University of Missouri — Kansas City. Before coming to UMKC he was Assistant Research Professor, University of Pittsburgh, Contract Team, Institute of Administration, Zaria, Nigeria; Research Associate, Research and Training Program, the International City Managers' Association; and Administrative Assistant Intern in the Office of the City Manager, Saginaw, Michigan.

Mr. Brown received his MPIA degree from the Graduate School of Public and International Affairs, University of Pittsburgh, 1964, and his B.A. from the University of Oregon in 1959.

He has developed and conducted management training and development programs for large cities and for directors of community action programs. He has presented papers at several national and international conferences, including a paper on "Applications of Organization Development Concepts in a Large City: The Kansas City Case." His publications include "Community Objectives: A Tool for Guiding City Development," and "Planning and Conduct of a Research Program."

Timothy W. Costello

Timothy Costello is a behavioral scientist and the former Deputy Mayor and City Administrator of New York City. He has recently (1969) assumed an academic position with the State University of New York at Buffalo coordinating a doctoral program in the "policy sciences."

He received his B.S. from Fordham University in 1937 where he was an honor graduate and his Ph.D. from Fordham in 1944 where he held the Walter G. Summers Fellowship. He also served as an intern in psychology at the Rikers Island Penitentiary. As a consultant to private companies, he has developed and conducted programs in management training and development, corporate reorganization and administrative improvement. He is coauthor of two widely used texts, *Abnormal Psychology* and *Psychology in Administration,* and has contributed widely to professional journals.

Timothy Costello has been active politically and has been a candidate for the City Council, Congress, and for President of the City Council. He is former chairman of the Liberal Party of New York State.

Daniel Ross Grant

Daniel Grant prepared the original draft of the "Plan of Metropolitan Government for Nashville and Davidson County" leading to adoption of the new "metro" form of government in 1962. He is a consultant to the U.S. Advisory Commission on Intergovernmental Relations. In 1963 he was the recipient of a Ford Foundation grant for a comparative study of metropolitan governments in Toronto, Miami, and Nashville.

Grant received his Ph.D. from Northwestern University in 1948 in the area of political science. At both the M.A. and the Ph.D. levels he was a Fellow in the Southern Regional Training Program in Public Administration.

Grant's publications include: "The Government of Interstate Metropolitan Areas"; *The States and the Metropolis; State and Local Government in America; Political Dynamics of Environmental Control;* and "A Comparison of Predictions and Experience with Nashville 'Metro.'"

Randy Hamilton

Randy Hamilton received his Ph.D. in political and social science at the International University, Zurich, Switzerland. He also has a master's in Public Administration and a master's in Community and Regional Planning from the University of North Carolina.

His practical experience in local government began with three years as city manager of Carolina Beach, North Carolina. He served four years as Associate Director of the National League of Cities (then American Municipal League) and six years as Municipal Management Advisor to the Royal Government Advisor to the Lord Mayor of Bangkok. In addition he directed a major United Nations project in comparative administration. His publications include one book and over fifty articles in professional journals.

He has served on the faculties of the American University, Washington, D.C., Thammasat University, Bangkok, San Francisco State College, University of Southern California, and University of California, Berkeley. He assumed the position of Executive Director of the Institute of Local Self Government and Special Projects Director, League of California Cities in 1965.

Senator Edmund S. Muskie

Senator Muskie is without peer in his concern for urban affairs and intergovernmental relations. He is Chairman of the Subcommittee on Intergovernmental

Relations, the Subcommittee on Air and Water Pollution and a Member of the Public Works Committee, Government Operations Committee, and Special Committee on Aging. In addition to those urban related responsibilities, he is Chairman of the Legislative Review Committee, Assistant Majority Whip, Chairman of the Subcommittee on International Finance and a Member of the Banking and Currency Committee.

Senator Muskie was the first Democratic governor elected in the State of Maine in twenty years (1954). He was elected to the United States Senate in 1958 and 1964. From 1946 to 1952 he served in the Maine House of Representatives and was Minority Leader during 1949 and 1951. Senator Muskie was a practicing attorney in Waterville, Maine. He graduated from Bates College in 1936 (Phi Beta Kappa) and from Cornell Law School in 1939.

Senator Muskie was Manager of the Demonstration Cities and Metropolitan Development Act of 1966 and sponsored the Proposed Intergovernmental Cooperation Act of 1967, the National Council on Intergovernmental Affairs Act of 1967, the Intergovernmental Personnel Act of 1967, and the Intergovern- mental Manpower Act of 1967.

Jesse M. Unruh

Jesse M. Unruh is Minority Leader in the California Assembly. He served as Speaker of the California Assembly for many years. He has provided the leadership to increase the capabilities of the Legislature to serve as an independent and strong branch of state government and has led the Assembly in meeting many of the challenges of the largest, fastest-growing state in the nation.

The Unruh Civil Rights Act of 1959 prohibits discrimination in the state's business accommodations and has been applied to housing as well. The Unruh Credit Act of 1959 protects consumers in the field of installment purchases. The fields of tax reform, public health insurance, recreation, rapid transit, education, and promotion of the arts have all been profoundly affected by Unruh legislation. Mr. Unruh is past President of the National Conference of State Legislative Leaders and an internationally recognized authority on politics. He is a Navy veteran and an alumnus of the University of Southern California.

Lawrence K. Roos

Lawrence K. Roos is supervisor of St. Louis County. From 1946 to 1950, he was in the State Legislature, Jefferson City, Missouri, as representative from the 1st District. From 1950 to 1962 he engaged in a successful career as a banker, serving as President of Mound City Trust Company and Chairman of the Board of the First Security Bank of Kirkwood, Missouri. During that time he took in a wide range of civic activities.

In 1962 he was elected St. Louis County Supervisor and was re-elected in

1966. In addition to occupying the office of St. Louis County Supervisor, he is a member of the board of directors of the National Association of Counties, Chairman of the East-West Gateway Coordinating Council, a council of heads of local governments representing the St. Louis metropolitan area, and is a member of the executive committee of the St. Louis Regional Industrial Development Corporation.

Thomas C. Kelly

Thomas C. Kelly is Administrative Officer to the Board of County Commissioners of Prince George's County, Maryland. He assumed this appointive chief executive position in 1963. Prior to that he was executive director to the Maryland Association of Counties and spent six years in the United States Navy as Intelligence Officer. He also taught government at the United States Naval Academy at Annapolis. He was educated at Westminster College in Pennsylvania's Georgetown University and received his Ph.D. in Public Administration at the University of Maryland.

Robert L. Williams

Robert Williams is Executive Vice-President of Hill Development Corporation. Before this he served five years as the Executive Director of the American Institute of Planners. He was Planning Director for the County of Alameda, California, from 1958–1963 and the city of Alameda from 1954–1957. He has also served as technical advisor to the Association of Bay Area Governments (ABAG) on regional planning. He holds the M.C.P. degree from the University of California (Berkeley). He has been active in the San Francisco Bay Area shoreline development program, rapid transit program, and open space program.

Mr. Williams is a Member of the Highway Research Board; Committee on Planning Transportation; Subcommittee on Organization and Administration; Member of the Advisory Committee to Urban DOC Project (demonstration project on computerized documentation and information retrieval); Member, Joint Committee on the Nation's Capitol; Member, Interprofessional Commission on Environmental Design; Member, NAHRO International Committee; and a Member of the Advisory Committee on the Problems of Metropolitan Society, United Presbyterian Church in the U.S.A.

Nathan D. Grundstein

Nathan Grundstein is well versed in both public administration and public law. In public administration he has published "Computer Simulation of a Community for Gaming" (coauthor), "Presidential Delegation of Authority in Wartime" and "The Development Administration Game: A Conceptual Formulation" (coauthor). His writings have also appeared in the *George Washington Law Review* and the *Journal of Public Law*. He received his Ph.D. from Syracuse University and obtained his LL.B. from George Washington University.

Grundstein is a member of the Michigan Bar Association, Detroit Bar Association, Institute of Management Sciences, Society of General Systems Research, and American Political Science Association. In addition, he is associated with CONSAD Research Corporation of Pittsburgh, Pennsylvania, and Management Improvement Incorporated, Manhasset, New York.

Grundstein is presently a cooperating faculty member at the University of Chicago, Summer Institute in Executive Development, and Center for the Advanced Study of Organization Science, University of Wisconsin (Milwaukee). He has also served on special education programs on the federal, state, and local level.

Dr. T. R. Lakshmanan

Dr. T. R. Lakshmanan, Vice-President of CONSAD Research Corporation, received his Master's degree in Geography and Physics from the University of Madras and his Ph.D. in Geography from the Ohio State University. He is presently Project Director of a study which CONSAD is carrying out for the Office of Economic Research, Department of Commerce, to identify the direct, indirect and induced impacts of federal procurement and to estimate and evaluate consequences on regional economies of alternate federal procurement policies. He is also currently engaged in designing a model for estimating and evaluating consequences of alternative policies related to housing and residential patterns in Calgary, Alberta, and Detroit metropolitan regions.

While with Alan M. Voorhees and Associates, Washington, D. C., he developed models of metropolitan development for several urban areas. Among these was a Market Potential Model of the Baltimore region, a model of the econometric variety for allocating economic activity to subareas of Connecticut, an operational model for estimating the impacts of alternative recreation planning policies for Connecticut, and assistance in the preparation of Study Design projects for long-range continuous, comprehensive planning programs in Baltimore and St. Louis metropolitan regions.

In India, Dr. Lakshmanan headed the transportation research group in the National Atlas of India, Federal Ministry of Scientific Research and Cultural Affairs, Calcutta. Previously, he taught for five years at the University of Madras in India. He has also served on the faculty of Johns Hopkins University and is currently on the faculty of the University of Pittsburgh.

Guy Black

Guy Black is Professor of Economics and Senior Research Associate with the Program of Policy Studies in Science and Technology at the George Washington University, Washington, D.C. Black received his Ph.D. from the University of Chicago in 1951 in the area of economics. He has served as Executive Secretary, President's Committee on the Economic Impact of Defense and Disarmament, and as a member of the Staff, Council of Economic Advisors. In 1964 – 1965 he was a Economist, Policy Planning Division, for the National Aeronautics and Space Administration.

Black has many publications to his credit, some of which are: "Substitution of Public for Private Research and Development Expenditures," "Systems Analysis in Government Operations," "The Effect of Government Funding on Commercial Research and Development" and "Innovations in Business Organizations: Some Factors Associated with Success or Failure of Staff Proposals."

Kent Mathewson

Kent Mathewson has been President of the Metropolitan Fund, Inc., Detroit, Michigan, since January, 1964. MF is an urban affairs research and action foundation for the 4,000,000 population Detroit metropolitan region.

Before joining the Metropolitan Fund, he was City Manager and Assistant City Manager of five U.S. east and west coast cities, 1939–1964. Salem, the capital of Oregon, was his last city manager responsibility.

Mr. Mathewson is a National Trustee of the Institute of Public Affairs, Washington, D.C., since 1961, and Chairman of the IPA Urban Affairs Committee. He is a member of the National Highway Research Board, Washington, D.C., since 1963, and of the Michigan State Library Board since 1965. In 1958 he was the originator of Oregon's Intergovernmental "Massive Cooperation" Program.

He has been Vice-President, International City Managers Association, 1961–1963; President of the Oregon, Virginia, North Carolina City Managers Associations. He was a member of the national board of the American Society for Public Administration, 1960–1963. He holds the M.S. degree in Public Administration from Syracuse University with a major in City Management.

Dr. Thomas P. Murphy

Dr. Murphy is Assistant to the Chancellor for Urban Affairs, Director of Graduate Public Administration Programs, and Professor of Public Administration, School of Administration, University of Missouri – Kansas City. He was Executive Director, Commission on Organization of Jackson County, Missouri. Before coming to UMKC he was Deputy Assistant Administrator for Legislative Affairs, National Aeronautics and Space Administration, and Staff Assistant to NASA Administrator, James E. Webb. His earlier experience includes work with the Federal Aviation Agency, the U.S. General Accounting Office, U.S. Air Force and Internal Revenue Service.

Dr. Murphy received his Ph.D. in Political Science from St. John's University, New York, in 1963, his M.A. from Georgetown University and B.A. from Queens College. His articles on political and urban organization have appeared in *Trans-action, The Economist, Ethics, Public Administration Review, Administrative Science Quarterly, Contemporary Review, Union Theological Quarterly,* and *Polity.* He is the author of a book, *Metropolitics and the Urban County.*